Breakthroughs

Classroom Discoveries About Teaching Writing

Breakthroughs

Classroom Discoveries About Teaching Writing

Edited by Amy Bauman and Art Peterson

National Writing Project
Berkeley, California

NATIONAL WRITING PROJECT, BERKELEY 94720

Contributing editors: Roxanne Barber and Rebekah Truemper
Special thanks to Peggy Trump Loofbourrow, co-editor of *The Quarterly* from 1996 to 2000.
Cover design and layout: Karen Karten

Support for the National Writing Project (NWP) is provided by a major grant from the U.S. Department of Education. The NWP publishes books for teachers to support its primary goal to improve student writing achievement by improving the teaching of writing in the nation's schools. All of the material for this book was originally published in the National Writing Project's journal, *The Quarterly*. For more information, please visit www.writingproject.org or write:

National Writing Project
University of California
2105 Bancroft Way #1042
Berkeley, California 94720-1042.

Library of Congress Cataloging-in-Publication Data
Breakthroughs : classroom discoveries about teaching writing / edited by Amy Bauman and Art Peterson.
        p. cm.
Includes bibliographical references and index
ISBN 1-883920-18-3 (pbk.)
1. English language--Composition and exercises--Study and teaching. 2. Language arts. 3. Creative writing. I. Bauman, Amy, 1960- II. Peterson, Art, 1933- III. National Writing Project (U.S.)
LB1576 .B598 2002
808'.042'0712--dc21
2002190885

CONTENTS

Section 1

We Started Talking, and It Hit Me
Colleagues point the way to teaching ideas

Let's Take Another Look at the Fish: The Writing Process As Discovery

Bob Tierney

How can writing help students move from learning facts to understanding concepts?

Beyond Rhetoric: A Reflective, Persuasive Final Exam for the Workshop Classroom

Sarah Lorenz

How can students be led to reflect on what they have learned in a way that commands their serious focus?

Teacherless Talk: Impressions from Electronic Literary Conversations

Elaine Ware and Karen Murar

How can we lead students to more in-depth discussions about literature?

Author to Author: How Text Influences Young Writers

by Dina Sechio DeCristofaro

How does the work of professional writers positively influence the composition of young writers?

Section 2

Those Words Just Jumped Out at Me
Reading inspires creative teaching

Staging Learning: The Play's the Thing

Jean Hicks and Tim Johnson

How can students ground their writing about important social issues in their own lives and voices?

Section 3

Okay. But What Now?
Teachers build on what they know

Section 4

I Was Doing the Laundry When ...
Teachers find inspiration in daily life

Section 5

I Had to Do Something!
Necessity inspires teaching invention

PREFACE

Each of the selections that appear in *Breakthroughs: Classroom Discoveries About Teaching Writing* was first published in *The Quarterly* of the National Writing Project, a journal by teachers of writing for teachers of writing.

ABOUT THE NATIONAL WRITING PROJECT

The National Writing Project (NWP) is a nonprofit professional development network dedicated to improving student writing and learning by improving the teaching of writing in our nation's schools. Founded in 1974 at the University of California, Berkeley, the writing project today consists of 175 sites at colleges and university campuses in 50 states, Washington, D.C., Puerto Rico, and the U.S. Virgin Islands. Using a teachers-teaching-teachers model that draws on the knowledge, expertise, and leadership of successful classroom teachers, the NWP annually serves more than 100,000 teachers, grades kindergarten through college, in all disciplines. Writing project sites work in partnership with schools, teachers, and students to develop programs tailored to the needs of their local communities. Readers will note that several of the writers in *Breakthroughs* pay tribute to and otherwise mention their local sites.

The summer institute, which is another term mentioned in the book, is the primary engine by which a local site sparks progress in the teaching of writing. Each summer, twenty to twenty-five successful teachers, grades kindergarten through college, are invited to participate in the site's four- to five-week institute. At the institute, the selected teachers share practices that have worked for them in their writing classrooms. These practices are presented in a workshop format, with fellow teachers working through the spotlighted strategy and participating in a discussion and critique of its implications and applications. Some of articles in *Breakthroughs* began as presentations to fellow teachers at summer institutes.

In addition to sharing their best practices, participants in the summer institutes also write, a requirement that grows from the NWP's belief that teachers of writing should write. After this writing immersion in the summer, many teachers continue to write, but this is not the only way that summer institute participants have been able to hone their ideas and practices. After these teachers complete the institute, they become teacher-consultants (TCs) for their local sites. The role of teacher-consultants involves many opportunities and responsibilities. Among them is the call for teachers to share their expertise with other teachers—perhaps as part of a workshop series, inservice, or other format sponsored by the local site—through which they can bring alive the writing project belief that successful teachers are the best teachers of other teachers.

Readers are encouraged to consider this partial and abbreviated description of the work of the National Writing Project as they read. The authors represented here are almost all teacher-consultants who have presented one of their strong practices at a local site's summer institute, going on to demonstrate their work in the schools, and then written about it in the form we have published in this volume. Readers who would like more information about the National Writing Project or would like to become part of this growing network of teacher-writers should contact us at our website writingproject.org.

ANOTHER WAY TO USE THIS BOOK

The editors of *Breakthroughs* made the decision to organize the book around this central question: Where do teaching ideas come from? However, readers looking for ideas related to specific writing process strategies may consult this alternative list of contents.

INTRODUCTION

Art Peterson

Albert Einstein never much liked the word *problems*. He would speak instead of *puzzles*. As you will see, the teachers whose writing we've chosen to include in this anthology of selections from *The Quarterly* of the National Writing Project have had their share of problems. In fact, that's the very reason we're spotlighting their stories.

But perhaps, in describing their struggles, we should defer to Einstein's word choice. Problems are global warming and way too many baseball strikes. Puzzles are the word jumble in the Sunday paper and Sherlock Holmes figuring out why the dog didn't bark in the night.

We approach puzzles with a sense of energetic play, with an attitude that says, "Hey, I can do this," that is often lacking when we take a hard look at problems. It is this optimism that a solution can be found that permeates the essays presented in this book.

Of course, Einstein's puzzle was a formidable project: he needed to crack the nut that enclosed the secret of the universe. By contrast, the difficulty that perplexes the teacher in room 254 may seem no big deal, but for the teacher and kids behind that classroom door, a breakthrough is no less relevant and the journey that led to it no less exhilarating.

Many readers may approach this text expecting these journeys of discovery to be of less interest than the practical end results. After all, we want to be able to flip on the television and watch an *I Love Lucy* rerun without enduring a lecture on the cathode-ray tube that made it all possible. Likewise, teachers, hungry for successful classroom strategies, could grow impatient with a recital of insights illuminated and glitches overcome. Rest assured that the editors are no more enamored of classroom shaggy dog stories than are most readers. The successful strategies are here and out in force. But in a time when there is an increasingly pervasive, if misguided, impression that "creative teaching" is an oxymoron, we think it is vital that we take a focused look at how accomplished teachers work.

The teachers represented in this book do not look for solutions in scripted lessons or in superficial inservice programs conducted by "trainers," pushing cookie-cutter learning utopias. They are teachers who stop listening when faculty meetings, intended to "address school problems," degenerate into gripe sessions at which the only viable solution seems to be a school without children.

These teachers know that they and their students need to be on the front line of educational solutions. They realize that the learning broth that is brewing right there in their classrooms can only be diluted by too many cooks operating from too great a distance.

This volume provides a forum for these teachers to demonstrate, in an era when the search seems to be on for teacher-proof answers, that teachers need not roll over and play the victim of forces beyond their control. Instead, these writers know that it must be their mission, and that of their creative colleagues, to invent better classrooms. As this is a charge all teachers, not only those represented in this book, need to accept, we have organized these essays to help readers answer the question "Where do creative teaching ideas come from?" In general, our answer is that classroom ideas are generated in the same way as other ideas. And each of the book's five sections focuses on one of these sources of creative thinking.

TALKING WITH COLLEAGUES

In the first section, "We Started Talking and It Hit Me," teachers show how colleagues have pointed the way to new teaching ideas. Talking with colleagues is, of course, what the National Writing Project is all about. We are the network that, through our institutes and inservice programs, promotes the idea of "teachers teaching teachers." But as useful as this slogan has been in explaining our work, it does not entirely capture the essence of what goes on when teachers build on one another's knowledge. It comes down to this: the teacher in the room next door may share an idea for helping students order their ideas within a paragraph; it works with her students and in her classroom, but it will not work in quite the same way with your students in your classroom. For this or any strategy to succeed, teachers need to bring their own creativity to bear, altering the approach or perhaps transforming it beyond recognition. Your colleague has not directed your work, but she has inspired your discovery.

It follows, then, that the strategies suggested in the twenty-five articles in this book are intended for inspiration, not mimicry.

BUILDING ON WHAT IS KNOWN

The second section, "Those Words Just Jumped Out at Me," highlights how reading the work of others can lead both teachers and students to deepen their insights by building on the work of others.

In 500 B.C. the Chinese discovered that moldy soybean curds could treat infection. Today we are able to genetically modify crops. These two breakthroughs are not unconnected. They are linked through the centuries by an expanding edifice of related ideas. The question that inspires here is "What's next?" It's said that an artist only goes to work on another composition when she is dissatisfied with the previous one. Conversely, the teacher who finds herself in a state of self-satisfied stasis is soon going to be wondering, "So what do I do with the next twenty years?"—a question right on the edge of teacher burnout. The teachers represented here refuse to stay bogged down in a teaching idea that is just working; they are always on the lookout for something that could work better.

READING WITH A PURPOSE

Management consultant Laurence J. Peter says, "Originality is the fine art of remembering what you hear by forgetting where you heard it." By Peter's definition, the pieces in the third section of our collection, "Okay. But What Now?" would not count as original. These authors, in fact, give scrupulous attention to crediting the inspiration for their ideas. The originality kicks in at step 2, when these writers transform the received wisdom, making it their own. They cobble together new classroom ideas from diverse selections of professional literature. Or they take a strategy that, according to a well-regarded authority, is *supposed* to work and tweak it until it does work.

Readers, as the modern view would have it, create their own texts. No one is better prepared to put this concept to practical use than the teacher-reader making meaning he hopes will improve his students' learning.

OBSERVING THE WORLD

It's a sad fact that too many people in the community at large hold to the mistaken view that teachers don't work much. ("But, you get all those vacations.") The truth is pretty much the opposite; creative teachers work all the time. We're not talking here about the equally erroneous stereotype of the teacher as drudge, committed to a lifetime of exposing with red ink every last tense shift in an undiminishing pile of error-laden juvenilia.

No, teaching ideas are everywhere, and creative teachers are always on the lookout. For the teachers represented in section 4, "I Was Doing the Laundry When . . ," the lightbulb can go on while reading the newspaper or pruning the azaleas or even browsing the aisles at Office Depot. To see one thing and think another: this is the mind-set of the creative teacher.

ACTING OUT OF NECESSITY

But now it's time to backpedal a bit. We want to make clear that these teachers are not just fooling around, indulging their creative whims in the manner of newlyweds picking out wallpaper. It's not "Gee, if I can come up with an alternative to the every Friday spelling test, everything is going be fun, fun, fun!"

The real situation is often a lot more bleak. It's the teacher who gets a knot in the pit of his stomach each morning on arrival at school because he knows he is failing. While most of the teacher-writers in section 5, "I Had to Do Something!" have not reached this level of desperation, their solutions are all inspired by the realization that something about their teaching needs to change.

The answers they devise appear to have a common thread, one that can inspire others who need to invent a way out of disheartening circumstances. Like the great conductors who know when to back off and listen to the orchestra, these teachers know when to pay attention to their students. As contributor Jan Matsuoka puts it, "Reviewing what I have done over the past two years, I am struck by the fact that every time I got in a jam, it was the students who helped me out of it."

Arthur Koestler has written, "Creative activity can be described as a type of learning process where the teacher and the pupil are located in the same individual." In our classrooms we need to remember that this aphorism holds as true for our students as it does for us.

Indeed, in all of the pieces collected in this volume, one is struck by the way the authors draw on the uninhibited energy of the young, a secret weapon that all good teachers know about. But the solutions presented here also depend on the disciplined intelligence of adults. Collectively, these pieces represent hundreds of hours of intellectual struggle, of wrong turns, of trial and error. For most of us, creative teaching isn't about the brilliant idea that occurs while eating an apple. It's about hard work. It's also a lot of fun.

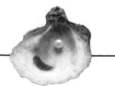

We Started Talking, and It Hit Me

Colleagues point the way to teaching ideas

Let's Take Another Look at the Fish: The Writing Process as Discovery

Bob Tierney

Written by Bob Tierney about his experience as a science teacher incorporating writing into the classroom. This article was originally published in the fall 1998 issue of The Quarterly.

The naturalist Louis Agassiz first came to my attention when I was a college biology student. Agassiz believed that students could best learn through their own discovery. The traditional lecture method left students, he believed, with much information but little understanding. Agassiz's approach to discovery learning intrigued me. Although my professors, who lauded his approach to learning, did not use Agassiz's methodology when attempting to teach me, I remember thinking at the time that if I ever had my own biology class, my students would learn the way Agassiz's students learned.

Unfortunately, as a beginning teacher trying to survive the bell-to-bell routine, I fell into the trap of giving product a higher priority than process. I was afraid to deviate from the cookbook labs, worksheets, and lecture approach sanctioned by administrators and used by some of my apparently successful peers. And although my evaluations indicated I was a good teacher, I knew my students were mostly memorizing facts and failing to gain understanding.

Then the successful launching of Russia's *Sputnik* in 1957 generated both panic and money for the American scientific community. Science teachers were able to get grants to attend special summer institutes at universities all over the country, and I attended some of these institutes. The summer institutes preached the same theme as Agassiz had: do not teach science as a body of knowledge. Approach science as concept. Have students hypothesize, experiment, and draw conclusions. Push students to think. It sounded fine, but lacking a vehicle to make it work, I went back to the tried and true classroom activities I had used before . . . and I felt guilty.

And then I had the opportunity to attend a writing project summer institute. The experience of collaborating with other teachers, considering others' methods as well as scrutinizing my own, openly discussing what works as well as what doesn't empowered me. The writing project gave me the courage, the vehicle, and the techniques to convert myself from a dispenser of information to a facilitator of learning. At last I felt I was on the course I had envisioned all along—a course guided by the thinking of Louis Agassiz and the National Writing Project.

~ *Bob Tierney, 2002*

*P*robably every science teacher has heard the tale of Louis Agassiz and the fish, but few have heeded its significance. It's a meaningful message, applicable for teachers across the curriculum. Louis Agassiz was a Swiss-American, nineteenth-century naturalist who proved there was once an ice age. Although famous for his work regarding glaciers, Agassiz was invited to the United States because of his writings about fossil fish. He spent the last part of the century as a professor at Harvard, and the Museum of Comparative Zoology there is now named for him.

One of Agassiz's students wrote an essay "A Pencil Is One of the Best Eyes" (Sparke and McKowen 1970, 87), about learning under the famous professor. According to the essay, Agassiz began one lesson by asking the student what he wanted to learn and how he intended to use the knowledge afterward. He then told the student to carefully remove a preserved fish from a jar and observe it.

"I will ask you later what you have learned," Professor Agassiz told the student.

The student gazed at the preserved fish. In ten minutes, the student had seen all that he thought might be seen of the fish. He looked, in vain, for his professor. Not finding him, he was forced to spend another half hour looking at the loathsome pickled fish. He then went to lunch. When he returned, the fish was still in the pan, and the professor could not be found. Bored and thoroughly sick of the smelly fish, the student pulled out a pencil and began to draw the fish. He discovered several new features of the fish. Finally, the professor returned. The student showed Professor Agassiz the drawings.

"That is right," Professor Agassiz said. "A pencil is one of the best eyes. Well, what is it like?"

Professor Agassiz listened attentively to the student's explanation of what he had learned, but to the student's dismay, he said, "You have not looked very carefully. Why? You have not even seen one of the most conspicuous features of the animal, which is as plainly before your eyes as the fish itself; look again, look again!"

The student observed the fish again but went about the task with a renewed vigor. He discovered one thing after another, realizing how just the professor's criticism was.

"Do you see it yet?" the professor asked.

"No," replied the student. "I am certain I do not, but I see how little I saw before."

"That is the next best," Professor Agassiz answered. "I will not listen to you now; put away the fish and go home; perhaps you will be ready with a better response in the morning. I will examine you before you look at the fish again."

So the student left the classroom without his notes or the specimen but required to search for the most visible feature the professor alluded to. He strolled along the banks of the Charles River, his mind focused on the fish and what he would explain to the professor.

The next morning, the professor greeted him cordially and seemed as anxious as the student that learning had taken place.

"Do you perhaps mean," the student asked, "that the fish has symmetrical sides with paired organs?"

"Of course, of course," replied the professor, obviously pleased, and he proceeded to talk for several minutes about the importance of the discovery.

The student then asked, "What should I do next?"

"Oh, look at the fish!" Professor Agassiz said and left the room.

An hour later Professor Agassiz returned and listened eagerly to any new discoveries the student made. "That is good, that is good!" Professor Agassiz repeated as the student explained. "But that is not all; go on, look at the fish."

For three days the student was forced to look at the fish without the use any artificial aid. "Look, look, look," admonished Professor Agassiz when the student asked questions.

On the fourth day, Professor Agassiz brought in a second fish of the same family and placed it alongside the first. The student was asked to point out the differences and similarities between the two. Another fish, and another were laid out until the entire family was before the student and the student understood the relationships between the fish.

"Facts are stupid things," Professor Agassiz said, "until brought into connection with some general law."

This story haunted me during most of my early career as a science teacher, resulting in a sense of guilt about my own teaching efforts. I realized I was a presenter of facts, wondering why the students never seemed to understand the concepts. I tested for knowledge of facts—knowledge the students retained just long enough to pass the multiple-choice examinations. It was education by checklist.

I had been a presenter of information when I needed to be a facilitator of learning. I had lots of facts, and if I ran out, I could always look up more. Later in my teaching career, after my exposure to the writing project, I realized the writing process is a discovery technique that can get students personally and emotionally involved, a way of getting them to "look once again at the fish." It is a means of accomplishing what Louis Agassiz had succeeded in doing with his students. I began devising writing assignments designed not so much to inform but to help students understand. I wanted my teaching to be more like Agassiz's and less like the questions at the end of the chapter.

On one occasion, my students entered to find that a leaf had been placed on each desk. "I want each of you to observe your leaf," I said. "But I want you to conduct this observation following my instructions."

I asked them to divide a piece of paper into four quadrants and number them one through four. "Now in square one, write a description of the leaf." When they read aloud their descriptions, I was encouraged by the variety of their perspectives.

Some focused on the facts before their eyes: "The leaf is green." "The leaf has veins."

Some put other senses to work: "The leaf smells like camphor."

One relied on a basic tool of science, the ruler: "My leaf is 6.2 centimeters long."

Another student made a comparison: "It looks like the teeth of a saw."

I next asked students to use square two to finish the following sentence: "This leaf is like_____ because . . ." They decided that the leaf was like:

a road map because the veins appear to be highways;

a canoe because of its shape and the fact that it floats;

the dress I bought for the prom because it is shiny green on the outside and dull green on the inside.

After writing these similes on the board, I asked, "Which of these represents the most far-out way of thinking about a leaf?"

The students were now at the center of the discussion, and I, like Agassiz, was taking a risk, unsure of what the students would come up with.

I remember on another occasion asking a writing project group at University of California, Berkeley, to create a leaf simile. The leaf, observed one writer, is like a "bedraggled, just-neutered dog: torn, wet, with a surface full of mold." We had a lot of fun with that one.

Back in the classroom, I asked students what it would be like to be whatever it was they chose as the most far-out metaphor. They were to imagine that life in quadrant three. As a group, we agreed that the prom dress simile was pretty far-out. Here are some of the ways students brought the dress to life. The leaf connection was not lost on the students.

By the end of the dance, I am bathed in sweat.

When the girl moves, I move.

I am making the girl more attractive, more noticed.

When I am exposed in just the right combination of light and shadow my texture and color can be extraordinarily beautiful.

Finally, I asked the students to use the fourth quadrant to again comment on the leaf. All along, they had listened to each other. This sharing was reflected in their responses. Now, also, they were asking questions about their observations.

Why is one side of the leaf darker than the other side?

How does the leaf breathe?

Does a leaf, like a prom dress, need to be cleaned? Is God the great leaf cleaner?

I then asked the students to write one sentence about something they believed to be true about the leaf, thus beginning a search for the truth that woud become the motto of the class. Then came the inevitable question: What do we mean by *true?* We defined truth as something that cannot be argued with. Sentences were scrutinized to see if they would be disputed, and if so, they are rewritten so that they are irrefutable.

For example, a student might write, "Leaves are green." After a discussion, the sentence might be altered to read, "Most leaves are green, but some can be red, yellow, or purple." A biology student might write, "The stomata controls the amount of air entering the leaf." After discussion, often a lively one, the sentence might be revised to read, "The opening of the stomata, under osmotic pressure, can regulate the amount of carbon dioxide the leaf gets." The students learn to differentiate between fact and assumption. This exercise pushes students toward specific thinking. Students will not write in a more specific way until they learn to think in more specific ways.

This exercise generates lots of questions about the object. Why do leaves turn color? Why isn't the underside glossy like the top? Are the veins of the leaf like the veins in our body? I build my upcoming lecture upon these questions, giving students some ownership of the presentation. If they accept ownership, they must also accept responsibility for learning, just as Louis Agassiz put that responsibility on his student. Agassiz didn't give the student facts. He facilitated the student's understanding. Students had been forced to think about the leaf, looking at it from different perspectives. I was showing, not telling, students more complicated ways of writing about the leaf.

Since this first adaptation of Agassiz, I have varied and expanded this activity using a variety of objects, sometimes even fish. I try to emulate Agassiz in other ways, too. Agassiz placed other fish alongside the fish his student was observing. Applying the Agassiz aphorism, "A pencil is sometimes the best eye," I frequently start a unit about the human eye by having students draw each other's eyes. Forced to observe closely, students notice similarities and differences that help them draw conclusions just as Agassiz's student did when asked to compare fish.

Just as Agassiz had his student think about the fish without his notes or the specimen, I often have my students do what I call a Neuron Note. The name is biological, it is jazzy, and it implies thinking. The students go home without their books or notes and write a summary of what they think they understand. I stress to the students that it is all right if they do not understand, but they need to realize they don't understand. Just as Agassiz's student said, "I see how little I saw before," the Neuron Notes help students identify what they do not yet understand. I give students full credit if they write their Neuron Notes and none if they don't. The following is typical of a Neuron Note by a general science student trying to express his comprehension of osmosis:

> Osmosis is to do with water and cells. Osmosis is the absorbing of water by cells, or pass through. I don't know what it does exactly once it's inside. Osmosis is not the only way, but the one that is used the most is diffusion. I would like to know where they got a name like osmosis for it? Osmosis is different than any other form, but still gets the job done.

15

When it occurs, water actually passes through a somewhat membrane so as to equalize the amount on both sides of the cell or whatever kind of membrane it is.

The lesson provides an insight as to what the students really understand. I can determine if they are really ready for a test. In the old days, I decided the test date months ahead, usually on a Friday, and gave the test whether or not the students were ready. I also complained, along with my colleagues, about how many students did not study.

In responding to the Neuron Notes, I try to emulate the one-on-one relationship Agassiz had with his student in the fish story. My students, at the beginning of the school year, provide me with a blank audiotape. I believe that the best response to student writing is the oral response, not the written reply. I put the tapes into bags, by period, and when they turn in a Neuron Note, I reach into a bag, find the tape, and then find the student's paper. As I read the paper, I talk to the student. I am able to coach each student, one on one, for the upcoming test. I congratulate the students on what they understand. However, I do not provide answers. Like Louis Agassiz, I ask questions that allow the student the exhilaration of their own discovery.

I later came to know some things about short-term and long-term memory and realized Louis Agassiz's teaching technique succeeded in imprinting his student's understanding into the long-term memory. Those early lessons of mine only ended up in the short-term memory of a student. Using the analogy of the computer, these lessons might have made it into their random access memory (RAM), but they were not getting into their hard drive. One way to place concepts of a lesson into the long-term memory of a student is to have the student associate the lesson with what she already knows. Another is to get the student emotionally involved. These writing exercises use both of these methods.

Some teachers, pressured to prepare students for tests that rely heavily on factual regurgitation, are struggling to help their students assemble facts into a comprehensible concept. When I ask myself how Louis Agassiz might meet this contemporary challenge, I can almost hear his ghost whispering in my ear, "Look, look, look again at the fish."

REFERENCE

Sparke, William, and Clark McKowen. 1970. *Montage: Investigations in Language.* New York: Macmillan.

Beyond Rhetoric: A Reflective, Persuasive Final Exam for the Workshop Classroom

Sarah Lorenz

Written by Sarah Lorenz about her teaching experience with high school juniors and seniors in Novi, Michigan, this article was originally published in the fall 2001 issue of The Quarterly.

Making new practices fit with old regulations is a problem that many teachers face. Some schools, for instance, still insist that all classes must include an objective final exam. For teachers using a writing workshop format, this can be a major obstacle—one I found myself facing. And even though my school was not terribly stringent about the final exam's form—I could assign a final project or use another type of assessment—I still felt as if we had finished the class with the portfolio and that the final exam was an afterthought. Still, since the exam accounted for 20 percent of a student's grade, I wanted it to be meaningful.

In conversation, a colleague told me about her reflective final exam. I took hold of her idea and developed it into the assignment that I describe in the following article. Initially, this test-assignment was a quick solution to the annoying end-of-the-term required exam. As such, it was an isolated task at the end of the year. But as I have reflected on and refined the process, I've begun to see the many benefits of an assignment that elegantly combines reflection, persuasion, review, craft, detail, and the course evaluation. I now see that it can be an integrated, important part of my practice. Now I talk more about this final project at the beginning of the year. I also allow more time for peer conferencing on the project and create a rubric with the students to achieve more consistent grading.

It is encouraging to find that new practices can sometimes fit in with the old habits of a school without being compromised. From that perspective, the reflective final exam paper introduces a new genre, teaches important skills in the use of evidence, neatly summarizes the year's learning—all while providing the necessary exam grade. This goes to show that we don't always need to start from scratch when we improve our methods and our schools. Inspiration—whether from old friends or old rules—can lead to creativity that results in something even better.

~ *Sarah Lorenz, 2002*

*I*t's five o'clock. I stagger through the front door carrying the mail, my lunch box, and my schoolbag, seemingly loaded with bricks. It's the end of a crazy exam day; grades are due tomorrow. I leaf through the mail, check the messages, talk to the cats, pour a drink, get comfy on the couch, and plow into the exams my sophomore and junior English students have just turned in. I can't wait to find out what my students have to say.

Believe me, it hasn't always been this way. Exams haven't always been high on my list of compelling reading material. In fact, this entire end-of-semester experience was often depressing. The problem was that I didn't know how to give an exam that was consistent with what I had been doing all year with my writing and reading workshop classes. I tried out some alternatives, such as creating objective tests over writing craft or asking students to report on authors they had read, but techniques such as these did not seem to mesh with what we had been doing. What I wanted was a final exam that served as a reflective review of the year, one that showed me what the students had learned.

I suspect that many teachers who have embraced the workshop model in their secondary classrooms often wrapped up a wonderful semester with great student portfolios but then, as I did, ran straight into a school requirement for an exam at the end of the term. For me, the traditional end-of-term exam was at odds with the workshop experience. But that was before one of my Eastern Michigan Writing Project colleagues, Michelle McLemore, helped me find a way out of this dilemma. Michelle, who also teaches high school English, has her students do a "detective story" exam in which they gather "evidence" of good writing in their work and present it to her in a conference. I decided to take this idea in another direction.

Now I ask my students to write a persuasive essay that tells me what grade they think they should get and then convince me that they deserve it. They must wax eloquent about how much they have learned from the class. They can pull from anything that we have done during the semester or year. The key to convincing me is the use of detail. They can't simply say they have improved as writers—they have to give examples and even quote their own writing. They can't just say their vocabulary improved—they have to use some of their favorite new words. And they can't just say something was helpful—they have to tell me why they thought it was important, how their thinking changed, or how they applied it in everyday life.

I give them a list similar to the one below to evoke ideas.

Write about:

• *favorite books you've read during the year and why you liked them*

• *poems that have led you to deeper understandings*

• *how your writing has improved, with specific examples*

• *new words you've acquired*

• *concepts or genres you've learned about*

• *editing skills you've mastered*

• *minilessons you have found useful*

• *writing prompts and revision techniques you particularly liked*

• *reading and writing habits you have developed or changed*

• *what you've learned from the class overall*

Since we have not studied the persuasive genre before, I work with the students to help them provide supporting details and examples to make their pieces convincing. As these students will have many more experiences with persuasive writing, this topic so closely connected to them, one with a very real purpose, seems like an ideal introduction to the genre.

The first inclination of many students facing this essay is, of course, to butter me up, to place at the center of their piece a thesis testifying to how great the class was, how great I am, how much they loved everything. Flattered as I may be by these testimonials, I won't really be convinced of students' growth until I see evidence of their learning—examples from their own writing, thinking, and living. This use of specific, supporting detail is difficult for students, and many write unreflective essays that simply repeat what I've told them during the year. Some essays are all rhetoric and no substance or, on the other end, occasionally give a bare list of topics with no persuasive appeal. For instance, one student wrote, "I also learned that many things can effect the quality of the poem. A few of these things are line breaks, shape of the poem, tone, fresh use of language, and literary devices."

While responses of this sort tell me the student was able to remember or refer to notes we used in our poetry study, they don't show if those devices were ever used personally. And tempting as it may be, I cannot allow a strong voice punctuated by humor to dissuade me from my insistence on specific examples.

*To move on to my next term, let's see if you know what a foot is, no I
don't mean the thing connected to your ankle. It's the smallest repeated
pattern of stressed and unstressed syllables in a poetic line. Believe it or
not this is a very helpful hint to remember.*

Though essays heavy with this kind of writing are not exactly what I'm looking for, I'm not gravely disappointed in them either. They do show evidence of
learning. But they don't get the highest grades.

I'm learning to better teach students to work with this format by providing
them with models and specific instruction. I ask students to tell little stories of
how they made a connection in real life with something they learned in class.
One student told how she felt a little surge of pride when she was the only one
in her family to know the answer to a *Jeopardy* question about literature. Another wrote of how she knew exactly how to answer the question on the ACT
about genre because we had talked about the concept so often. And there were
students who made larger connections between what we had learned and their
own lives:

> *One of the authors that you read from said something along the lines of
> "being aware of details, don't forget to live," this has helped me to notice
> things in a different way. I remember flipping through a magazine a few
> days ago and looking at a few pictures and thinking about what great
> poems could be made out of them. Even when we were in Washington,
> D.C., I saw people and could think of how they might be feeling and why
> and create a poem in my mind. Such as when I saw an elderly woman
> standing in front of Robert F. Lee's house in Arlington, I would find
> myself thinking of her "overlooking the solemnly quiet cemetery. All the
> white blurring together in a bare blanket of glory for the deserving sol-
> diers. Her eyes were remorseful, as if she had lost something and didn't
> think to regret it until it was too late. She was standing there alone, but
> not lonely. She had stopped being lonely." It was sad to think of, but was
> an amazing moment for me, to be able to see someone and make up a
> past and be able to remember it.*
> ~ Stephanie

Of course, topics on which we had spent the most time in class come up
frequently in the essays. This past year, my sophomores and juniors did a genre

study on poetry that lasted most of second semester, so they wrote a lot about poetry in their essays, telling how their perspectives on poetry had changed and giving examples from their own work. Krist said, "You showed us that poetry isn't all common sense; it's our dreams gone wild." He quoted from his response to a dream-write in which he used alliteration inspired by a *National Geographic* picture: "Monkeys—hairy furry flamboyant hanging on powerful power lines with a sunset that's powdery pink."

Students spent a lot of time revising their poetry, putting to work poetic devices. Camelle referred to her inclusion of metaphors in a revision of her first poem:

> *The volleyball flew over the net. There's really nothing much to read into—so let's compare it to something descriptive: The volleyball flew over the net like an asteroid flies through space. Doesn't that sound much more descriptive? It gives life and meaning to your statement.*

Trae cleverly demonstrated his understanding of figurative language by incorporating an example of these devices right into his sentence:

> *Using similes and metaphors is like breathing to me. . . . I have noticed a great difference in my writing and so have my parents. They can tell the difference because when they read my poems they asked me did I copy them from somewhere. . . .*

Other responses, while not rich in content, were startling in their level of understanding. Melissa talked about our Socratic Seminar discussions of poetry, which were difficult for her to jump into even though she saw the value. "Some of the poems you had us decipher were tough," she said, "but I think we did a good job of digging in to dead people's souls and finding out their deep, dark secrets."

One of the best features of this project has been the way it clarifies the use of minilessons in my classroom. My lesson on the use of the thesaurus, for instance, made an impact in ways I had not anticipated. Students wrote about learning new words and using the thesaurus, and they commented on some of the extra advice I included in the minilesson as well as how their new skills made them feel. Dylan wrote, "Words like *skinny* and *dull* are now replaced with *gaunt* and *somber*. I kind of like how these words enhance my profile from an intellectual perspective."

Camelle said:

*But Mrs. Lorenz did tell us to make sure that we don't use the thesaurus
as a way to use big words and confound everyone, but to use rich words.
Like instead of saying fast, you could say abruptly. Abruptly sounds better, and it doesn't confound anyone.*

Some minilessons were very short and focused on practical matters of usage
or common errors. "I learned a ton of stuff this year. I even learned that *a lot* is
two words," wrote Sean. The very practical lessons, things I never recognized as
content but just as stuff I'd throw in for free, were now recorded as minilessons,
and this helped us recognize their value.

Many students referred to a minilesson I'd given on writing sympathy notes
as one of the best, which was a real surprise to me. Students talked about terms
that we learned: "I had never heard of a line break before February 23, 2001,"
said Chris, and Aaron revealed some interesting wordplay that had been going
on inside his head:

*An outstandingly helpful minilesson was #9, which talked about repeti-
tion and personification . After learning about these techniques, I created
my own tool, Personificaucasian, which gives Caucasian-like characteristics to an animal, object, or concept.*

Has anyone ever found material like this on a multiple-choice exam?
Writing-craft lessons came up in the essays. We had had many minilessons
on the use of specific detail, so I was gratified to find many students mentioning
it in their essays.

*Now, when I write something, I don't just say the room was dark. I
would describe the eerie glow it had about it, the dancing shadows on
the walls, and the creeping feeling of doom all around me.*
　～ Nate

*Instead of telling the reader that you're eating fruit, tell the reader that the
juice from the oversized pomegranate was dribbling down your chin.*
　～ Stephanie

*For example, don't say your "car." Say something like "my gleaming red
hot rod convertible."*
　～ Chris

You can never use too much detail. Details are the insides of the story. Without them, we would all be lost. Be specific. Instead of saying "there was a pretty flower by the windowsill" say "there was a radiant geranium sitting on the windowsill's left." Now you know what kind of flower it is, where it is, and what kind of "pretty" it was.

   ~ Beckie

Beckie provides here the kind of example that I try to share with other students. She not only develops the concept with an example but goes on to analyze the reasons for using detail.

Students talked about books they had read during independent reading, an area of learning I had never even tried to assess on the final exam. While many of these comments tended to be more general than I would have preferred, they did give me a clear idea of the variety of learning that was taking place during independent reading time. Nate admitted, "*Slot Machine* was the first book that I have ever laughed out loud while reading." Andy revealed that he had read over seven hundred hours this year. And Alex, who avoided reading at all costs in the past, wrote how he had changed:

I figured out what kind of book I like to read. I like to read factual books. . . . After all that reading, my imagination, once a non-existent part of my life, started to unfold. My concentration level grew after that, and I started using the right side of my brain.

Other students wrote in convincing detail about what they had taken away from our writing conferences:

You were looking at one of my poems that had no feeling or thought behind it. Then you brought up Emily Dickinson and how she only hints at something else for the reader to find. It's really incredible how she does that, so I went and read a few of her poems. It took awhile to digest them and go over them again to figure out. But once I figured out one or two of them, I realized what you were talking about. I then thought about how amazing it would be to have people reading those kind of poems, making them sit down and try and get into your mind, your innermost thought, and why you wrote that. I know I'll never be Emily Dickinson, or even close to it. But that really inspired me, and gave me something to work towards.

Elsewhere in the essay, she reflected on her writing process:

Emily Dickinson wrote, "The brain within its groove / Runs evenly and true; / But let a splinter swerve, / 'Twere easier for you / To put the water back / When floods have slit the hills . . ." I feel like this is me, when I get distracted.

> ~ Stephanie

Lying on my couch, beaming idiotically, I feel like maybe I am doing something right after all.

As my students have worked with this end-of-the-term persuasive essay format, the benefits to them have become increasingly clear. But I also benefit. I often would come to the end of the semester wondering despairingly, "What did we accomplish?" During the year, I would create new lessons based on errors I saw in students' writing or on topics that arose serendipitously, so it didn't always feel like I'd covered a lot of weighty topics in depth. Some minilessons were so short and focused—like the use of *a lot* or the use of the thesaurus—that I frequently felt as if my direct instruction was haphazard and random. This is not as much of a problem now. As I've introduced the persuasive essay final, I've also required students to record all minilessons in a special section in their learning logs, and this is one of the main sources they draw from when they write their persuasive papers. It helps them take minilessons more seriously during the year, and it offers a substantial review at year's end, which is, after all, the purpose of an exam. Further, students and teacher alike realize that we really did cover a lot during the year. It's great to go from wondering, "What did we spend all our time on this year?" to thinking, "Wow—we really did cover a lot of ground."

This project has other benefits. It provides a way of thinking about language arts skills that gives a bigger picture than the reflective piece typically included in portfolios. Portfolio reflections still have a place, of course, but they are highly focused on the pieces included in the portfolio and don't usually address the class as a whole. Reflection of any kind is often difficult for students, and teachers' demands for reflection on portfolio entries can be vague and frustrating. While the persuasive essay is also reflective, it has a very direct and businesslike purpose and audience—it's for me, and it's for a big grade. That may not seem very kind and gentle, but it's honest, and it sure gets great results.

The review is also valuable because the students think about how much they have learned and grown in the workshop format. Because workshop is different from traditional teacher-directed classes and is very student centered, kids sometimes don't realize that they are learning or even doing work. Nate said, "The methods of teaching were such that it gave the illusion that we were not really being taught. . . . In a way, we taught ourselves with the assistance of a teacher." Students often comment that they are surprised at how much they've gained. As Adam admitted:

> *I'm ashamed to say it, but here it goes. I like writing. Yes, it's true. The student with the absolute worst attitude in the school towards anything involving ink actually enjoys putting the stuff down on paper. Especially poetry. (Don't tell my friends.)*

On a practical level, this is an assignment that can be done during the exam period itself, but it is better done outside of class as a take-home exam. Either way, I provide students with a prewriting assignment or worksheet. In class, I go over the minilessons and other material that we have covered, and I provide models of the type of writing that is appropriate. I use old essays that received an A. I explain to my students that A papers are rarely under four pages typewritten and often up to eight pages, because of the level of detail required to persuade me of A quality. If students are to explain the content learned over an entire semester or year and include detailed examples in a persuasive format, they will need to elaborate. It's possible to do this in fewer than eight pages, but that means very tight, clever writing—something that takes as much time as writing more.

Interestingly, I've found that students are usually accurate and honest when giving themselves a grade. Their assessments almost always come close to mine. Students who put a lot of time into their writing do so on this essay as well, so they ask for a good grade and, as a rule, get it. Students who don't put the time in write shorter essays with less information. But usually they recognize this and ask for a B or C—grades that often reflect their previous work.

Settling down to read these exams, I realize the personal mental health benefits for me. It's a great way to combat end-of-the-year fatigue, and it helps me understand what students have found important and memorable about the class, even as, on this last day, they learn a few more things about the process of writing.

Teacherless Talk: Impressions from Electronic Literary Conversations

Elaine Ware and Karen Murar

This article, written by Elaine Ware and Karen Murar about their collaborative teaching experience with high school juniors and college freshmen in Pennsylvania, was originally published in the summer 1998 issue of The Quarterly.

No matter how well intentioned we are as teachers, teacher-directed classroom discussions about literature are often reduced to an exercise in which the teacher asks a question, a student offers an answer, and then the teacher responds, often evaluating the response in the context of some preconceived notion about the work. It's all an orchestration of predictable idea sharing, with the teacher as choreographer of this literary vocal dance. In such a scenario, clearly the student is demonstrating what she knows rather than engaging in the natural give-and-take of real literary conversation. The teacher controls such communication, and usually only a small percentage of the class is comfortable enough to participate.

In contrast, our experience has been that when students take responsibility for creating their own questions about the literature, they move away from concerns about symbolnegro, language usage, and plot to more psychological concerns about why characters act the way they do and how characters' behavior may be similar to actual people the students know. In other words, students become involved in a more animated dialogue driven by students' personal needs and connections with the literature rather than enduring an academic discussion of literary conventions, which so intrigues teachers.

And so we authors—one of us teaching high school and the other teaching at the college level—started talking. And as we expressed to each other joint concern about the limitations of the traditional classroom in encouraging student-guided literary discussion, we quickly realized that computer technologies offered exciting possibilities for more enriching, authentic interaction for students. As a result of this conversation, we chose email as the vehicle that would both join two physically remote audiences and minimize the insecurities of face-to-face social dynamics. The success of this project has resulted in a five-year collaboration that expanded from an email-based endeavor to one that now includes video conferencing, Web page creation, and electronic publications. But the highlight of the project—through these technology partnerships—was that it freed the students to engage in truly independent conversations that spotlighted student voices and ideas.

~ Elaine Ware and Karen Murar, 2002

ear Dave, Mary, Melissa, and anyone else who might be watching over your shoulder (unbeknownst to you, of course),

Well, we were all just sitting around here twiddling our thumbs, and we realized that we all had this uncontrollable urge to email each and every one of you! At present, we don't feel like delving deep into August Wilson's Fences . . . so we won't. What we will do is tell you a little bit about ourselves, do a little dance, and make a little noise. Can you feel the beat? OK, well, I guess as I'm typing all these ramblings at present, I will go first. My name is Barry, and I am 16 years old (ain't life grand?). I am 5 foot 9, have brown hair, and have no visible scars. I enjoy playing chess, basketball, and street hockey (even though that particular sport has drawn more of my blood than any hospital will do prior to my death). I can't think of too much else to tell you right now, so I will now turn the keyboard over to John, mad accomplice that he is...

Hello, I'm John. Aren't these icebreakers strange? Well, I'm older than Barry (though not by much) and taller (by a lot). I have some small visible scars. I like Star Wars and Jack Kerouac and, oh yeah, comics too. Also of interest, Barry and I both work on a fanzine. It's pretty cool.

Well, folks (Hey, it's Barry again...) that's about all there is for now, so I suppose we shall retire for the evening. You folks take care and drive safely...

   ~ Barry and John

Hi Barry and John!

I'm Melissa, but I'm sure that came up across the top of this email. I'm an art major here at IUP. Specifically, my major is graphic design. Sorry I didn't get back to you sooner, but this is a very busy week for me. I have a humanities lit. test at 8 a.m. tomorrow. Then, I have a huge geography test on Friday. I studied for about three hours tonight. Well, I'm 5'6" (the last time I looked at my driver's license anyway) and I enjoy, well that's a tough thing to say. I work 2 jobs. Between classes, I work at Housing and Residence Life here on campus; then I work at the Ice Center on the weekends. And with being an art major, I don't have much free time. Well, I'd better go, it's 12:09 a.m., and I have a long day tomorrow on campus. Feel free to email me whenever you want. I check my email everyday, except I slack a little on the weekends with it. Talk to you later.

~ Melissa

With voices as distinctive as these, juniors at Gateway High School in Monroeville, a suburb of Pittsburgh, Pennsylvania, and sophomores in introductory literature at Indiana University of Pennsylvania (IUP), fifty miles away, began an email collaboration to discuss August Wilson's *Fences*, a play set in Pittsburgh in the late 1950s that focuses on the social and familial barriers experienced by the play's African American protagonist, Troy Maxson. The idea for this project came about when we—their instructors—met while participating in the Western Pennsylvania Writing Project Summer Institute. Through the institute, which each summer brings teachers together for several intense weeks of professional development and collaboration, we were reminded of the benefit of community in regard to reading, writing, and thinking. Based on our experiences there, we developed an idea for bridging our two schools to make students feel that they, too, were part of a wider community of readers and writers.

THE CAST

GATEWAY HIGH SCHOOL JUNIORS

Barry, Carol, Danielle, Derek, Faith, Jan, Jane, Jarad, Jeff, Jessica, John, Jordan, Kathy, Kelly, Megan, Patsy, Rochelle, Roxann, Sandra, Tricia, Selma, Surinder, Vincent

INDIANA UNIVERSITY OF PENNSYLVANIA SOPHOMORES

Amy, April, Beverly, Brad, Candace, Celia, Dave, Jason, Julie, Linda, Mary, Melissa, Michelle, Nadine, Pete, Samuel, Sharri, Susan, Sylvia

The idea began to take shape when, in comparing curricula before the start of the new school year, we discovered that both of us planned to teach the August Wilson play that first semester. With topic in hand, we discussed format and quickly settled on using email. Using email would get rid of most scheduling and logistical problems. But beyond this, we would soon discover, it would also prove to be a freeing, safe environment for the students. Email empowered students to analyze literature through cooperative peer dialogues.

With our overall plan carved out, we incorporated specific dates for the project into our academic calendars and went to work on the details. Because the high school students did not have school access to email, students who lived in the same area formed teams, receiving parental permission to use home computers. The college students had email access at four campus computer labs. A master list of email addresses was then compiled. (We suggest that teachers initially test the email addresses to ensure that connections can be made.) Our project required that a minimum of three exchanges of email correspondence take place within two weeks.

Rather than the typical teacher-led discussion, the project fostered student-generated conversation minus teacher facilitation. Students analyzed other literary pieces in class while they independently worked outside of class on the email project. Formal class discussion of the play did not occur until after students completed all email correspondence. However, as teachers, we functioned as troubleshooters when students made us aware of any problems they encountered with technology. Although we established the literary and technological framework, the literary conversations centered on student ideas rather than teacher instruction. Students were encouraged to write about anything in the play that they found interesting.

Since teachers were not the primary audience for the email discussions, students adapted their language and use of email technology to suit peers. Once the icebreakers established personal connections, students entered a language comfort zone, one much more akin to spoken conversation than to standard academic writing. Many students actually referred to their online communication as "talk." The college students tended to be spontaneous communicators, composing online, while the high school students first wrote individual reactions to the play in a dialectical journal and then further developed the interpretations in their emails. The student literary conversations that resulted—without teacher intervention—displayed the reading strategies teachers strive to achieve in the classroom, namely, predicting, questioning, clarifying, connecting, interpreting, and evaluating, all discussed in further detail in the following sections.

PREDICTING

Our students' predictions of the outcomes of Wilson's play were the result of close reading rather than haphazard guessing. Their predictions also revealed our students' knowledge of plot patterns, consistent characterizations, and social dynamics. Jason, for instance, in his first email forecast an important role for the character Troy:

I believe that in Fences, *Troy will be the character that we will want to follow and pay attention to. He sees the world as it was when he played baseball. He still has an open wound about how he was cheated out of money and how he was viewed as lower class because he is black. We see his inability to deal with the reality that the world is changing and that the black man is now starting to have equal rights and opportunities. We see this attitude when Troy and Rose discuss the future of Cory [their son]. Cory has Troy's athletic ability and has the potential of becoming a great ballplayer. . . . Troy's attitude is something that I believe we will want to trace and keep track of. He might change and let Cory try out for football or [he might] choose to not see the world as an ever changing and evolving place.*

Predictions, a component of problem solving, also served to motivate student reading, as illustrated in Amy's email:

The character that will really get hurt in the play is Cory. He has a chance to become something and Troy is trying to stop him. There seems to be resentment between Troy and Cory due to the fact that Cory has a chance that Troy never had. I am interested in getting right on to the next act so that I can see the continuation of this little saga.

Not all students articulated the evidence upon which they based their predictions as clearly as did Jason and Amy, but others were quite adept at internalizing clues that might foreshadow later events in the play. For example, Jessica, Rochelle, and Jane closed an email by asking, "Is something going on between Troy and that Alberta chick? Just wondering. Adios!"

QUESTIONING

Most students believe that asking questions suggests a vulnerability or lack of intelligence. In most classrooms, the teachers ask the questions—usually not a recipe for a real conversation. Student email questions, however, circumvent the need for teacher-centered questioning. Students engage in honest question-and-answer dialogue with a small group in a supportive social milieu. Email promotes risk taking as students experience the metamorphic process of shaping ideas through dialogue. Megan and her team experienced freedom to admit a lack of understanding when they asked Julie and Brad:

What do you think Gabe symbolizes in the play? We can't seem to figure out the purpose of him being there. He says all those weird things like

blowing the horn when it's time for judgment, and Lyons king of the
jungle. We know it's important, but we don't know why or how.

The freedom to question also frees students to explore alternative answers. At first students seemed cautious about their own insights, but confidence grew as they explored each others' ideas. They were liberated to dig deeply, without thinking they had to have all the answers. Real learning is, after all, the posing of a question and the search for an answer.

In our email collaboration, students employed questioning as an invitation. As Celia wrote to Kathy and Faith:

How do you feel about Troy and the way he treats his family? Do you
think he treats Rose with respect? Is he a loving father and husband?
What are your thoughts on Lyons and how he is always borrowing mon-
ey from Troy?

Such questioning promoted the conversational quality of dialogue since it is flattering to be asked, "What do *you* think?"

CLARIFYING

As students conversed, they engaged in many clarifying strategies. Specific textual references and quotations often supported and illuminated their assertions. While many students realized the need to explain and support their statements, others learned this lesson from their email partners who requested clarification, such as Nadine who wrote to Jan and Selma, "I didn't understand what you were getting at with Troy's fight against discrimination. In your next response, could you go into further detail?"

When the students replied to Nadine, they explained, "You mentioned that you didn't understand Troy's fight against discrimination at his level. Basically, we mean that Troy is not a Civil Rights activist or anything, but attempts to fight against the discrimination in the society around him that affect him, like his workplace and baseball." In the classroom, students might become defensive when asked to clarify their statements, but in the context of email, students accepted such requests as a normal part of interpersonal communication.

CONNECTING

Email provided students opportunities to connect literature to their lives, knowledge, and opinions as they might in ordinary conversation. Dave wrote to Roxann and Danielle, "Fences is starting out to be a very interesting play because of the native setting in Pittsburgh. That got my interest right off the bat." Wilson's references to specific places that students knew firsthand energized their attitude toward the entire project. As well, Wilson's baseball references to Josh Gibson, the Babe Ruth of the Negro League, inspired historical connections as students discussed prejudice issues of the 1950s. Beverly shared with Patsy and Jarad that she

> thought there was a deep-rooted prejudice towards white people and vice-versa throughout the play. . . . There is also much bitterness between Troy and the baseball league. I don't really know much about the negro baseball league so if you have any information you could pass down I would really appreciate it.

Elements of the play motivated students to research racial inequalities of the time period. They discovered information about the local Homestead Grays, whose players, like those of other Negro teams, were prohibited from playing in the all-white National Baseball League. Students also came to realize that the personal struggles of Satchel Page and Jackie Robinson within baseball mirrored the larger civil rights struggle within American society. Vincent and Surinder commented:

> . . . if blacks ever tried to challenge the inequities in sports, as well as all other aspects of African American life, they would greatly suffer. This brings up an important concept in the story: sports truly represented all aspects of life. The conflict in this story is not simply Cory's desire to play sports versus Troy's desire for him to acquire a secure job. Cory wants to challenge the discrimination prevalent in the time, whereas Troy truly cares for [his son] and wants to protect him from any danger that he may face in challenging that authority.

Jessica, Rochelle, and Jane connected the microcosm of the play to the macrocosm of society with this email:

> We felt that this [the play] also symbolized the slow progression of blacks through the 1950s and 60s. They didn't just all of a sudden break free of

the cycle of prejudice and segregation but made small improvements one step at a time over the generations.

Kelly, Carol, and Jordan reflected on the importance of such sharing:

Samuel, thanks for telling us some historical information about the time period the play was written in. It gave us a broader view of the play by helping us look at the events of the play in connection with the events going on in the world at the time.

The students also vicariously related to characters and contemplated their own values, peppering the correspondence with gender connections. One young man, Pete, empathized:

The story was really good, I thought. I felt bad for Cory. . . . I am sort of like him in athletics and I would have wanted the chance to go on and further my education and do what I have fun doing, too.

The women reacted strongly to Rose's actions as a 1950s woman and the sexual stereotyping regarding her role. Sylvia believed that "Troy was way out of line when he expected Rose to handle the 'other woman' thing just fine and be rational about it. . . . I know that I wouldn't be." Tricia's enthusiastic sanction "Go, Rose!" resulted in Melissa's response:

I agree with Tricia . . . I'd be so disgusted . . . I couldn't bring myself to talk to him either. . . . I was shocked when Troy asked Rose to raise the baby with him. . . . I don't get the impression men ever even thought about helping with a baby back in those days.

Kathy and Faith also reacted to the gender issue:

He treats his wife like a possession. Although it coincides with the attitudes of the time, it should not be an excuse. He cares about her but thinks of her as an inferior. He calls her "my woman," a very sexual comment. Similar sexual comments demonstrated a lack of respect for her.

Student email included literary connections as well. Sandra, whose first language is Spanish, compared Troy's friend, Bono, to "Don Quixote's Sancho Panza, his . . . sidekick who supports Troy's drinking and laughs at Troy's stupid jokes." Brad made another parallel: "The father-son relationship in *Fences* is almost exactly the same as the father-son relationship in *Death of a Salesman* because both sons are unemployed, lazy, and immature for their ages." Understanding family relationships in *Death of a Salesman* also served Dave in understanding family relationships in *Fences* when he proposed:

> *In* [Death of a Salesman] *the boys were raised full of hot air, to think they were perfect and better than anyone else, that they were always going to be top dogs. In* Fences, *it is clearly the opposite. Troy tries to teach his boys a hard work ethic . . . he discourages Lyons constantly for playing music and tells him to get a REAL job . . . Troy also discourages Cory. . .*

Melissa explored the same link:

> *I also think Lyons is a lot like Biff in* [Death of a Salesman]. *Did you guys ever read that? Well, in case you didn't, Biff is a man in his late 20s, early 30s, who doesn't know what to do with his life. He bounces from job to job, never really amounting to anything. Lyons reminds me of this because his only job seems to be playing in that band at the bars.*

Other students related their knowledge of television genres to their reading of the play. Three female high school students wrote:

> *The second act of* Fences *seemed like a soap opera. Troy was having a child with another woman while still living with Rose. Cory gets into a fight with Troy and leaves home. Troy dies.*

Two other high school juniors wrote, "Act I seemed very tranquil to the almost soap-opera like Act 2." Making such connections resulted in the students' own valuable contributions to the dynamic literary conversation.

INTERPRETING

Students' freedom to choose their topics for discussion led to rather fluent and creative interpretations of Wilson's characters, symbols, and theme rather than the sometimes mechanical and stilted literary analyses students produce in formal papers. Whereas students in the traditional classroom feel the need to prove that they have read the selection and understand the terminology by regaling the teacher with plot summaries and technical definitions, email frees them to share their interpretations and naturally apply literary terms as they communicate. The following exchanges illustrate student focus on characteriztion in *Fences*—in this case an analysis of a particularly enigmatic Gabriel who has a metal plate in his head as a result of a World War II injury:

> *Hi guys! It's us again. We're ready to start our second analysis of* Fences. *Let's start with an overview of Gabriel's character. We think it would be safe to assume that Gabe is comic relief. For example, when Troy told Rose about his affair, Gabe entered the scene. The scene was extremely tense, but Gabe added a distraction that allowed the reader to have an aesthetic distance from that very serious conversation. Gabe asked silly questions such as, 'Are you mad at me, Troy?' These questions seemed so out of place in the midst of the conversation taking place . ... We can't believe what Troy did to Gabe!!! How far will Troy go for Gabe's money?*
>   ~ Danielle and Roxann

> *Dear Danielle and Roxann,*
>
> *Hi again . . . I agree with what you said about Gabe. Troy committed him for the money. The way he treated him was wrong. I think Gabe needed Troy's love and Troy ends up contradicting himself. He says he needs to be free, but Gabe ends up locked up. That was wrong . . .*
>   ~ Candace

Most students discussed the motivations and psychological problems of the main characters. In addition, without being given specific instructions to apply critical theories, students experimented with feminist readings of the hus band-and-wife relationship, Marxist inquiries into the economics of the manual labor force, new critical interpretations of theme and imagery, new historical investigations into the Negro and National Baseball Leagues, as well as other approaches, thus bringing multiple perspectives to the play.

Building on the literary concepts learned in the classroom, students quite willingly took risks when presenting their ideas. Only occasionally did a student indicate insecurity about an interpretation with a statement such as Michelle's: "Boy, did I have to dig deep for that one. I hope you have not lost all faith in my intelligence." More often, students saw their exchanges as chances to work together, to interpret together, as Linda expressed when she wrote:

> *If either of you have more questions, feel free to email me anytime. You don't have to wait until you have your whole response. By doing this, it might help all of us to better understand this play.*

Collaboration was evident as our students socially constructed the meanings of the text during the give-and-take of email interpretations. Students not only eagerly shared their analyses but also frequently requested feedback about the plausibility of their interpretations when they asked, "Do you agree with the points I have made?" or remarked, "Well, let me know what you think of my response." Inviting constructive criticism revealed that students were willing to consider the opinions and evidence of other students in their ongoing analysis of Wilson's play. Jeff and Derek illustrated this when they commented to Sharri, "Jeff and I will look at what you've said and add it to our insight of *Fences*. You have some pretty interesting stuff written down, and I'll take it into consideration."

EVALUATING

Responding to interpretations naturally led to peer evaluations. Students often saw their views mirrored back in different words, thus validating their original ideas. Such agreements often resulted in elaboration that strengthened an interpretation. Here, for example, is Nadine introducing her interpretation of a fence as symbol:

> *I think that [a fence] represents something different for each member of the family. Rose wants her husband and son to work together and build a fence around their house. Troy and Cory, on the other hand, are putting off building this fence. I believe that Troy doesn't want the fence because he will feel caged in like prison . . .*

Jan and Selma reply to Nadine:

> *We agree with you about the symbolic title. In addition, we have found fences to symbolize the way that Troy has built up barriers against expressing emotions and/or feeling the pain around him.*

While agreement and elaboration were most common, students did feel free to interpret the text from multiple perspectives that sometimes led to disagreement. Disagreements developed students' critical thinking skills because they had to reconsider the text and pull out more persuasive evidence. Students also developed tact and diplomacy, despite their opposing viewpoints, as Jason illustrated in his response to Jeff and Derek:

40

Now about the part of showing us social classes that I read in your last email, I find that if in fact the author wanted to give us a taste of social structure and classes, he would have done it differently. I am no analyst so don't take my words as law or what is right. I have been wrong before. I think though if he wanted to get across the social classes and how the different classes were treated, he would of given us another family or neighborhood to compare the social conditions with. I just don't see this happening. He concentrates on this one family and their troubles, which brings me to believe that the main theme is embedded within the family and how it operates or how it is dysfunctional. The conflict between Troy and his children support the idea of family related crisis and hardships.

CONCLUSION

The email project socially liberated our students from constraints that tend to stifle individuals in usual class interactions. Students who might usually hesitate to be active discussion participants experienced a lack of self-consciousness in email and a motivating comfort level. Some of our students, however, were novice email users who felt frustrated by the new writing experience, as Susan explained:

I felt that the total atmosphere of trying to sort through my thoughts in a computer lab was very wrong for me. I would be thinking about what I wanted to write, and all of a sudden, something would go wrong with the system, or my screen would do something weird, or anything else that could possibly go wrong. I can't work with distractions, and when I'm forced to, my work suffers.

Certainly teachers as well as students are in a period of transition as they learn to use email to expand the classroom. Until computer classrooms with email access are routinely available in all schools, teachers will receive mixed feedback about email projects, as April illustrated:

In general, the whole email idea is good. It forces people to learn how to do it, and it keeps communication lines open. The biggest problem was availability of computers. If you live off campus and don't have a hook up at home, it can be an annoying challenge.

While a few students expressed reluctance, others, like Brad, acknowledged the possibilities such technology now offers:

The mind-boggling innovation of email has gone far beyond what I had originally thought it would turn out to be. Here I am, now, giving my assessment of computer communications, when apparently it was yesterday that I sat in my grade school class learning how to "load" on an old green screen Apple computer. I couldn't even imagine back then that technology would lead to this.

For most, bridging the two schools birthed an excitement for addressing a new audience, an audience that did not prejudge the writer. Most students responded enthusiastically:

These email sessions are very helpful in deeply delving into the story because they make us analyze not only our views on the play, but also the views of three other people. It really feels like we know the characters because of all this analysis, and we have such strong feelings towards them.
        ~ Danielle and Roxann

Melissa seems to have opened up a good dialogue between the three of us and the students from IUP. She's brought up many good points from Fences *and showed us a different way to think about some points from the story. It was interesting.*
        ~ Barry, John, Tricia

Imagination coupled with today's ever-expanding technology offers unlimited possibilities for improving our classrooms. Students can now converse without time and distance restraints. Networking students and teachers across states and even countries can make the classroom one of the most exciting places to be. As Barry, John, and Tricia concluded, "Hoorah Hoorah for email!"

Author to Author: How Text Influences Young Writers

Dina Sechio DeCristofaro

Written by Dina Sechio DeCristofaro about her teaching experience with fifth grade students in Scituate, Rhode Island, this article was originally published in the spring 2001 issue of The Quarterly.

A few years ago I had the opportunity to join a teacher research group, the basis of which was exploring classroom issues in depth. I had already been conducting my own classroom research informally for some time, as I wanted to make my writing workshop more effective, but I saw the research group as an opportunity to look at my teaching in an organized, structured way. So, along with twelve other teachers, I eagerly joined the group.

Within the structure of the group, I began to think about the student writing samples that I had been collecting for the last few years. I looked at the collection again—each piece intriguing for one reason or another—and wondered about the connections I saw between the students' writing and the books we had read in class. Recognizing the importance of providing good models for children, I regularly used literature during writing lessons, but I had not thought much about the specific effects that practice might have on the students' writing.

My research question was taking shape: How does the work of professional writers influence the composition of young writers? Over the course of the next year, I recorded many different links between student writing and the work of professional authors. At the same time, through the group, I began making connections with other researchers pursuing related topics. Specifically, I noticed a connection between my study and the work of two other teachers from our site. In 1998, out of an ensuing collaboration, we presented a workshop about our research entitled "'Can We Copy?' Studying the Intertextuality of Our Classrooms" at the annual National Council of Teachers of English (NCTE) conference in Nashville, Tennessee.

Out of these collaborations—with the teacher research group as well as with the more intimate group—came this article. It was my first foray into writing about my work for publication, and I was pleased to have it published in the National Writing Project's journal, *The Quarterly*. But even more rewarding was the positive experience of our collaborative efforts. In many ways our work together reflected the same issues we were exploring independently in our students' work. And although the word *intertextuality* was new to me, exploring the concept with colleagues opened the door to a new perspective on collaboration and borrowing that helped me reframe old ideas about originality and plagiarism. And best of all, as I listened to my colleagues' discoveries, I found that I, like my students, was able to move with more authority and conviction into the territories I was exploring.

~ *Dina Sechio DeCristofaro, 2002*

The writer studies literature. . . . He is careful of what he reads, for that is what he will write.

~ Annie Dillard

everal months into my exploration of how my fifth grade students' reading was influencing their writing, I conducted a survey. I asked questions like, "Where do you get ideas for your writing?" "Do you ever get ideas from stories you read?" "Have you ever tried to copy a famous author's style?"

More than half of the students commented that they got ideas from reading. Some said ideas came from movies or television, and many were influenced by their friends' ideas.

And while students generally agreed that it was okay to get ideas from an author for their writing, I was surprised by several of the responses regarding the question about copying an author's style. To these students, the idea of copying was not acceptable. Simon wrote, "I never cheate." Jack stated, "That's playgerrisum."

I know that in some way I am responsible for those attitudes. Earlier in the school year, I had spent several weeks teaching the process of how to write a research paper for social studies. I had emphasized the importance of paraphrasing when taking notes. I told them not to copy. Simon and Jack had confused copying, a practice I very much discourage, with a practice I encourage: an immersion in the work of accomplished writers that allows students to assimilate the skills, ideas, and creative direction of these authors either consciously or by osmosis.

Since 1994, when I became involved with the Rhode Island Writing Project, I have been researching the reading-writing connection. Even before this involvement, I knew that I could help students understand such features as story elements and writing strategies through illustrating these elements in the work of professional authors. For instance, after explaining the concept of internal conflict during a writing workshop focus lesson, I might select *Ira Sleeps Over*, a picture book by Bernard Waber. In this story, the protagonist is a young boy who is invited to sleep at his friend's house. He struggles with the question of whether or not to bring his teddy bear with him, afraid his friend will laugh if he does yet afraid to sleep without the bear. For some time, I had used picture books to provide students with effective examples of writing features such as imagery, characterization, and setting.

Now I wanted to look in a more formal way at the link between the reading my students were exposed to and how they were writing. What effect, I wondered, did the books students were reading and the stories they were experiencing through read-alouds have on their writing? When I began my research, I suspected I would find that students borrowed topics, used particular words, or emulated what I loosely refer to as "author style." After looking at the writing more analytically, I was able to see more clearly a host of connections between the authors' works and the subject, tone, genre, diction, and rhetoric of my students' work.

SUBJECTS

One read-aloud that had an impact on student writing was *Grandad Bill's Song*, by Jane Yolen. In this moving story, Yolen's protagonist mourns the loss of his grandfather as other family members share their memories of the man as they knew him. Dealing with the loss of a loved one as it does, *Grandad Bill's Song* can be a difficult story to read aloud. The last time I read it, I had to ask a student to finish the reading because I was too choked up to continue. Some of my students experienced the same emotional reaction, and we had a lengthy discussion afterward about why some of us responded the way we had. We talked about death. We talked about how a good book can make you cry sometimes. It was a powerful literary experience for them and for me.

When writing workshop commenced, I did not require students to write on the topic of death and loss. Writing workshop for me is about choice, and I know my students appreciate this crucial element of our writing environment. ("This class is like 'Choose Your Own Adventure!'" Dylan blurted out one day.) But, without prodding, Anna began "All About My Great Grandpa." Unlike Yolen's story, Anna was reporting not a firsthand experience but a secondhand memory of her great-grandfather's death as it was related by her mother, who was ten years old when the man died. When Anna shared that memory, students were moved by her story, and, at the same time, Anna's friend Sheila opted to write about her grandmother who had passed away the previous year. In both these cases, writing topics were chosen as a direct result of the students' exposure to *Grandad Bill's Song*.

TONE

Another book I selected to read aloud was *The Stinky Cheese Man and Other Fairly Stupid Tales* by Jon Scieszka. Scieszka adopts a tone of irreverent humor to parody the genre of the classic fairy tale. Most students love his approach. As I shared this book, I spotlighted some of the elements of the fairy tale that Scieszka was treating lightly. The book includes stories such as "The Princess and the Bowling Ball" and "The Really Ugly Duckling." The students had previously heard other Scieszka books, including *The Frog Prince Continued* and *The True Story of the Three Little Pigs*.

That week, again without my intervention, two students began writing tales similar in tone to Scieszka's. Marty started "Chicken Licken Gets Fried," a humorous account of his title character's ill-fated trip to Kentucky. Tammy worked on "The Princess and the Porcupine." I was amused at how the attitude of Scieszka's work was reflected in Tammy's writing:

> *Once upon a time, there was a stupid prince who was looking for a stupid princess. Now he was not just a person who was called names. He was really stupid. He decided that if he wanted a pure princess who was kind, he had to see if she could feel a porcupine through ten mattresses.*

> *He found a princess who was kind and loyal, but he needed to do the porcupine test. He found a porcupine, ten mattresses, and told the princess she had to feel the porcupine. Well, that night, the porcupine jumped out from under the mattresses, bit the princess on the butt, and ran away.*

> *In the morning, the princess said, "Yeah, I felt the porcupine. He bit me."*

> *The princess left and the prince lived unhappily ever after.*

During peer conferences, a few other students became interested in Marty's and Tammy's writing. They asked if they could form a small group and work together. I was beginning to see a pattern that would occur repeatedly as I observed students making connections between reading and writing. The children were being influenced not only by the professional writers they were reading, but also by the writing of their classmates. The short stories that resulted from this venture included "Lucky Ducky and the Four Eggs," "Hippie Locks and The Three Bears," and "The Melted Cheese Man and the Nachos."

I was noting something of a chain reaction. Marty and Tammy were inspired by the original stories I read, and other students were motivated to similar projects after listening to Marty and Tammy read their creations. In *Writing: Teachers and Children at Work*, Donald Graves suggests, "No distinctions should be made between the reading of children's writing and the writing of professionals. Both are treated as important writing" (1983, 76). When Marty and Tammy shared their stories aloud, their texts were important enough to inspire their classmates.

GENRE AND STYLE

For children, alphabet books are a familiar genre. Most kids experience them in their earliest years, but Jerry Pallotta's books make clear that there are alphabet books and there are alphabet books. His informative texts are colorfully illustrated, with one alphabet letter per page, a structure that is easy for children to imitate. Here are a few excerpts from *The Ocean Alphabet Book* by Pallotta:

> *E is for Eel. Eels are slimy! Eels are long and thin like snakes. If you do not like to hold snakes, then you probably would not like to hold Eels.*

> *We cannot think of any fish whose names begin with the letter X! Can you?*

> *Oops, we found one! X is for Xiphias gladius (pronounced—Ziphias). This is the scientific name for Swordfish.* (Pallotta 1986)

Borrowing Pallotta's take on the alphabet genre, Joel wrote "ABC Sports," which includes the following:

> *H is for the Hartford Whalers. The Hartford Whalers are a hockey team, even though they are not very good.*

> *Q is for Quarterback. A Quarterback is a position in football. The Quarterback throws passes and hands the ball to the running back.*

> *T is for the Texas Rangers. The Texas Rangers are a baseball team in Texas. They are having a heck of a season.*

> *X is for the X Cleveland Browns. They are the X Cleveland Browns because they moved to Baltimore.*

Joel illustrated his alphabet book with the help of two classmates. Other alphabet books started popping up: "The Animal Alphabet Book," "The Fruit and Vegetable Alphabet Book," "The ABC Book About School." Were they modeled after Jerry Pallotta's books or Joel's? I believe that both authors influenced the students in my class.

Looking beyond Joel's borrowing of Pallotta's form, I see that Joel also emulates Pallotta's conversational style. Some of his pages, like the one about the quarterback, simply give information, as Pallotta does with his page on the fiddler crab. On another page Pallotta informs his readers that eels are slimy and that they might not want to hold one. Joel, in a similar fashion, gives his opinion about a particular hockey team (who happened to be having a less-than-perfect year). He later lets us know that the Texas Rangers are "having a heck of a season," and he also has some fun with X, as Jerry Pallotta did in his book. Shelley Harwayne notes that students "frequently choose to borrow language patterns from individual picture books" (1992, 298).

SILENT READING INFLUENCES PUBLIC WRITING

I was seeing ways that students, after hearing stories read aloud, are influenced in making decisions about subjects, tone, genre, and style. But much of the reading students do in my class is silent reading in books of their own choosing. I was curious about the effect that reading in this context has on student writing. When A.J., an avid reader, shared his story "The Cry of the Wolf" during a conference, I tried to plumb the sources of this sophisticated piece of writing. Here are some paragraphs from A.J.'s work:

> The young wolf sat on a rock sniffing the wind as it blew across his wet nose. He could pick out the sticky-sweet smell of the Spruce Tree. But the strongest smell was the approaching snow.
>
> Without warning one of the pups from his pack knocked him from his rock. A second pup joined the playful fighting and nipped at his fur.
>
> The wolf allowed the pups to charge into him. The[y] weighed only forty pounds, much too small to really hurt him. Besides, it was his turn to watch them while their parents rested.
>
> Just then, a piercing howl interrupted their playing. Fifty yards away the alfa male was pacing nervously. Back and forth he went. Suddenly, he

stops. His body was stiff, his ears shot forward. He stopped to look at the mountains. Then he raised his head and howled. His mate joined him, their voices blended in an eerie cry up the mountain.

The caribou herd, their only source of food, was a gray smudge in the distant light. The caribou had also smelled the snow and were moving to a new feeding ground.

I discovered that A.J.'s piece was generated by reading, but not a single piece of reading. Graves states that "when information is the classroom focus, and literature is the center of activity, children will work with a broad assortment of reading materials" (1983, 67).

When I asked A.J. about his process when writing this piece, he told me he had originally become interested in the topic of wolves from a book he had borrowed from the library. After he decided to write this story, he borrowed several more books, some of which he read during reading workshop but most of which he read at home. A.J. also looked for information in *National Geographic*. He read some fiction as well, mostly books by Gary Paulsen, and he had just finished *Call of the Wild* by Jack London. In writing workshop, A.J. was able to dig deeply into his own literary resources in the way Harwayne describes: "[Students] need to call upon their own internalized sense of what good writing is and to recall those works that have affected them as readers. They need to form mentor relationships with the writers they admire, trying to do what these writers have done" (1992, 154). It is evident that A.J. formed those mentor relationships and also knew where to find information that makes his writing more effective.

In an equally challenging endeavor, Sam attempted to write a story like *Hatchet* by Gary Paulsen. In *Hatchet*, the protagonist, Brian Robeson, flies in a single-engine plane to visit his father. When the pilot has a heart attack and dies, Brian must land the plane and then survive alone in the wilderness. His only aid is a hatchet his mother gave to him before he left. Sam's story, "The Knife," relates the adventure of a boy named James who gets knocked unconscious while walking in the woods with his dog. When he regains consciousness, he realizes he is lost and must survive on his own. Fortunately, James remembers that he has his pocketknife with him.

Looking at Sam's writing, I saw obvious similarities to Paulsen's work. Although Sam intentionally set out to write a story like *Hatchet*, he was not cognizant of all the parallels between his story and Paulsen's. Here is an excerpt from Sam's piece:

> Then he sensed what he needed most. Food. He looked at the bushes.
> What he saw was beautiful. Berries were everywhere. For the next hour
> James ate as many berries as he could. When he couldn't eat another
> berry he crawled into his shelter and fell asleep.

Though not verbatim, the passage reflects Sam's connection to Paulsen's text in several ways. The idea itself is taken directly from *Hatchet*. Paulsen writes,

> The slender branches went up about twenty feet and were heavy, droop-
> ing with clusters of bright red berries. They were half as big as grapes
> but hung like grapes and when Brian saw them, glistening red in the
> sunlight, he almost yelled. . . . there was such a hunger in him, such an
> emptiness, that he could not stop and kept stripping branches and eating
> berries by the handful. . . .

Sam's diction and sentence structure are also reflections of Paulsen's style. The word shelter, for instance, is used several times in *Hatchet*. One-word sentences appear often as well. Paulsen writes, "And now, he thought, if I just had something to eat. Anything." In an earlier scene, he writes, "They would find him. Maybe not tomorrow but soon. Soon. Soon." Sam writes, "Then he sensed what he needed most. Food."

Typically in fifth grade, I would be emphasizing the need for students to avoid sentence fragments. I did not teach Sam how a fragment can, in fact, become an effective structure. Gary Paulsen did.

In all the situations I have mentioned, the students were aware, at least on some level, that they were emulating a particular author. When I asked Tammy where she got her idea for her story "Evil Time," however, she said the idea just came to her. She was not aware of how much her story resembles Avi's *City of Light, City of Dark* until I brought the similarities to her attention during a writing conference. In Avi's book, the characters are in search of a token that will save the people from darkness. Tammy's plot revolves around finding the Golden Mushroom so Time will not be frozen forever. In *City of Light, City of Dark* a text within a text appears, explaining the treaty between those who hold the power and the people who must search for the token. Tammy also effectively uses a text within a text in her writing, as shown in figure 1.

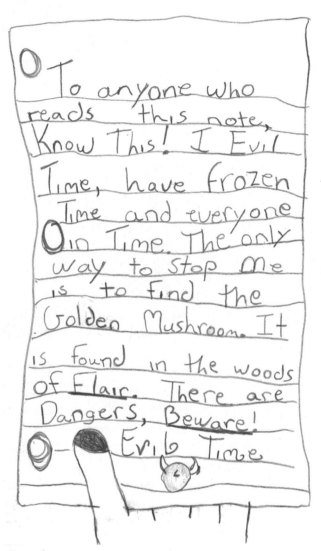

Figure 1

Tammy was surprised to see how much her story was like Avi's. I was not. She had read Avi's book twice.

Even though I was becoming increasingly aware of the ways professional writers influence some students' writing, I was also coming to view the whole phenomenon of borrowing as more complicated than I originally had seen it. Why do some students appear to make connections between reading and writing while others do not? Interestingly, both Simon and Jack, the students who considered borrowing as copying and plagiarism, had difficulty reading. As I think about it, I cannot recall having any outstanding writers who were struggling readers. Perhaps this will be a topic for further study. I am also curious about how much borrowing was conscious and how much was not. While I strongly believe that students should choose their own writing topics, I wonder if their topics are just as likely to choose them. Student texts are affected by many factors: conversations, teacher modeling, student writing, and, of course, reading. It appears that some students are very much aware of their borrowings. Most, though, are not cognizant of such intertextuality.

As a result of my classroom research, I have strengthened my belief in the reading and writing workshop as an effective model of classroom instruction. When students are immersed in a literature-rich environment, they are exposed to many teachers of writing: the authors I read to them, those they select to read on their own, and the student authors in our classroom. Student writing takes on characteristics of all those authors. According to Zemelman and Daniels,

> Researchers and teachers are discovering more of the connections between reading and writing. Of course, reading provides specific data and topics for immediate writing projects, but it can do much more than that. At a deeper level, immersion in certain kinds of reading helps all writers assimilate the tone, flavor, structure, norms, and rhetorical strategies of particular genres of writing, a prewriting activity that's no less effective for being osmotic and unconscious. Further, reading helps students identify themselves as fellow writers. (1988, 143)

Finally, if writing is so strongly influenced by what students read and by the stories they hear, surrounding children with quality literature should be our first objective. As Graves writes, "All children need literature. Children who are authors need it even more" (1983, 67).

REFERENCES

Avi. 1993. *City of Light, City of Dark*. New York: Scholastic.

Dillard, Annie. 1989. *The Writing Life*. New York: Harper & Row.

Graves, Donald. 1983. *Writing: Teachers and Children at Work*. Portsmouth, NH: Heinemann.

Harwayne, Shelley. 1992. *Lasting Impressions: Weaving Literature into the Writing Workshop*. Portsmouth, NH: Heinemann.

London, Jack. 1960. *Call of the Wild*. Racine, WI: Whitman Publishing.

Pallotta, Jerry. 1986. *The Ocean Alphabet Book*. Watertown, MA: Charlesbridge.

Paulsen, Gary. 1987. *Hatchet*. New York: Puffin Books.

Scieszka, Jon. 1992. *The Stinky Cheese Man and Other Fairly Stupid Tales*. New York: Viking.

———. 1991. *The Frog Prince Continued*. New York: Viking.

———. 1989. *The True Story of the Three Little Pigs*. New York: Viking.

Waber, Bernard. 1972. I*ra Sleeps Over*. Boston: Houghton Mifflin.

Yolen, Jane. 1994. *Grandad Bill's Song*. New York: Philomel Books.

Zemelman, Steven, and Harvey Daniels. 1988. *A Community of Writers: Teaching Writing in the Junior and Senior High School*. Portsmouth, NH: Heinemann.

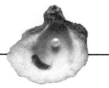

Those Words Just Jumped Out at Me

Reading inspires creative teaching

Staging Learning: The Play's the Thing

Jean Hicks and Tim Johnson

This article was written by Jean Hicks and Tim Johnson about their teaching experience with middle school and high school students in Louisville, Kentucky. It was originally published in the summer 2000 issue of The Quarterly.

How can students ground their writing about important social issues in their own lives and voices? We know the answer is not in textbook assignments or in one-size-fits-all writing prompts. It is in the daily lives of our young writers. We strive to engage students in a process that helps them identify the issues that concern them, filter their reflections through their own experiences, and use these experiences to articulate their perspectives.

In 1997, as a new director of a writing project site, I set out to find tools to help students write short, dialogue-filled scripts about their lives. While immersing myself in relevant professional materials, I was inspired by *Puppet Plays*, a timeless video featuring third grade writing project teacher Margaret Grant of Missoula, Montana. Grant suggests that partners can construct a dialogue using strips of paper that they attach quickly to a blank script.

Grant's strategy for physically producing scripts provided a way to manage the writing, but it didn't tell us how to find relevant content for the plays, especially plays that could be drafted quickly. That missing piece was supplied through the conceptual work of Errol Bray in *Playbuilding: A Guide for Group Creation of Plays with Young People*. One of Bray's ideas is to create a class play with a number of scenes that all focus on a single theme. The serendipitous combination of these two resources resulted in a strong demonstration lesson that we have used in many professional development sessions. We have honed it in classrooms with middle and high school students, and our colleagues have used this activity successfully with students in upper elementary grades as well.

Below, we join a scene in progress, developed using the process we call Post-it Note Playwriting.

~ Jean Hicks, 2002

*D*amon grabs a stapler, flips it open, and begins to talk into his car phone. He and Chris are in the front seat (two wooden chairs), and two other students, Brandy and Crystal, who are playing the roles of their dates, are in the back (two more chairs). Chris interrupts Damon's improvised phone conversation:

CHRIS: *It's been a long day. Let's go clubbin' tonight.*

DAMON: *What club should we go to?*

CHRIS: *What about the Ghetto Rose?*

CRYSTAL: *No, we're not going to the Ghetto Rose. Let's go to Club X-Cubed.*

BRANDY: *Yeah, we don't wanna go to the Rose because they always shootin'. We goin' to Club X.*

CHRIS: *Naw, man, they don't even serve liquor there.*

DAMON: *Plus the chicken wings are terrible, too!*

CRYSTAL: *Damon, you are always worried about the food!*

BRANDY: *We ain't even gotta go to no club. Let's go out to eat or somethin', since can't nobody come up with which club to go to.*

CHRIS. *Well, I guess we can go to Club X. But first, let's drink this fifth of Hennessey.*

In less time than it takes to watch an *NYPD Blue* rerun, four African American high school seniors created four characters, each distinct, each with accompanying body postures and accents. In slice-of-life vernacular they crafted a drama, highlighting the tension that, to their minds, exists between males who desire to be boastful and live on the edge and females who assert quiet wisdom and urge caution.

These lines were scribbled on Post-it notes as part of a process that allows an entire class to draft and perform scenes for a thematic play during a ninety-minute period. This particular scene was one of several that explored, from the unique perspective of the writers, facets of peer pressure. All of these scenes give students a chance to voice, in a nonthreatening way, issues important to their lives.

INITIATING THE PROCESS

We begin by inviting groups of students to work together to create scenes for a thematic play using a method that we adapted, as mentioned above, using the work of Errol Bray. The idea is to create group interest by having the class brainstorm topics, choosing one of particular interest to them. Once the students select a theme on which to concentrate their writing efforts, each small group creates its own unique dramatization of an aspect relating to it. A single theme, such as jealousy, might be treated in as many different ways as there are groups.

Thus the structure of a theme play differs from the more familiar exposition: rising action, climax, falling action, and resolution. Instead, the theme play depends on the cumulative effect created by looking at a single issue from a variety of angles. We have sometimes introduced our students to this concept by discussing with them the structure of movies and plays like *Twilight Zone* and *Plaza Suite*—works that involve a collection of vignettes under a larger umbrella theme. Each group's task, then, will be to develop a scene, illustrating one facet of the theme.

CHOOSING THE THEME

In choosing a theme, different approaches seem to work for different age groups. Middle-schoolers and even ninth-graders often have a difficult time distinguishing between a topic and a theme. When students come up with topics, such as sports, instead of themes—those global abstract concepts that connect topics—we brainstorm with them, pushing them to larger ideas:

JEAN: *So everybody has had some experiences with sports? Do you play them or watch them? [Several voices respond: "Play." "Watch." "Both."] So why do you play and watch? What makes sports interesting to you?*

DONNIE: *Somebody's gonna win.*

JEAN: *And somebody will lose?*

DONNIE: *Yeah.*

JEAN: *Why do you care? Why does anybody care?*

SHONTAY: *'Cause we like them. 'Cause it's a surprise.*

MICHAEL: *'Cause they've worked for it, they've earned it. You wanna see who's the best.*

JEAN: *So what's really behind the attraction of sports? Is it what they play or how they play?*

DONNIE: *Kinda both, but more how they play.*

JEAN: *Why?*

MICHAEL: *That's what you can't know. You can know a team's good, but they could be against somebody better or against somebody who is just getting better, but you don't know it until they're pitted against each other. That's the fun.*

JEAN: *Would it be fun if everything were made equal and everybody played the same? Or if you always had a really strong team always against a really weak team?*

DEANDRE: *Naw, man, who'd care? Teams gotta be able to compete or there's no point.*

JEAN: *Oh, so it's competition that makes sports what it is.*

DEANDRE: *Yeah.*

JEAN: *So could that really be our theme, competition? Do you see how that's bigger than just "sports"? What else involves competition? Do people compete for grades? When I was in school, everyone was out for the top score. You wanted to do better than the next guy. Do you compete for grades?*

ANNELLE: *Grades? Not much. But sometimes I compete against me, against how I been doing.*

JEAN: *What else do people compete for?*

VARIOUS STUDENTS: *Jobs. Money. Prizes.*

JEAN: *What about things that you can't touch? What about attention? How do people compete for attention?*

Our discussion continued as we examined each of the topics on the board: sports, teachers, school, bullies, brothers/sisters, summer vacation, music, and having fun. Our discussions of a new topic borrowed from things we'd noticed earlier, which helped students broaden their understanding of the concept of theme. For example, our discussion of sports helped us see that a fight with one's sister connected to the larger theme of sibling rivalry.

Older students work through the theme selection process much more quickly, easily generating abstract terms important to them when asked to suggest themes. They'll suggest, for instance, alienation, racism, peer pressure, and love. The brainstorming that follows allows them to make these abstractions concrete, as they work from the more general topic to a more specific situation that represents a possible approach to a dramatization of the theme.

RACISM

economic: *discrimination and segregation on the job*

educational: *attendance quotas*

voluntary: *blacks have black friends, whites have white friends*

PEER PRESSURE

sex, breaking the law, conformity vs. being yourself, drugs, alcohol, clothes, music

Specific topics, such as first day of school, first dates, and family reunions, can be fun to experiment with but tend to elicit stereotypical responses unless they can be related to larger themes. Relating them to a particular theme helps the students begin to focus on a particular approach to dramatizing the situation they finally choose. This helps them in determining a more significant purpose to their writing. In this way, the first day of school can be presented as a child's coming to see the importance of family support when she or he faces new situations. Since the idea is to have groups develop scenes that could be presented consecutively, abstract themes provide the widest array of possibilities. One of the most successful thematic plays developed through this process focused on the generation gap. We tried to avoid the predictable kinds of commentaries that involved adults downplaying teens' life crises. One scene provided a gap-narrowing counterpoint, portraying today's teens making the shocking discovery that some of their music was played thirty years ago. The most effective effort, however, involved one character berating another over loud music, strange hair, short skirts, late nights, and loose morals. The audience was surprised to learn in the last line of the scene that they'd seen a teen lecturing her newly divorced mother.

CONNECTING TO THE THEME

After the theme has been established, students usually write for about ten minutes, summoning memories, ideas, and experiences related to it. We put the emphasis on the personal. Left to their own devices, inexperienced writers often resort to reproducing television and movie scenes they have seen. Borrowing from the media feels safer; as writers, they will not have to further develop characters or plots or defend the quality of either to their peers. When students frame their connections in personal terms they eliminate this temptation and promote the kind of risk taking that leads to growth in writing.

While we have sometimes had students share their writing in small groups, it speeds the process to ask instead for five or six students to share with the whole class. Involving everyone in the discussion helps the students focus on a narrow slice of the theme that might make a good scene. As each student shares, we invite the class to help create a title for the material being read and identify a specific aspect of the theme it embodies. In one middle school class that was considering the theme of sibling rivalry, potential scenes included:

I Had It First (competing for family resources)

Calling In the Troops (tattling to Mom or Dad or caregiver)

More Than Sticks and Stones (name-calling, teasing, ridiculing)

Battle Scars (wounds that recall famous brother-sister fights)

Ganging Up (one sibling is always the underdog; leads to explosions)

Fooled Ya (practical jokes, taking advantage of a sibling, especially younger ones)

He Ain't Heavy, He's My Brother (happy ending—I can beat him up, but you'd better not!)

STARTING THE SCRIPT

We encourage groups to form quickly, perhaps at tables or by way of the natural clustering that occurs as teens choose their territories in the classroom. Groups of three of four seem to work best, although older students have successfully involved as many as five or six actors. Sometimes groups form around one of the scenes we brainstormed earlier. Most groups choose one of the scenes named during our exploration of the theme, although some come up with a new angle that wasn't on our original list.

Next, each group member develops a character. The member will choose a name, age, persona, and so on, subject to revision as the dramatization progresses. Allowing the students to change helps them enter the writing phase willing to take greater risks. They realize they can "edit" their characters and their dialogue, situations, and so on. Since they have selected the scene together, their choices are necessarily limited to characters that might logically be found in the situation. They pick up on this with little or no direction, perhaps because characters typically arise from their own lives. In the passage at the beginning of this article, for example, the class had chosen the theme of peer pressure. Damon, Chris, Crystal, and Brandy knew they wanted to develop a scene exploring the issue of teen drinking. They quickly decided to become couples who were double-dating, in part because there were two guys and two girls in the group, but also because they knew from experience that the pressure to drink would be greater in a group setting. They could just as easily have elected to develop a much different scene that included different characters such as a bouncer, bartender, or liquor store clerk.

Although we suggest that the groups develop the situation first and then the characters, some do the opposite. We don't object, since part of the purpose of the exercise is to encourage students to try something new, decide what is or isn't working, and make the necessary adjustments to the material. Often a scene must be changed because students decide the characters don't fit, or a character is changed because the group has become more enamored of the scene they developed than of holding on to a particular character.

One caveat is that a scene must take place in a single setting and that it lasts between a few seconds and a maximum of ten minutes. The characters can enter and exit as needed or be on stage simultaneously, but the action must be confined to one place and one short time period. These rules make it possible to develop and share the play quickly, and they also eliminate some of the problems that students create for themselves by trying to make their scenes too complex.

After group members have developed their characters or scenes, they put the Post-its to work. We give each student in the group about six colored Post-it notes. The lined index-card type is perfect. It's simplest if each character has a different color, so we buy the packs that have yellow, green, pink, orange, and blues (available at office supply stores). It has proven to be key for each student to physically hold his or her own Post-its.

JEAN: *Okay, you've each got your character, right? Who's who?*

ROB: *I'm Jack, the gang leader.*

JEROME: *I'm Tony, his brother.*

JEAN: *Younger or older?*

JEROME: *Two, three years younger, I guess.*

ANGEL: *I'm Desiree, Jack's girlfriend.*

JEAN: (handing each a stack of Post-its) *Here's orange for Jack's lines, green for Tony's, and yellow for Desiree's. That way you can tell your lines apart at a glance and move them around or throw them away if you change your mind. So how will the scene start?* [Silence.] *Who'll speak first?*

ANGEL: *I could come up and say, "Hey, Jack, you were s'posed to pick me up after school today!" I could be kinda mad.*

JEAN: *Okay, put that down on your note. What will you say, Jack?*

ROB: *I don't take nothin' from her, so I blow her off.*

JEAN: *How?*

ROB: *I can say, "You know I've got better things to do than play taxi for you."*

JEAN: *Write that down.*

ROB: *She's not finished yet.*

JEAN: *Doesn't matter. You can each write at the same time, as soon as you have a line you want to try. That way no one has to sit around. Just say the line out loud. Then somebody else in the scene can be thinking of a response. Plus if they've heard it, they can help you if you forget exactly how you planned to say your line. So Jack's got better things to do; what could come next?*

ANGEL (putting her first line on the blank script): *I could come back with something like, "Yeah, well you've got plenty of time to . . . hmm, what would he be doing?"*

ROB: *I'm hangin' out, makin' plans, figurin' how I'm gonna stay on top.*

JEROME: *Maybe some other gang is challenging us, movin' in on us.*

ANGEL: *No, I've got it. Rob's been seein' some other girl, at least that's what I hear. "You've got plenty of time to go over to Renee's. Destiny saw you there last night, so don't be lyin' to me."* [She writes that on her yellow Post-it.]

Rob and Angel write back and forth, pressing their green and yellow rectangles on the master script. Suddenly Jerome interrupts. "Where's this leave me? I'm gonna join Lisa's group."

ANGEL: *No, come on. You could try to keep us from fighting. How 'bout that?*

JEROME: *How? What would I say?*

ANGEL: *Maybe you've got a crush on me, and you get mad at Jack for treatin' me so bad.*

ROB: *And I beat you up for lookin' at my woman.*

Angel and Rob start writing back and forth again. Once again Jerome is silent, but he scribbles a few words on one of his Post-its.

ANGEL: *Hey, Teacher! We need some more paper, some more yellow and orange.*

JEROME: *Hey, I've still got four Post-its left. How 'bout letting me talk for a change?*

ANGEL: *Okay, okay! I'm sorry, I just get goin' and forget. Why don't you tell Jack what you think of him right here?* [She peels off some other Post-its and sets them aside to reposition after Jerome inserts his line.]

We've discovered that these notes literally give kids a voice. In the complex peer relations that sometimes silence adolescents in the classroom, this simple drafting tool makes legitimate their right to enter the dialogue. Post-its become their tickets into the conversation. As Jerome put it: "Hey, I've got four Post-its left. Let me say something next!"

Not all students will stand up for themselves, of course. Walking around the room, we can quickly count Post-its and intervene, if necessary. Whether a student's lack of involvement stems from personal choice or from the group's exclusion, our gentle pressure usually turns things around: "Hey, Jerome, you'd better get busy or Angel is going to have a monologue."

In addition to the Post-its, we've learned to provide each group with several large sheets of paper so that everyone can see the entire script as it develops. Students are tempted to divide the sheet in half and reserve one side for stage directions; or they may spend time thinking of a title for the scene so they can scrawl it across the top of their sheet. We tell them to focus on characters, setting, and dialogue. The rest can wait for the revision.

LEARNING CRAFT AS WE DRAFT

It should be clear that this process teaches some quite specific skills.

Using Post-its helps students make concrete the difference in punctuation styles between plays and other literary genres. But the dialogue-writing format of playwriting can carry over to other forms, particularly the understanding that one separates speakers by paragraphs for the sake of clarity.

The activity also makes visual the concept of writing as a recursive activity. When students hit a snag, we suggest they go back and read their parts aloud. Sometimes a new line or direction will arise as they hear themselves in the scene. Revision is quick; lines can be peeled off and placed elsewhere or discarded completely. The process demonstrates that revision is not confined to the end of the writing process.

The activity also encourages students to take a close look at language, a task in which it can be difficult to engage learners. Tim overheard the conversation of one group in which students were discussing the authenticity of the dialogue that they had written so far: "He sounds like some guy from the East End. Don't nobody sound like that where I come from."

Tim did not solve this problem for them. He said, "I wanted them to develop a procedure for working together, to negotiate differences of interpretation, and wanted to leave the process in their control."

Young writers often realize that something doesn't "sound" right, but they don't always have the language for expressing why. That gives us an opportunity in a lesson such as this to talk about word choice, dialect, and the way our speech patterns reveal our regions, backgrounds, and sometimes even our ages. Kids begin adopting the persona of their characters and, in the process, learn a lot about character development. They experience the way other characters' reactions help define the character, discover that the way they speak reveals almost as much as what they say, and learn that their dialogue must advance the scene as well as impart key information by making known the characters' actions. The drafting process in playwriting also teaches that we don't have any trouble keeping track of characters if they are truly delineated by the writer; we know who said what based on the words. Although the color-coded Post-its certainly help, they shouldn't be necessary in later drafts when the voice of the character is well established.

In the scene-drafting process, students also learn about dramatic conventions. Staging considerations, for example, may mean that characters need to talk about having done something rather than acting it out. Background or events that precede the action currently taking place on the stage are difficult to present to an audience. For example, in "The Ghetto Rose" scene at the beginning of this piece, we know that the characters have been in Club X-Cubed before because Damon says that the chicken wings are terrible there. We don't need to show the characters at Club X eating those wings; we can just embed that experience and information through dialogue.

Walking through a scene can help inexperienced writers discover what Damon knew intuitively: the folly of trying to act out everything one says. The middle school writers of the following exchange had not yet learned this lesson:

T. T.: *Hey, Roxie, remember, we're gonna pick up Darrell and Kenny today. Go get your purse and let's head out.* [Roxie walks offstage and air-steps her way to her room and back.]

ROXIE: *Oh, let's go get them at their house and pick them up. Come on, let's go get in the car.* [They move left and pretend to sit down in the car, two chairs they have pushed together.] *Where we going after we pick them up?*

T. T.: *We're going to the movies, remember, dodo brain. You have such bad memory loss.*

At this point Jean intervened.

JEAN: *Hey, guys, let's stop here and talk about what works and what doesn't when you're staging a scene. What does the audience absolutely have to know?*

JONATHAN: *That they're gonna go to the movies?*

JEAN: *So what kind of action does that require?*

DEIDRE: *Them talking.*

JEAN: *I think so, too. What action takes up time, doesn't really need to be shown?*

T. T.: *Roxie getting her purse?*

JEAN: *What else?*

DEIDRE: *Them getting in the car?*

JEAN: *So could the whole conversation happen in the car? If we have to know that she has her purse, how could you handle that?*

ROXIE: *I could say something like, "Oh, no, where's my purse at? Oh, here it is, on the floor."*

JEAN: *That's right, you could just talk about these things instead of trying to show them all.*

Exchanges like this—beneficial as they are—help students discover that the play form has its limitations, largely because it is essentially dialogue. The more students experiment with drama, the more likely that they will hit a point where they're uncomfortable with this limitation. "How will they know what he looks like or where they are, unless I tell them?" a student will ask. We help them to understand that in drama, these duties fall to the set designer and the costume designer.

The centrality of dialogue can create another difficulty. Students who have been schooled in the dictum "show, don't tell" are now being confused by our insistence on a seemingly opposite principle, "tell, don't show." We do still expect dialogue to be rich in detail, but we forbid the use of narrators. The quickest way to make a student scene lose its freshness and, indeed, appear puerile is to allow writers to fill in the blanks for the audience: "Now he goes to his granny's to ask for money." If it isn't possible for the request to happen in the single-setting scene, then it must be worked into the conversation, not announced by an intrusive voice. Students sometimes resist the thinking that such rules require, but we've discovered that working with these restrictions both produces stronger drafts and, at the very least, helps some writers come to value the power of description in other genres.

THE FIRST RUN-THROUGH

Each group needs to perform its scene for the class. They can present their work as reader's theater, each actor stepping up to read at the appropriate moment. Or they can plan to walk through the scene as time permits; scripts can be photocopied or students can simply work off the script, improvising rather than reading word for word. One group decided to divide up their script, since the Post-its are easily removed, so that each character could hold a page with only his or her own lines. Members quickly discovered they needed to insert the last few words of the previous line as a cue; after that, the process worked fairly well.

Groups are instructed to jump up when their scene seems to naturally follow the one they've just seen. This helps us talk later about juxtaposing scenes with opposite points of view and combining or omitting scenes that really have the same message.

We keep the props simple—a table and a few chairs are usually handy to serve as cars, sofas, store counters, and the like. Sometimes we've had a box of hats and scarves available to help students take on the persona of their designated characters.

DEBRIEFING AFTER THE SCENE

Talking about the facet of the theme that the scene portrays helps the group start to think about the play as a whole. This is also an opportune time to point out dramatic devices that the group might use to their advantage. For example, in "Ghetto Rose," would it have been appropriate for us to see the girls get out of the car and leave their boyfriends drinking in the front seat?

TIM: *Is this a positive or negative message about drinking?*

DAMON: *Positive, because the girls left.*

TIM: *True, they did. But what image is the audience left with?*

CRYSTAL: *The guys tipping up their bottles, saying they'll just hang out together.*

TIM: *So they won. Your last image makes them the winners. How could we make the young ladies seen as the winners?*

DAMON: *Stop the scene with them walking away?*

TIM: *Exactly. You need to stage it so we're looking at the girls at the end.*

DAMON: *Or what if we keep it like it is but add the sounds of a car crash as the lights go out?*

TIM: *That would do it!*

This kind of debriefing also offers an opportunity for assessment and allows the whole class to share in peer review by asking clarifying questions and commenting on the scene.

REVISION SERENDIPITY

Sometimes a student will be absent when a scene is written and return at the time the scene is presented. There's usually some confusion, but we've learned from this experience. We now schedule a session during which the writers watch their creation being performed by students who have never seen the script before. Not having the context that the writers have, actors who go into the reading cold will quickly discover some of the problems: "Hey, this isn't going anywhere. There's no conflict," eighth-grader Shanea exclaimed as she read her lines. The writers had to agree. They'd gotten so caught up in their characters' chatting with one another that they'd never really gotten to the point. When another group of writers watched as performers stumbled over some of their lines, they knew they needed to rephrase some wordy and confusing sentences and add a few stage directions.

PRODUCTION NOT THE GOAL

After the initial drafting and rehearsal, students are invited to shape their separate scenes into a short theme play, ordering the different plays for effect and perhaps adding some type of opening and closing to the grouping.

But the process is as important as the product. Students have learned to function in a collaborative writing experience. This same experience is not as

71

easily carried out when writing in other forms. Also, they've learned the particular conventions of the dramatic form and writing strategies, such as oral rehearsal, peer review, and so on, that they can apply independently in other writing situations. A nice byproduct is that a few students invariably get hooked on playwriting and pursue it during subsequent workshop time.

Whether or not the students' scenes move into the production phase, the activity has allowed them to learn far more than techniques of dialogue writing and skills of collaboration. Wagner reminds us that oral language is the seedbed for later growth in literacy (1998, 34). She notes that drama in particular supports students' acquisition of a standard dialect and helps them develop fluency in both reading and writing. Like Wagner, we've discovered that playwriting takes learners down many paths to greater literacy. It's not so much about the genre or the product as it is about creating a culture that supports the thinking and learning of writers. In our classrooms, we stage learning, not productions, because we know that when we teach the writer, the writing will come.

REFERENCES

Babbitt, Natalie. 1975. *Tuck Everlasting*. New York: Farrar, Straus & Giroux.

Bray, Errol. 1994. *Playbuilding: A Guide for Group Creation of Plays with Young People*. Portsmouth, NH: Heinemann.

George Mason University and Fairfax County Public Schools. 1984. *Puppet Plays: Writing and Revising with Partners*. Program 5 in video series, *Teachers Teaching Writing*. Distributed through ASCD/NCTE.

Hicks, Jean. 1998. "Post-it Note Your Way into Playwriting." *Louisville Writing Project Network News* 18 (1): 11.

Wagner, Betty Jane. 1998. *Educational Drama and Language Arts: What Research Shows*. Portsmouth, NH: Heinemann.

Episodic Fiction: Another Way to Tell a Story

Pen Campbell and Dan Holt

This article was written by Pen Campbell and Dan Holt about their experiences teaching high school in St. Joseph, Michigan. The article was originally published in the summer 2001 issue of The Quarterly.

Until I encountered John O'Brien's story "Birds," my fiction writing left much to be desired. My tedious and mechanical stories suffered from weak plots, weaker characters, and general verbal dysentery.

I wanted to create seamless movies with my short fiction, but the moments of narrative magic in my work seemed to be floating in a sea of words that trivialized the impact of my stories. That was before O'Brien showed me the way. In "Birds," he tells the story of a man who learned through a lifetime of interaction with birds not to mistreat animals. The episodic approach the story takes gives the reader images but leaves out the narrative bridges, allowing us to connect the dots. O'Brien produced a wonderful mosaic that gave a clear and poignant picture of a changed man. I knew immediately that I had found a fiction approach that would work for me.

I found that by isolating the images and story high points and by forming these into vignettes and linking these episodes with a common theme, my stories became vibrant, sparse, and poetic. My prose suddenly became powerful instead of weak because I squeezed all the excess out of it. Putting my stories into episodes was like panning for gold, sloshing the creek water about, eliminating everything but the nuggets.

I've used this approach to teaching fiction writing for twenty years—first with my high school classes and now with my college classes—all with continuing excellent results. My college writing students, who have had exactly the same problems with fiction writing that I have had, like the episodic approach as much as I do. Students who are intimidated by constructing the classical story find the episodic form more doable because they can write it in pieces. Each scene is an episode, another step toward a finished story.

This article lays out the specifics of how I, as well as my colleague Pen Campbell, a high school teacher, make use of episodic fiction as a teaching strategy.

~ *Dan Holt, 2002*

*a*s Dan states above, "Birds," by John O'Brien, was different from any story he'd read before. Unlike a movie or traditional short story, in which elements of the story line are connected by transitions to tell a story in a linear fashion, O'Brien's "Birds" seemed to him to be more like a slide show or even a music video. Separate episodes were individual images juxtaposed, to be woven together by the reader into a story. He found the form intriguing and decided to try his hand at it to see where it would lead.

At the time, he had two different stories in progress, neither of which was working out: one about a man who, while visiting his parents in Arizona, struggles with the decision of whether or not to leave his wife, and a second story that grew out of a newspaper report about a man whose horse had broken its leg in the desert and subsequently been killed by coyotes. Experimenting with the episodic form, Holt combined these two stories into "Ten Stories About Coyotes I Never Told You," presented on pages 77-83. In doing so, he took as a model for his own story one additional element from O'Brien's "Birds" beyond the episodic form itself—that of a repeated motif occurring in each episode.

"Birds" is not really a story about birds. Rather, it is a story about a man coming to a decision concerning himself and the sanctity of life around him. Each of the episodes of the story features a bird, not as a symbol but more as a repeated motif– perhaps the way Alfred Hitchcock's cameo appearance was featured in each of his movies. Holt used the repeated motif in "Ten Stories . . . ," which, despite its title, is not really about coyotes, though one appears in almost every episode.

Pleased with having solved the problem of the two balky stories, Holt sent "Ten Stories . . ." to Stuart Dybeck at Western Michigan University, who had suggested the O'Brien story to him in the first place. Having sent it with no more purpose than to say "Thanks—I enjoyed the story and fooled around with the form; here's what I got," Holt considered the matter closed. Several months later, however, when he received a copy of a magazine in the mail, there in the table of contents he found his name and "Ten Stories About Coyotes I Never Told You." Dybeck had sent the story on to his friend John O'Brien, editor of the *Great Lakes Review*, who promptly published it in that journal.

Since his introduction to episodic fiction, Holt has introduced many others in turn to the form: students in his high school creative writing classes, participants in both invitational summer institutes and advanced institutes at Western Michigan

University's Third Coast Writing Project, and participants of the 2000 Festival of Writers sponsored by the Louisiana Writing Projects State Network.

EIGHT RULES ABOUT EPISODIC FICTION I NEVER TOLD YOU

1. The work involves a dynamic character, one who changes in fits and starts throughout the course of the story.

2. Episodes vary in length.

3. Episodes are roughly chronological but not specifically so.

4. Episodes may or may not be multigenre, but the language is often rich and poetic.

5. A single unifying device runs throughout the story, appearing in each episode.

6. Episodes are not related directly by cause and effect; instead, all are related to a central theme.

7. If a traditional short story is a movie, moving in a linear fashion from beginning to end, an episodic story is more like a slide show or a music video.

8. And finally, to borrow a rule from George Orwell, "Break any of these rules sooner than say anything outright barbarous."

FOLLOWING THE RULES

First Holt wrote "Ten Stories . . ."; the rules came later when it was time to introduce episodic fiction to his students. In a way, teaching the rules is nothing more than articulating the process of how to take an interesting piece of literature and use it as a model—an effective technique writers have been using as long as there have been stories.

The protagonist/narrator of "Ten Stories . . ." is a man whose marriage has broken up, and his response has been to go home to his parents—and paint the corral. Throughout the story, we share his experiences—though not his thought processes—as he comes to a decision about his marriage. In the end, on his way home to resume his marriage, he views from the departing plane the corral he painted in episode one. At that point, most likely, the title clicks into place for the reader. The "you" in the title to whom the stories are addressed is his wife. These are stories he told her after he returned home.

None of the episodes is very long, and they vary in length from three lines of manuscript to perhaps a quarter of a page. The first three episodes are arranged in roughly chronological order, though one does not precipitate the next. They are not related by cause and effect. Actually, the order in which they are told could indicate simply the order in which they were recalled. The first three are memories about the protagonist's time away from his marriage. Episode four is a flashback to childhood, and the image of the four boys tormenting the old coyote ups the emotional ante of the story. Episodes five, seven, and nine together are the retelling of a single incident, fragmented by the insertion of episode six, "Cheating at Golf," and eight, "Go with God." The last episode follows the others chronologically and brings the reader full circle.

Each of the ten episodes is prose, rich with sensory images. All episodes but episode seven, "Screams," and episode ten, "Chasing Chickens," contain a coyote—as promised by the story title. Seven is the shortest, most intense episode, and on one hand there's the least room here for the device of the coyote. Then, too, the missing coyote may heighten the tension of this climactic episode, causing us to glance over our reading shoulder for that "flash of gray." We don't see the coyote in "Chasing Chickens" either, and as the protagonist flies over the desert landscape, he imagines chickens running in circles—chased, we suspect, by the unseen coyote.

In some ways, perhaps the inclusion of the unifying device in episodic fiction is a little like rhyme in poetry—we have to be careful with it and be sure it isn't allowed to take over or muscle us into bad decisions, especially when we're

TEN STORIES ABOUT COYOTES I NEVER TOLD YOU

BY DAN HOLT

I. THE WHITE FENCE

When our marriage broke up, I went home and painted the entire corral. I don't know why it was so important, but it was. I had to get home and grab a paintbrush and stand in the Arizona sun and paint the corral. I painted it white; so white you couldn't look at it for very long.

"Jesus, is that fence white," my father said.

"Whitest damn fence I ever saw," my mother said.

They stood, arm in arm, framed by a rose arbor. I wanted to cry, they looked so good. They looked so good standing there that I wanted to cry and maybe paint the fence again. After all, I had the time, another coat wouldn't hurt.

"That's true," my father said. "The chicken coop could stand a coat, too."

I heard a coyote yelp in the distance.

just getting started. That's where the beauty and utility of rule eight comes in. As George Orwell says, "Break any of these rules sooner than say anything outright barbarous."

So is this a story about coyotes? Is the coyote a symbol, and if so, of what? These questions would undoubtedly come up in a classroom discussion of this story. Rule six says that all episodes should be linked by a common theme. In the first sentence, we have a man reacting to the turmoil in his marriage. We could look at the story as a process, with each episode contributing a piece to the process of the protagonist's decision. The episodes fit loosely together in this way, not always proceeding from each other but clustering about the common theme of coming to know what we want to do in our own lives.

II. MORNING RIDE

There were partridges near the barn, and it was still cold enough that I could see my breath. I kneed Poco's belly so that I could tighten the cinch. He blew hot smoke and danced away from me.

The desert was green that December, and the earth was a rust color, especially with the red sun coming over Hat Mountain throwing a tint on everything. At the end of the graded road behind the barn were two wrecked cars. They were rust color, too.

I took my hands out of my pockets when the sun started to warm me up. I thought that it would be nice just to keep riding, deeper and deeper into the desert. I felt so good about the riding and the sun that I wanted to glide in a walking trot all the way to Mexico.

I caught, out of the corner of my eye, just a flash of gray.

IN THE CLASSROOM

One of the attractions of the episodic form is its versatility. While it came to Holt's attention first as fiction, it wasn't long before the form began suggesting itself for use in other types of writing as well. It is a natural for personal narrative, and students who have collected freewriting responses to prompts designed to encourage personal narrative are likely to find a rich collection of possibilities from which to develop an episodic piece.

The form is student friendly in other ways as well. The very nature of episodic writing breaks up the task of the whole piece into parts, encouraging students with their "do-ability." The often-troublesome details of transitions and unity of time and place become more manageable when the story is told episodically. The structure of episodes also encourages students to think in terms of scenes in constructing their stories.

As we know, the move from personal narrative to fiction is a short step. Sometimes a student may begin a piece as personal narrative and, with later revisions, turn it into a piece of fiction. Holt points out that encouraging students to search for the roots of fiction within their own realities often yields realistic stories that touch the reader with their authenticity. Even personal narrative, when told episodically, is more likely to be driven by character development than by plot since the episodic story does not consist of a single cohesive chain of events.

An excellent example of such an episodic personal narrative is "It's Not Funny Anymore," written by Andy Myers while he was a student in Holt's creative writing class. (*See page 84.*)

FOLLOWING THE RULES

"It's Not Funny Anymore" follows the rules. The protagonist is a dynamic character, maturing throughout the story. In the first six episodes, the protagonist is most likely between ages eight and ten, and these episodes have no specific chronology but serve to introduce the grandfather, his humor, and his importance in the boy's life. At the beginning of the seventh episode, the protagonist has become an adolescent, and his growing maturity in the following episodes corresponds inversely to his grandfather's growing frailty. Once the protagonist hits middle school, the episodes, which vary in length, are recognizably chronological.

III. COYOTES ARE AFTER MY MOTHER'S CHICKENS

I hung around the house, standing in the kitchen, watching Mom wash the dishes. She was talking to me.

"How's your job? Are you happy? Are you going back to her?"

I was sticking a butter knife into the toaster.

"You know that's plugged in."

"What?"

"You know that's plugged in."

"What's plugged in?"

"The toaster you're sticking the knife into."

She was looking out the window over the sink as she said that, and suddenly she stopped pulling glasses out of the suds and leaned forward to get a better look at something in the backyard. She was standing on her toes and then she said "Shit" and ran to the utility room, grabbing a .22 automatic out of the closet, and ran out the back door.

I followed her and saw her fire three shots at a disappearing coyote.

"I'll get one of them yet," she said.

"When did you start saying 'Shit'?" I asked her.

Andy uses effective language throughout the prose episodes, creating clear and moving images. The episodes are formatted without the numerical labeling or titling of "Ten Stories . . . ." White space on the page separates one episode from the next. The unifying device of a joke or reference to one appears in each episode. While the unifying device is more intrinsically a part of the story than Holt's coyote, the story is not about jokes. Each episode relates to the central theme of the protagonist's relationship with his grandfather and the inevitability of change that time brings to that relationship.

IV. CHASING AN OLD COYOTE

I was twelve when we caught a coyote in the open, four of us chasing a coyote across a dried-out cotton field. He must have been old or sick because he couldn't outrun us. So we kept him in the middle of the field and then tried to run him over until he caught a hoof in the side. He stopped trying to run from us and just sat down in the middle of the field. We kept riding around him, Indians circling a wagon train, but he wouldn't run anymore. I guess he just decided it wasn't worth it.

RESEARCHING EPISODICALLY

At Lake Michigan Catholic High School, students in Pen Campbell's senior English class spend the year exploring issues of social justice. Throughout the year, they read literature and view films in various genres, examining them through discussion and writing. In late January students choose a research question to investigate in depth over the next three months. At the end of the year they present a portfolio of work that includes a visual piece, a traditional research paper, and either a multigenre collection or a piece of episodic fiction, all of which grow from their research.

As they read, discuss, and study various forms, they respond to prompts designed to help them create characters through which they can voice what they are learning about their research topics. Sometimes the prompt is a piece of literature students use as a model. Sometimes Campbell offers prompts that have successfully generated personal writing. Students put themselves

V. POCO THROWS ME

I was thinking "coyote" to myself when Poco jumped sideways. He was jumping and bucking. I pulled his head up and kept him from throwing me, but he kept jumping, first sideways and then he lunged forward, the bit in his teeth. The leather cut into my fingers.

"Shit."

Poco wheeled on his hind legs and reared.

"Son of a bitch."

We went down backward. I jumped to the side; he hit, rolled on his back like one large rocker off a chair.

in the place of someone affected by the topic they are researching, and through those eyes, in that voice, they respond to the prompt. Writing letters or journal entries in the voice of a character often yields excellent material for the students. After collecting a number of these responses in their daybooks, students have a body of drafts from which to choose pieces for further development.

"Through the Eyes of a Haitian Mother: An Episodic Short Story" grew out of Campbell's student Katie Imach's research on conditions in Haiti. (*See page 87.*) After reading the work of novelist Edwidge Danticat early in the school year, she became especially interested in questions of a woman's life in Haiti. Katie has taken the episodic fiction form in a slightly new direction by using a variety of narrative forms to create her story.

FOLLOWING THE RULES

"Through the Eyes of a Haitian Mother" is a multigenre episodic story. In the first episode, prose rich with images, the protagonist is introduced in third person. In the next, we hear her voice as she writes a letter to her daughter, and in the third episode, we delve deeper into the protagonist's thoughts and feelings about her life through a poem. The short journal entry of the fourth episode, with its matter-of-fact acceptance, develops our sense of the dreadful realities under which the protagonist lives her life. The final episode combines the third-person prose of the first with the protagonist's voice in a poem that ends in prayer.

These episodes may be chronological, though the theme around which all the episodes cluster speaks of an endurance that negates the importance of which event came first. In the same way, the change in the protagonist, which we would expect, becomes secondary to the fact that she endures. Her dynamism

VI. CHEATING AT GOLF

My dad wanted me to play golf with him on Saturday. The golf course was the only place where he could talk. There was something about sitting on a bench in a lime green cardigan, waiting for two or three foursomes to get off the tee, that really opened him up. He told me the story about the time he and Ed from the shop tried to hit a coyote on the fourth fairway.

I broke 100 that day but cheated a lot. We both did. If there was a tree in the way, we'd move the ball, or kick it out of the rough, or sometimes put the ball on a little tuft of grass so we could hit a wood. Sometimes, we'd even forget a stroke. All in all, we cheated about the same.

"I don't know if I want to go back," I said to him while we were waiting to make our approach shots to the eighteenth green.

"What do you mean, you don't want to go back?"

81

is grounded in that endurance rather than in an overt change or epiphany.

The unifying device in this story is more subtle than in "Ten Stories . . ." or "It's Not Funny Anymore." In each episode, a sound of sorrow or of trouble reiterates the theme of the story. As readers, we may not be conscious of these sounds in the same way we become conscious of the coyote or of the jokes in the two earlier stories. Imach's use of sound is an effective use of sensory images, but if the repeated motif blends so smoothly into the story that it isn't noticeable, does it still have a purpose? Perhaps the question it brings is really about the purpose of the coyote, the jokes, and the sounds. Sometimes the repeated motif serves more as a cattle prod to the writer than as a beacon to the reader. The challenge becomes fitting the coyote in; rising to that challenge, we tax our writing brains, which is always good exercise for us.

Rule seven says if a traditional short story is a movie, moving in a linear fashion from beginning to end, an episodic story is more like a slide show or a music video. "Through the Eyes of a Haitian Mother" does have that episodic, music video feel, and it also has a feeling of authenticity that is present despite the fact that this is not the personal narrative of the writer. The student author is not a Haitian mother, but in presenting her research as reality through the eyes of a character, she has clearly demonstrated her new knowledge of the topic. And isn't that, after all, why we research—to understand something we didn't understand before?

VII. SCREAMS

He broke his leg when he went down. He kept trying to get up and kept falling down again. His wild eyes looked so large and white. I ran down the riverbed, not wanting to look back at him thrashing in the sand. I didn't know horses could scream like that.

VIII. GO WITH GOD

The Mexicans came out of nowhere, out of the desert, just appeared in the driveway. One had a red rag around his head; the other had a hat pulled over his eyes, and they were both soaked from a shower. I found out later that there were others, whole families, hidden not far away.

My father saw them first and walked out to talk to them, his hands stuffed in his pockets. I could see him shake his head and then point across the desert to the west. Mom was holding the .22 and checking to see if it still had bullets. And just like that, they headed across the desert in the same direction my father had pointed, walking under the "Vayas con Dios" sign over the driveway entrance.

"Who are they?" I asked my father when he came back to the house.

"They call them Coyotes," he said. "They bring people to the promised land."

IN THE END, IT'S STILL STORYTELLING

Getting started on episodic fiction is a little like being pregnant. Suddenly, you look around, and, although you never thought about it at all before, you begin to see pregnant women and babies everywhere. The same thing happens with episodic fiction. As a matter of fact, a number of people have pointed out the similarities between the episodic form and the nonlinear communication that is becoming more and more prevalent in our digital age. Internet sites, magazines, and even textbooks present a mosaic of information on each page, encouraging a randomness of order through which students move with increasing adeptness. *B* no longer necessarily follows *A* as a matter of course, and episodic fiction reflects that change nicely.

But in the end, no matter how you get started with episodic fiction, and no matter how you play with it or what new twists and turns you give it, it all boils down to another form of storytelling. And ultimately, that's what matters—telling the story. How you tell it—how you get there—is not as important as the fact that you're telling it. But, as getting there is half the fun, episodic fiction is an incredibly flexible, creative form—and one you and your students will certainly want to try.

IX. CANIS LATRANS

I didn't see them until I was almost on them. They were standing like gray plaster statues, so still. I remember thinking that only wild animals can stand that still. I also remember thinking that if I could get close enough, I could see my reflection in their eyes. I picked up a rock and threw it at the largest coyote. He moved just enough so that the rock missed and then he froze again. We stood a little longer: one specimen Homo sapiens, sub species of the order Primate and approximately twenty specimen of Canis Latrans facing one another in a dry riverbed in a desert.

Finally, they moved off toward the spot where Poco lay, exhausted.

X. CHASING CHICKENS

My parents stayed in the departure area until I was in the plane and the doors closed. I looked for our house and found it by looking for Hat Mountain and Winslow Peak, the red tile roof of the house drawing my attention. The empty corral didn't look white from the air. I imagined chickens running in circles in the backyard.

IT'S NOT FUNNY ANYMORE

BY ANDY MYERS

In the fall, I used to rake the leaves with my grandpa in his backyard. We would go around the whole lawn raking them from underneath the trees, the bird feeders, and from behind the barn. We would also, very carefully, rake them out of the garden he grew so proudly, which was filled with parsley and rhubarb.

We would rake the leaves in rows across the lawn instead of piles. He always thought that method was the best. He kept me laughing the whole time we raked, telling me jokes that he had memorized from one of the many joke books he had on his shelves. He always told me the same one about the belly dancer, and I could never remember the punch line.

~

"Ginny, what's a four-letter word for Greek cheese?" My grandpa only asked for help on his crossword puzzles when he absolutely needed it. He did the crosswords out of the paper, and I would work right along beside him in my crossword puzzle book. He bought the book for me for my eighth birthday along with the Book of 1,001 Jokes and Riddles. I would usually finish my puzzles before him, but his were a lot harder.

~

On the playground at E. P. Clarke Elementary School, out by the Redwood Climber, I told my friends the joke about the four-legged canoe my grandpa had told me the weekend before. I didn't tell it as well as my grandpa did, but the guys still liked it and laughed all recess. After that day, I started telling them all of the jokes and stories that my grandpa had told me. All the ones I could remember that is.

~

Grandma had sent me downstairs to get the Christmas cookie cutters one Saturday morning before Christmas. Normally I hated to go down to the basement alone because my grandma ran a doll hospital and everywhere you looked there were broken dolls and dismantled doll parts laying around. I wasn't as scared as I usually was this time because I knew Grandpa was down there doing his genealogy studies. The other part of the basement was my grandpa's library. It was filled with tons of old books and newspapers, mostly stuff relating to our family or the Civil War.

I slowly made my way down the steep linoleum steps and into my grandpa's study. I peeked around the corner, hoping he would see me and fire off a joke or riddle, but he didn't. He was sitting behind his old green desk, reading a decayed yellow newspaper. His bifocals were slid halfway down his nose, and he was chewing on a fountain pen; I was shocked at the way he studied that paper. It was really the first time I had ever seen my grandpa not joking or without his usual fun-loving smile. He didn't seem quite the same.

~

We met my grandparents at church on a rainy Sunday morning in the early part of April. As my grandpa greeted me he said, "Hi-ya Chester ol'top. Glad to see you back. It's been ears and ears, but I still nose ya." As he said it, he touched every body part he mentioned on me. I laughed all through church and asked him to do it about a dozen more times that afternoon.

~

"Holy mackerel!" My grandpa exclaimed as I hit the wiffle ball over the fence with my big red bat. It was my first home run of the afternoon. It landed in the Burkel's back-yard. There must have been a hundred wiffle balls we left in her backyard because my brother and I were always too scared to retrieve them.

My grandpa held my waist as I leaned over the fence to corral the ball. I grabbed it; and as he pulled me over, my shirt got caught on the fence. "Wait, Grandpa, I'm stuck," I said. He replied, "No, you're Myers; I'm stuck." My grandpa's last name was Stuck. I'll never forget how much we both laughed.

~

In the Upton Middle School cafeteria, I noticed I wasn't the one telling the jokes any-more. It was another boy who everyone thought was hilarious. He told one of the same jokes my grandpa told me. I hated him because of it, but I eventually got over it.

~

When we opened presents on Christmas Day at my grandparents' house, my grandpa always wore the Santa Claus hat. He would hand out each gift, and when we were without presents, he would re-supply us. That Christmas, my aunt thought it would be funny to wrap one of my presents in a Tampon box. Evidently the look on my face was the highlight of the day.

~

A couple of months after my grandpa's stroke, my mom visited him. She found a notebook with "Don's Notebook" printed really large on it. In the notebook were some basic characteristics to remember family members by: Andy = oldest, Josh = tallest, Karen = girl. I remember making fun of this notebook to my friends. That's the one joke I wish I could have taken back.

~

At the beach last summer, my girlfriend told me she liked me because I was always kidding around. She said I was quick witted. I told her I loved her that day. We were together about every single day after that.

A couple of months ago, I came home after being out with Lori around 12:30 a.m. The usual group of guys were over to spend the night. They were mad that I always went with her and never hung with them; I told them I would rather spend time with

85

a pretty girl than sit around my basement making fun of each other. They all agreed with me, and we had a good time after that.

~

My grandpa was admitted to the hospital again in September. My mom, brother, sister, and I went to visit him one chilly morning after church. He didn't look very well. He was dressed in his white hospital shirt and propped in his bed. I noticed a sign that hung over his bed which read "Legally Blind." I guess it was there for the nurse's sake. I felt like crying as we left his room without even attempting any sort of joke or riddle to make him smile.

~

Christmas Day a few weeks ago, I saw my grandpa for the first time since I had been up to the hospital in September. I was too busy I always told myself, trying to make excuses for forgetting him. I tried to soak up as much about the day with him as I could because I was feeling absolutely awful for neglecting him. I sat in the living room with him as he tried to pet the dog, trying to carry on conversations.

He didn't wear the Santa Claus hat this year. Nor did he hand out a single present. He sat in his special chair with his cane draped over his knee, struggling to open his own presents, often times being the butt of a joke cracked by my aunt or uncle. Most of the time, everyone laughed except for me. I remembered when I used to laugh with my grandpa playing baseball, raking leaves, doing crosswords, and I was not about to start laughing at him.

~

I stopped over at my grandparents' house the other day to check on them. The three of us talked for over two hours. I could tell that it made their day that I came by. It made my day as well. As I left, I gave them each a hug and told them I loved them. As I grabbed my coat and headed for the door, I turned back and told my grandpa the joke about the belly dancer, the one he had always told me, hoping to get a laugh out of him. I did. He had forgotten the punch line.

THROUGH THE EYES OF A HAITIAN MOTHER: AN EPISODIC SHORT STORY

BY KATIE IMACH

SOUNDS

What scared her the most in the muggy Haitian nights were the sounds—the eerie sounds of the night that bore into her brain and allowed no time for sleep. The sounds that echoed, night after night with their deafening rhythm. They came from so many different places, and yet all had the same story. The story that had been passed on for generations.

Children crying because of lack of food, their stomachs contracting to their full extent. An empty look in their eyes that shows so much agony in one glimpse. A stare that tells of their pain and anguish.

Children crying as they hold their bloody mother or brother in their arms and weep— begging the Lord to make their loved one come back. Such anguish experienced that they close off in their own cocoon, a cocoon of silence which they suffer in.

The sounds of soldiers, with their cocky commands beating down upon the people, the people they are supposed to be protecting, and the ever so frightening sound of gunfire, gunfire, gunfire.

Where are the sounds of laughter? Where have they disappeared to? She tries to remember that precious sound, but it is drowned out by all the others.

~

LETTER TO DAUGHTER

Dear Faith,

I can feel that your prayers have been with me. As you have probably heard, the bombing has stopped! The tanks that had come into Port-Au-Prince two weeks ago finally left. Of course, the signs of their presence still remain.

Some buildings have been bombed, many houses have bullet holes in the windows, and wounded people walk the streets, but overall not that much damage has been done. It was a lot worse last month.

As usual, we don't know which party inflicted all this destruction. I don't understand how there can be so much chaos without any ramifications. Aristide tries his hardest, but it's hard to pacify our country. We are all so tired and feel that we can't trust anybody anymore. I want to believe he will make a difference, but I don't want to be disappointed once again.

Do you remember the little boy with big green eyes down the street? The one that was always after Maggie? Well, we attended his funeral today. He got his legs blown off by the terrorists and the hospital was very full, so by the time the doctor was available, he was already gone. His poor, poor mother. This is the second child of hers she lost. *The other one she miscarried a few years ago. He was such a promising child—wanted to be a doctor, and would have made our whole community proud.*

I'm so happy you finally got out. You have such a great future to look forward to in America. I would have left, but I feel I belong here. My blood is all Haitian, and it doesn't want to depart from its homeland. I don't want to abandon my people, especially at my age. I'd rather have a young one leave because at least they have a hope for a future. Me, I just live from day to day and pray that the Lord watches over our souls.

Take care of yourself and know that your mama loves you. You are making us all so proud.

Love,
Mama

~

STORY OF MY LIFE

I cried when my daughter was born
tears of sorrow
for the life I have brought her into
She doesn't deserve this
No one does

So alone
Sick of the same spiraling circle
of events
that affects every generation of my country
my women

My grandmother and mother
so strong
yet so ignorant to the fact
Things don't have to be this way

Poverty . . . virginity tests . . . abuse
rape . . . depression . . .
Political instability . . .
The story of my life

Scared of walking down the streets at night
and during the day
scared of my own country
punished for being a woman

So many responsibilities,
so little respect

"Tears from my eyes,
made me realize
all the pain inside"
Pain that I had swallowed for so long
a big lump in the throat
that grows and you ignore

I want to be strong
I don't let those tears shed freely
So tired of crying . . .
too tired to cry anymore

~

JOURNAL ENTRY

It happened again last night. I woke up to the sound of gunfire and ran next door to
Namphy's house, as I always do. I found his wife there, a small shadow curled in the
corner, crying, sobbing, her whole body heaving with sorrow. "They took him away,"
she said. Namphy was taken prisoner by the soldiers. Why? Nobody knows, but he
probably won't return. They never do.

~

WONDER

This warm and starry night is eerily silent as she ponders her life and this war, which
has never ceased to control and limit her. She has never known peace and wonders
what life would have been like under different circumstances.

I wonder what it's like to go to sleep,
knowing you'll soon see the light
of a tranquil dawn

I wonder what it's like to let your children play outside,
careless and free,
without worrying you'll never see them again

I wonder what it's like
not to hear the splatter of bullets every day
echoing through the alleys

I wonder if this will end
this insanity
That's all I pray for

RESOURCES

While they may not all offer examples that follow our eight rules exactly, the books below are ones that may be useful in beginning to think episodically.

Barry, Lynda. 1999. *The Good Times Are Killing Me*. Seattle: Sasquatch Books. A blend of coming-of-age social commentary and a fantastic multigenre research example in "The Music Notebook" section, this book is a gem. It would make a nice pairing with another coming-of-age episodic story, that by Cisneros.

Cisneros, Sandra. 1991. *House on Mango Street*. New York: Vintage Books. Available as an audio book read by the author. Would pair nicely with Barry.

Cormier, Robert. 1999. *Frenchtown Summer*. New York: Delacorte Press. Cormier's own memoir in verse.

Dresang, Eliza T. 1999. *Radical Change: Books for Youth in a Digital Age*. New York: H. W. Wilson. http://slis-two.lis.fsu.edu/~inst/RC2.htm. Check out Dresang's website, and be sure to take a look at the Book Updates and the archived updates for excellent reading recommendations.

Hesse, Karen. 1999. *Out of the Dust*. New York: Scholastic Press. A young girl's struggles during the Dust Bowl, told episodically in verse.

Kitchen, Judith, and Mary Paumier Jones, eds. 1999. *In Brief: Short Takes on the Personal*. New York: W. W. Norton. This is a marvelous book to use for models of short personal narrative essays.

Romano, Tom. 1995. *Writing with Passion: Life Stories, Multiple Genres*. Portsmouth, NH: Boynton/Cook. Filled with ideas and examples, this book encourages an entirely new approach to research writing for many of us.

Rylant, Cynthia. 1990. *Soda Jerk*. N.p. A wonderful little book, an episodic story in poetry of a young man's adolescence in a small town.

Sones, Sonya. 1999. *Stop Pretending: What Happened When My Big Sister Went Crazy*. New York: HarperCollins. A young girl's telling of the title situation in verse.

Stern, Jerome, ed. and introd. 1996. *Micro Fiction: An Anthology of Really Short Stories*. New York: W. W. Norton. Another interesting form especially useful in episodic writing is micro or flash fiction. Pieces done in this form are very, very short stories of approximately 250 words and are, in a way, a hybrid of fiction and prose poetry. The book includes excellent examples.

Let's Talk: Building a Bridge Between Home and School

Catherine Humphrey

Catherine Humphrey wrote this article—originally published in the summer 2001 issue of The Quarterly *—about her teaching experience with high school seniors in southern California.*

At the time I conceived the ideas in this piece, I had been thinking for some time of ways I could better work with my students' parents to focus on our mutual concerns about their kid's learning. I had heard much from my National Writing Project colleagues about parent journals and classes intended to assist parents in helping their kids with learning as well as other ways of connecting school to home. But my personal breakthrough came the evening I was reading to my husband, Ted, the notes I had taken that day during a talk delivered by Dr. Maria Montano-Harmon. Montano-Harmon, an expert in sociolinguistics, had been working for a week with teachers in our district to help us find ways to improve what she called "quality verbal interaction" between our students and the adults in their lives. She defined quality verbal interaction as an "exchange back and forth on an idea level," and she said there was not nearly enough of it between kids and adults. Personally, I did not think I was doing badly communicating in this way with my students. I enjoyed, and was good at, asking, "What do you think?" questions. I loved the back-and-forth with the kids, but I saw my students for only an hour or less a day. How about the other adults they encountered, particularly their parents?

Talking with Ted about this, I began to realize I could help my students have quality verbal interaction with their parents, and I, in turn, could use these adults as an untapped resource in my classroom. Parents, I now understood, should be a primary source of this kind of communication. This was something that could be taught. I would try it.

~ *Catherine Humphrey, 2002*

"*P*ick up your socks." "Turn down that music." "Get home at a reasonable hour." These may all be necessary demands when a parent is instructing a teenager on the nuances of reasonable social behavior, but imperatives like these hardly qualify as what the sociolinguist Maria Montano-Harmon labels "quality verbal interaction." According to Montano-Harmon, quality verbal interaction is talk between young people and adults about ideas. When a parent or teacher asks a question that begins with "What do you think about . . . ?" the adult has initiated an opening for this kind of conversation.

According to Montano-Harmon, the average quality verbal interaction in the United States today between parent and child is seventeen seconds per day. She argues that extending the time of an idea exchange to twenty minutes per day would make a substantial difference in a youth's critical thinking skills. She claims that this exchange does not even need to be twenty consecutive minutes but can be in five- or ten-minute increments.

After experiencing Montano-Harmon's thinking in the context described above, I realized that parents were an untapped resource for both my students and me as we established a learning community based on the exchange of ideas. As a teacher, I savor these exchanges with my students, and now I wanted to invite parents to join in the conversation.

Working with my two senior classes, I selected a thought-provoking editorial from the January 29, 2000, *Los Angeles Times*. The essay, "Hold Parents Liable for Learning," by David E. Kahn, an English teacher at Fremont High School in south-central Los Angeles, made the argument that "poor parenting" is the "key factor" in our "educational crisis" and "tragic failure rate." The class and I read and discussed the essay's key points. I asked my students to take a position in agreement, disagreement, or partial agreement with the author. Kahn's radical suggestions included mandatory parent orientation sessions and ongoing parent participation—at least three hours per month—lending assistance in campus beautification and repair, tutoring, or yard and hall duty. Parents would pay for children's missed school and/or failure. "School would be free only as long as Johnny is attending and passing."

Students' pens flew as they summarized and responded to Kahn's argument. In self-selected groups, they shared their written work aloud with each other, agreeing and disagreeing with Kahn, making assertions, backing up their opinions with examples and evidence, coming to conclusions. I wanted them to take home some of the energy we were generating. What would their parents think of Kahn's proposals? I asked students to discuss his arguments with their families and bring their parents' ideas back to class.

I was delighted when many students arrived in class the next day with stories of lively and thoughtful conversations with their parents. Amy's mother surprised me by writing her ideas as an "essay" and giving it to her daughter to bring to class. Her mother wrote, "I agree wholeheartedly with Mr. Kahn, even though some of his suggestions are off the wall. But he does have the basic concept. . . . Parents, take responsibility for your children and stop passing the buck." She concluded her paper with a plea for her two daughters to have "good, strong, responsible" teachers, "to help me in my goal of raising well-rounded, educated girls." I made comments (not corrections) on the paper, inviting Amy's mom to continue the dialogue, and sent it back home with Amy. This exchange particularly pleased me because, based on high absenteeism, missed assignments, and incomplete written work, Amy had just finished the first semester in our senior English class with a D-. Now in our first week of the second semester, Amy finally seemed interested in writing a paper of her own after observing her mother sending an "essay" to school.

Encouraged, I sent a second editorial home with all my seniors, "A Martinet Helped Us Learn," by ninth grade teacher Gail Saunders (*Los Angeles Times*, January 29, 2000). When Amy's mother responded again with an essay, Amy was hooked. In Saunders's opinion piece, she argues that the mean, "Marquis de Sade of physical education" teacher she had as a student in school did her and her classmates a favor by "making" them participate. "As long as you were not comatose or in the hospital, you would be in class participating." The student with the note from home and a finger in a splint was still "seen dribbling a ball around the court that day." With a series of examples, Kahn demonstrates that in her student experience "no one questioned authority . . . none felt abused," and "none of the parents ever complained," because students and parents knew "it was good for us . . . we learned not to be wimps, and we learned not to blow small incidents out of proportion. We didn't whine about our rights because the teacher didn't talk to us like the maitre d' in a five-star restaurant, and we didn't try to get her fired because of it. We simply learned to tough it out." Saunders concludes that learning to "swallow our lumps and move on" builds character instead of encouraging whiners.

Students and parents had a lot to say in responding to Saunders's argument. Perhaps surprisingly, most agreed with her. Amy, working on her own essay, armed with her mother's response and their conversation, said to me, "We'd all get better grades in here if we did this kind of writing workshop more often." Amy was finally writing more than a few simple sentences and trying to pass it off as an essay; she began to write paragraphs, and for the first time she filled an entire page. Amy discovered for herself that writing is the communication of ideas, and by June she passed her senior English class with a C.

I learned from this experience that for Amy to become interested in participating in writing assignments she had to believe that the writing she did was "real." When she saw the example of her mother's engagement, she became engaged. She particularly enjoyed watching me write comments on her mother's papers and then acting as messenger between us.

Not every student shared the essays with a parent. Some even put up an intellectual argument against their parents' involvement. Daniel, for example, gave feisty reasons for his parents' lack of participation. A long-haired transfer student from out of state, Daniel argued against Kahn's suggestion of making parents liable for their student's academic performance. Daniel wrote, "Students must take responsibility for and take the consequences of their own actions." In a carefully reasoned essay, Daniel argued for abolishing grades and for establishing small, individualized study groups in which students "graduate themselves as soon as they think they are ready to use their education in the outside world." In keeping with this line of thinking, he refused to take the editorial home, stating his education was his own responsibility, not his parents'. Nevertheless, he contributed positively to the discussion in his small group when other students described conversations with their parents.

The reluctance of some other students to share these essays with their parents was based more on family chemistry than on intellectual conviction. Jason asked me if he could stay after class because he wanted to tell me his mother's reaction to a particular article. He added that he hates asking his father's opinions because his father "always has too much to say." In fact, many students wrote that their parents talked too much or talked "at" them rather than "with" them. And not all parents were willing to contribute. Brian's mom said, "Go ask your neighbor." Cory's mom said, "Do your own work." However, my hope remained that if I encouraged an exchange of ideas at home, parents and students would learn to engage more often in "quality verbal interactions," a process that

I believed could increase students' abilities to think critically and to articulate well-reasoned opinions.

Since something new and valuable seemed to be happening as a result of the bridge building in my two senior English classes, I decided to take another step: I would involve my ninety-one junior advanced placement composition students in an assignment of quality verbal exchange. My assumption was that the parents of these students would be eager to talk about ideas with their bright, highly motivated children. I sent home the same kind of prompts that students would experience when they took the advanced alacement composition exam. One of these was the following aphorism from Henry David Thoreau:

> *"Many men go fishing all of their lives without knowing that it is not fish they are after." In a well-thought-out essay, examine the accuracy of this aphorism in modern society. Concentrate on examples from your observations, reading, and experiences to develop your ideas.*

I asked students to talk about this statement with their parents and to write a nongraded narrative in class about their experience. Then, several days later, students would write a graded essay on this prompt. In this first attempt to send a "talk" assignment home with AP students, more students than I expected wrote that they did not share their prompts with their parents because their parents didn't speak English, were too busy, or (in the students' opinion) wouldn't be interested. Many others, based on their own narrative reports, did not have a positive experience, and some of their reflections were heartbreaking. Several parents did not understand the prompt or became critical of the student's response. The following two student narratives reveal very different outcomes:

> *I was very disappointed when I talked to my parents. They never went below the surface to see the true meaning. I did not benefit from the experience. As I became angry my parents became furious, and I got nowhere. They weren't willing to listen to my ideas. They still think I can't write even after I have shown them my improvements. The final results included a weak essay, upset parents, and a week indoors without privileges.*
> ~ Charlotte

> *At first I was reluctant to share the AP prompt with my mother who was home at the time I began my homework. This was because I assumed*

that she would not understand the prompt because English was not her first language. Yet when I interrupted her watching television to discuss Thoreau's quote with her, I was pleasantly surprised to see her turn off the blaring television and direct her full attention to me. I had never realized or even dreamed of how much attention she would give to me. We discussed the prompt and she at first didn't understand Thoreau, so I gave her my interpretation of it, and we built upon that. She talked about setting well thought out goals instead of working foolishly and impulsively toward it. It was a different, yet interesting experience to discuss my homework with my mother.

~ Joanne

Joanne's comment that she had never "realized or even dreamed how much attention" her mother would give her made me realize that there was more going on in this interaction between parent and child than I had originally planned for. While my initial motivation had been to elicit parental support for their children's academic performance, I was beginning to see an unanticipated and—possibly more valuable—outcome. These discussions were building bridges not only between home and school but also within families.

For example, Stephanie wrote:

I told my mother and step-dad that for homework I had to talk with them about two essay prompts from English. They said okay, but as the weekend went by they were busy and I was busy. Then yesterday I told them we had to talk about it. First my mother questioned why and isn't that my job to think of ideas on my own. So I read the prompt. At first my mom said she didn't know and that her brain hurt and that is the reason why she doesn't want to go back to school. But after awhile we started thinking and came up with some good ideas. My step-dad kept asking what an aphorism was, but he gave me ideas too. It was fun bonding with my parents. I don't get to do that at all, which makes me sad, but I got to show my parents how hard this class is and how I think. It was a priceless moment.

Some students came away with a revised respect for their parents' intellectual ability:

I thought over the prompts with the help of my mother. She was an incredible help. I had no idea my mom was so smart.

~ Melinda

To my shock, my mother responded with a thoughtful and reasonable answer. . . . I turned to my father now, hoping to stump someone with this question. . . . I could not believe my father even had a reasonable response to the prompt. . . .

~ Jason

This newfound enthusiasm for parents' abilities was only slightly offset by a few students who reached an opposite conclusion:

In discussing the Thoreau quote with my parents, I came to a harsh realization. I realized that my parents would fail AP English.

~ Krisante

In general, it was clear that many students were returning from these discussions with ideas for fresh ways to approach the prompt.

At first [my father] applied the quote to his occupational background. This confused me, but only because it made me think he misunderstood. I allowed him to continue though, and the more I listened the more sense he began to make. I felt bad for undermining him, which taught me a valuable lesson.

~ Casey

That night at the dinner table I happened upon a break in conversation in which to introduce the question, and I did. My mother slowly finished chewing her food and followed it with a brief pause. She then made what I believed to be a wondrous and insightful interpretation in the context of various forms of literature and movies in popular culture.

~ James

I shared my prompt on Thoreau with my grandmother. My parents happened to be very busy this weekend so I brought Thoreau up when I was talking to her. Thoreau was very interesting to my grandma; she had never read anything by him before but seemed intrigued. She is a very spiritual and religious woman and was very much in agreement with

Thoreau and added her own religious tone to it as well. Talking to her
helped me think of different ways of approaching this prompt.
   ~ Heidi

Parents as well as students grew from a discussion of Thoreau's aphorism:

When I showed my dad I expected him to not get it. My dad is very bad
in English, but extremely smart in the maths and sciences. He took a few
minutes to read them and said, "Well I can't write on many things but
this would be easy for me." I just looked at him because I thought maybe
he was being sarcastic (as he is a lot of the time) but he was very serious.
He said he could do it because he has had many experiences with things
that relate to the prompt. Now he wants to copy down the question so he
can take it to work.
   ~ Jen

I was concerned, however, about some of the students who, like Charlotte, had trouble approaching their parents and those whose parents, for whatever different reasons, responded negatively. Kevin told his mother he needed help on something.

She asked what I needed help on, and when I told her that I needed her
help on English, I saw the life drain from her. I explained that I needed
to engage in "quality verbal interaction" on the Thoreau quote. At this
moment she cringed and closed my door and walked away. About an
hour later she came back and tried to help. My dad wouldn't even let me
ask him for help.

I came to realize that some parents were truly baffled by the concept of suddenly joining our classroom discussion. I saw that we needed practice setting the stage for meaningful student-parent talk. So the next year I started "training" the parents in September at back-to-school night. I discussed my desire to extend the conversation of ideas from the classroom into the homes. Hearing it from me, parents were excited. They want to help their teenagers learn, and they know that the question "Have you done your homework?" does not go very deep, but they often don't know what else to say or ask. Talking with parents, I explained some of Montano-Harmon's research about the value of quality verbal interaction, about her view that students needed more conversations with adults on an idea level as they developed language and critical skills. Despite this positive response, I was aware that not all parents attend back-to-school night, so I also wrote a series of articles about reading and then talking about ideas in the home that was published on the front page of our parent newsletter, *The Eagle Eye*. This newsletter is mailed home every six weeks with a graded progress report to the parents of all our students (3,200 students this year). I explained my idea of sending prompts, editorials, or topics home for "talk" and summarized Montano-Harmon's research on quality verbal interaction and my desire to build a bridge between classroom ideas and talk in the home.

I took additional steps to make this process more comfortable for parents and for students. First, I allowed more time—two weeks—for this conversation between parent and student to take place. When students had not been able to talk with their parents, it was often because they had little time together. I wanted to take the pressure off.

I also prepared students for the possibility that they would not necessarily get a positive response. I assured my classes that their responsibility was to give a conversation a try. I let them know that they would not be graded down if for some reason parents were unable to talk with them.

At this point, parental response remains mixed. In some families it is understandably difficult to get a foot in the door.

> *Instead of an explanation I have received a tired look and explanation of tiredness. I persisted [in] my inquiry and was yet again received by glazed eyes and "I don't know, I'm too tired." I whined "but mom . . ." and again repeated my question and attempted to initiate a conversation. Once again to no avail. It's not a lack of communication or a dearth of family love, but my parents really were exhausted and intellectual conversation after their already mentally strenuous day would have been impossible.*
> ~ Jason

Other conversations took the student and the parent in directions neither I nor they would have guessed:

> *It could be that my mom has such a deep connection to Thoreau's quote that it has a painful meaning. She sounded like Amy Tan's* Joy Luck Club *mom. Indeed, she told me that she had not found what she was looking for in the U.S., and may choose to move back to Taiwan when I enter college. The quote from Thoreau is insightful in developing the idea*

*about one's search for his or her role in society. Even a failed attempt to
talk with my mom about Thoreau's meaning opened up a new perspective in my life as I try to find what my purpose is.*

　∼　John

However, since I have been providing more direction for parents and for
students, there has been a general change for the better. Now that I allow a window of two weeks for conversations between parent and student and the free-
writes that describe what happened, these narratives are much more extensive.
Last year, not one of my ninety-one students wrote more than half a page. Last
year's formal graded AP essays written in class on the Thoreau prompt were not
particularly stronger than their essays had been on AP prompts they had not discussed with their parents. However, this year, when I asked students to explain
to me in a freewrite what happened when they shared the Thoreau prompt with
their parents, all students wrote at least a page, some two or more pages, and
almost all described analytical discussions. I attribute the marked difference in
the quality of shared discussion to my clearer explanation to the students and
parents of what I was hoping for, as well as the two-week window that I accompanied with reminders of the upcoming deadline. Even students unable to connect with parents now seemed to have lots to say.

Molly began:

*Talking to my parents is one of the hardest things. We usually do not
have a normal conversation without arguing. So, upon having to discuss
this prompt with my parents, I was praying we were not going to break
out in an argument about who was right.*

Her narrative continued for two and a half pages and included comments
made by both parents and her commentary on their ideas. Although Molly saw
herself as "suffering" through the discussion, she and her parents were holding
a discussion at an idea level. As with other students, she narrated her parents'
responses—even if negative—analyzing and synthesizing their ideas.

I continue to send ideas home for discussion. The results suggest that students do want to talk with their parents about ideas, are pleased when their
parents will listen to their ideas, and are fascinated by the discoveries of family
stories they have never heard before. In addition to building a valuable bridge
between our classroom and their homes, idea-based discussion strengthens the
bridge between parent and child.

TIPS FOR QUALITY VERBAL INTERACTION

1. Prepare parents if possible through parent newsletters, notes home, and back-to-school nights. Let parents know that the goal is quality verbal interaction, not being right or being wrong. These conversations about ideas may be only a few minutes at a time and still be effective.

2. Prepare students for a variety of parental responses. The goal is conversation about issues and ideas. Even if a parent doesn't want to talk at a particular time, it is worth the attempt.

3. Give a several-day window for conversation; even a week is not too much time, as parents and students both keep very busy schedules.

4. It does not matter what language parents and students use for quality verbal interaction. Conversation does not have to be in English to be effective.

5. Do not grade students on their parents' response. Allow students to discuss their experiences in small groups, and have students write a description, reflection, and/or analysis to the teacher.

6. Keep a sense of humor.

7. Praise students for making an attempt and reporting what happened.

8. Praise parents for responding.

9. Provide several opportunities for take-home conversations throughout the year.

10. Use prompts that encourage discussion of ideas and issues, not right or wrong answers.

Kyle's Surprises: Anecdote as a Strategy to Strengthen Student Writing

Edward Darling

Written by Edward Darling about his teaching experience with a high school student in Vermont, this article was originally published in the summer 2000 issue of The Quarterly.

From the day I first read Ken Macrorie's *Writing to Be Read,* I was motivated to try with my students the form Macrorie calls a "case history." In developing these histories Macrorie urges writers to think seriously about stories, "details that reveal the essence" of a situation. When I thought about his advice, I was reminded that much of what I have read that has stayed with me has been connected to a story or is a story. So I wanted my students to choose an important chunk of their experience and develop it by telling stories that elucidate and support it. Many students elected to write about their jobs, an area of their lives that seemed rich with possibilities. But their first efforts were little more than lists of work routines, and I began to conclude that I didn't know how to teach this kind of writing. Maybe Ken Macrorie could pull this off, but I couldn't. When I saw Kyle's piece about working at a home supply store, however, I decided to give it one more try.

I worked with Kyle in the way I describe in the article, and his piece changed the way I and all my students since have looked at case histories. When I took his case history into a class to read and talk about, I found his piece provided the key that opened the gates to this type of writing, and ever since case histories have been one of the most success-ful projects my students work on.

Stories are central to Kyle's piece. The editors of *The Quarterly* inserted the word *anecdote* as they prepared this piece for publication. The con-notations of *anecdote* and *story* are different to me: *story* seems to carry more weight, but *anecdote* suggests "fun," and that is certainly appropri-ate for Kyle's piece.

If I were to write a case history of how I wrote this piece, I would include the help I got from writing groups at a summer institute of the National Writing Project in Vermont and at a National Writing Project writing re-treat in Santa Fe. I am indebted to many conference partners.

~ *Edward Darling, 2002*

I first learned about case histories in 1995, reading Ken Macrorie's *Writing to Be Read*. In chapter 8, Macrorie suggests the following assignment:

Write a case history of some job, process, action—what happened through a period of time. An hour working with a computer, a day in the body shop, one swimming lesson you gave a five-year-old, one vacation day when you did "nothing" for eight hours. If possible, take notes as you go through the experience, or right after the act, and record details you can remember.

Choose an action that is fun or misery for you, exciting or boring. Speak factually most of the time. . . . Make your readers respect you as an authority on this action by the way you reveal it in intimate workings, but remember not to lose them in meaningless technical terms.

Pack in the detail but make it add up to reveal the essence of the job, or your feeling toward it. (1984, 71–72)

I decided to try a Macrorie case study with my high school students. I did not know what to expect, but I did know there was often a gap between a teacher's best-laid plans and the less-than-fulfilling products that sometimes emerge from these creative teaching ideas. As I perhaps should have anticipated, most of my students wrote pieces that were mainly lists of generic activities and routines with no sense of the writer's involvement. However, one piece, "A Day at a Home Supply Store" by Kyle Ransom, seemed to have a skeleton structure on which we would be able to build. His draft gave a sense of what it was like being in the store. He wrote about the beginning of his work shift, getting ready for work, the way he went about arranging potting soil and light bulbs for display, his break, running the cash register, and getting ready to go home.

As my students always have a chance to revise their work, I decided the class should take a look at Kyle's piece to see what could be done with it. As we examined his writing, we wanted to know if there was material he could add about arranging the lightbulbs and if there were any interactions between him and customers or fellow employees that could be considered part of his job. Kyle said he could add material about bulbs and interactions, but he didn't let on what these would be. Further, he did not revise his case history during the course, a September-to-January semester elective for juniors and seniors. The syllabus provided a few open weeks during which he could have worked on his case study, but he did not choose to work further on it. And were it not for an unusual circumstance, he would never have developed it.

Kyle had joined the course three weeks late, at the end of September after the class was well under way. He wanted to change his schedule and assured me he would make up the work he had missed. By the end of the course, though, he hadn't made it up. I gave him an incomplete rather than a low grade because he had done so much good writing about his family, his opinions, and a fellow employee at the home supply store. We arranged to meet for weekly conferences until he made up all the assignments.

In the first conference I asked why he hadn't revised his case history, and he said he preferred to write opinion pieces. Then I pushed a little bit. I said I thought his case history had potential and a revision could be part of his makeup work. We discussed what had been said in class after the reading of the first draft, and I asked him to tell me about how he arranged the light bulbs. He did. I was impressed by the variety of bulbs his store sold and his knowledge of them. I encouraged him to add this material, even though in the first draft he had written: "It's hard for me to go into detail on how I organized them all [the light bulbs], but I can say it took me over two hours." I reminded him that he had said there were stories involving fellow employees and customers he could include.

The second draft, which he brought to the second conference, included more detail about the light bulbs as well as a story about a customer who had wanted help finding Christmas lights. This story was my first surprise in my work with Kyle, and it confirmed my feeling that he was carrying around more stories and details than he was owning up to. The story hinged on a misunderstanding: he had thought the customer wanted him to get an older, more knowledgeable employee to help her, when she had actually agreed that he should help her. This story took me deeper into his experience. There was drama in the misunderstanding and feeling in Kyle's uncertainty about what the customer wanted, in his need to remain polite, and in his failure to help her.

I asked Kyle if there were more stories like that, and he told me one. As he talked, I wrote notes to give him after the conference. He said,

> Customers come in not knowing exactly what they need, and they ex-
> pect you to pull a bulb out of a hat—they'll say something like, "I need a
> round bulb to fit a lamp this size," and they hold out their hands about
> two feet apart to show you.

A woman came in and asked for a bulb for an oven, but she didn't know what size bulb she needed or what make her stove was. I said, "It shouldn't be too hard to figure out." I'd seen one in my oven. So I picked one out. It was a standard size. But she thought it wasn't what she wanted.

I didn't think she knew what she was talking about, but I remained polite. I told her I'd get another one, but she said she didn't want one and that she lived too far away and she left without getting one. One of the guys I work with said the one I'd picked out would work.

This story was my second surprise. I asked him if he had still more stories. If so, he should incorporate them into a third draft.

He came to the third conference with a third draft in which he had added more light bulb detail and three more stories, including this one:

Two other employees were fixing the eight-foot-long fluorescent bulbs on the ceiling, the longest size we sell.

"Hey, you want to do us a favor," one of them called to me, "Bring these two burned-out bulbs to the back room for us?"

The doors that go to the back room are double doors . . . the type that swings both ways. The bulbs were too tall for me to walk through the doors with them standing vertically, so I turned them around so they were horizontal and tucked them under my arm. . . . I approached the doors wondering how I was going to pull this off. When you push the doors open, they swing right back towards you. My plan was to kick the doors open hard so they would open all the way, then run through fast so the bulbs would make it all the way through without getting hit by the doors that would be swinging back. . . .

I kicked the doors as hard as I could, they flew open, and I charged like I was using the light bulbs to joust. I was almost through when the two doors hit the wall, snapped back, and closed right behind me, shattering the last three feet of each bulb.

This story and the others he added also surprised me. They were full of drama, irony, misunderstanding, emotion, and tension between adult customers and a teenage employee as seen through a teenager's eyes. Kyle had written three of the stories mainly as dialogues: he was using voices besides his own to tell his case history. The writing in these four stories contrasted with the narrative of his first draft, which had become a frame within which to tell the stories.

Kyle's complete text (see the sidebar beginning on page 110) is designed to show his process of adding material. The production of the piece, however, was more complex than that. He had to rewrite the part about the swinging doors to make it clear. He also had to deal with a problem related to the four stories, only one of which had occurred during the shift he wrote about. In a discussion of case histories in *Telling Writing,* a book for college-age students, Ken Macrorie suggests that writers might include "facts from several different days' experience and put them together so they appear to belong to only one day. That's not necessarily presenting the case falsely, if you're trying to show what the whole experience has meant to you" (1985, 61).

This option of using material over a longer time span than a day increases a writer's choices, and it was an option Kyle took advantage of. In his piece it seemed improbable that all four stories would have occurred within one four-hour shift. This problem led to the technique of telling a story within a story: occurrences on this shift reminded Kyle of occurrences from the past, and he told about them at opportune moments in the narrative. Kyle was relying on an ancient storytelling technique, applying it to a piece of nonfiction.

Kyle and I also discussed how his case history could be told either in the past or present tense. The immediacy of the present tense, he believed, was more likely to involve readers in his narrative.

I was so impressed with Kyle's third draft that I asked him if I could take it to my second-semester writing class so the students there could read it. We were pleased when they delighted in it as much as I had. And a couple of weeks later I was surprised again when these students turned in their own case histories. I could see Kyle's work had influenced them: several were rich with details, stories, and dialogues. Kyle's work had set a standard. It was published in our class magazine and has continued to influence writers ever since.

After "A Day at a Home Supply Store" became such a hit in my second-semester class, I wanted an edited version for the future, and I asked Kyle if he would meet with me for an editing conference. That summer we worked on the piece together for the last time, editing and cutting. If I were to confer with Kyle again, I would recommend more cuts, especially in the part where he shows how he arranged the light bulbs. That's an example of losing readers in something like the "meaningless technical terms" Macrorie warns against. I had recommended that Kyle include this material because it gave a more complete picture of his work, and its inclusion had seemed so hard-won that it never entered my mind that readers might find it unimportant. And details about his break and other tasks could be thinned. Following Macrorie's admonition to "tell the truth," I had wanted Kyle's experience to be as inclusive as possible, when I could have been helping him to think about what was significant and encouraging him to engage his readers by being selective without violating the truth.

I never asked Kyle why he didn't think of including his four stories when he wrote his first draft. Maybe it was because he had never read a case history that included stories. In contrast, the writers who have come after him have read his piece and others like it and have seen the value of stories immediately.

As I look back over the history of Kyle's piece, I wonder if I should have kept suggesting he come back to it if, as he told me, he preferred to write about his opinions. While I console myself that my suggestions and recommendations were not requirements, I know that a student may interpret a teacher's advice as orders. I hope Kyle felt he was free to not work on his case history if he wanted to write something else. Whatever his reasons for writing his three drafts, he opened up new territory for me and my students that neither he nor I would have predicted.

In the preface of *Writing to Be Read*, Macrorie points out that a book on writing ought to include examples of the writing the book discusses and recommends. My experience with using Kyle's case history as a model has led me to conclude the same thing about teaching: my teaching ought to include examples of what my program and recommendations have produced. When I started publishing class magazines, I thought they would be a way for students to see their work in print, to read each other's pieces, and to preserve their writing. I wasn't aware that these magazines could become major texts in future writing classes—another surprise that grew out of using Kyle's piece as a model.

Donald Graves, speaking at convention of the National Council of Teachers of English, asked his audience, "What gives you energy?" The question took me back to the days when Kyle and I talked about his case history, and the way he kept strengthening his drafts as we talked, enlivening his work with these surprising revisions. Surprise can be reward enough, but I see now that the surprises in this case led to discoveries about a writer's experience and beyond that to discoveries about writing and teaching.

Because of the circumstances of Kyle's situation, I spent far more time with him than most teachers are able to spend with most students. But this investment of time resulted in a piece of work that, as a model, has helped many students write with authority about jobs, volunteer work, athletic contests, sports practices, classes in school, and workouts in gyms, to mention only the more popular topics. Students discover they have a wealth of material to select from and an informed interested audience in their classmates who have had similar experiences. For several years now, I have depended on Kyle's surprises to show students the way.

Oh, and there is one last surprise: Kyle is now a teacher. Or maybe that is not so surprising.

KYLE'S SURPRISES: STUDENT WORK

Here Kyle reveals how anecdotes added in successive drafts ($1 = \square$, $2 = \bigcirc$, and $3 = \star$) turn a bare bones essay into one humming with life.

A DAY AT A HOME SUPPLY STORE

BY KYLE RANSOM

☐ *I make my daily walk up the stairs to the employee bathroom, unlock my locker, and tie my green apron behind my back. My apron is furnished with all the "luxu-*
☐ *ries" an employee could desire: knife, tape measure, pen, pad of paper, price list,*
☐ *and a set of keys which unlock the back gates and the kerosene pump. I'm ready for another night shift. I punch my time card and head downstairs to the main*
☐ *floor.*

☐ *Every night my manager gives me my assignments. The list of things to do always varies. Sometimes it's little things, like restocking merchandise or putting price*
☐ *stickers on different items. Other times, I'll be assigned bigger projects, like orga-*
☐ *nizing parts of the warehouse, or setting up a display somewhere in the store. In addition to doing my assignments, I often have to "cover the floor." This means*
☐ *I have to watch my department for customers to help, and answer the calls that come in for my department. More often than not, the department I work in is*
☐ *called the seasonal department. We have all the outdoor items like gardening*
☐ *supplies, accessories for wood and coal stoves, kerosene heaters, grills, Christmas lights, anything that is seasonal.*

☐ *Today I have been assigned to two main things. First I have to stock bags of*
☐ *potting soil. After I am done with that, I have to organize the light bulbs in the*

☐ electrical department. And if things get busy, I will run one of the cash registers up front. There are always two going, but when it gets busy, I open a third.

☐ I begin stocking the potting soil. There are three sizes of bags: eight, sixteen, and
☐ thirty-two quarts. I have a limited amount of shelf space, and I have to set them up so that all the shelf space is used, while keeping in mind neatness, organiza-
☐ tion, and easy customer access.

✶ While I plan the display in my head, an old man approaches me and mumbles something in a raspy voice. It is hard for me to understand him, but I'm pretty
✶ sure he says, "Where do you keep the vice grips?" I point him to the hardware department. He nods, thanks me, and walks in that direction.

✶ A few minutes later, he comes back. I am bent over, opening the boxes of potting soil. He taps me on the shoulder. I turn around, surprised to see him back.

✶ "Boy," he says in the same raspy voice. "You are so out of touch. You stopped sell-
✶ ing bicycles five years ago! Don't you pay attention?"

At first I am bewildered. Who said anything about bicycles? Then I realize what
✶ has happened. Vice grips. Bicycles. If you say them fast, they sound the same. I cannot help but laugh.

✶ "I'm sorry sir. I thought you said 'vice grips.' My mistake."

✶ "Yeah, right," he says as he walks away. "Nice try. Like they really sound the same."

☐ Back to the potting soil. The space I have to work with is three shelves high, each shelf four feet long. I have three different sizes, so I give each size its own shelf. I
☐ put the thirty-two quart bags on the bottom shelf, because they are heavier and it will be easier for customers to get them. I stack all the bags from biggest to small-
☐ est, so the eight quart bags are on the top shelf. Now, on to the light bulbs.

○ Thinking of light bulbs reminds me of a customer who came into the store a while ago. She stopped me and asked, "Excuse me, do you work here?"

○ "I sure do. What can I do for you?"

○ "Can you get me someone who can help me with the Christmas lights please?"

"Well ma'am, that would be me. I'd be glad to help you"

○ "Aren't you a little young? I was looking for someone a little older."

○ I was insulted by her comment, but I was still polite. "I'm the one in the seasonal department tonight, so I'm sure I'll be able to answer any questions you might
○ have, and if I can't, then I'll get someone from electrical to help you."

○ The woman seemed to be sticking with her supposition that I was too young to help her. "Maybe that would be a good idea," she said.

○ *"Okay," I said. I turned to get someone else to help her, and as I was walking away, I heard her behind me.*

○ *"God, how rude."*

○ *I stopped in the middle of the aisle and turned back to see her standing with a disgusted look on her face. Sensing a complaint, I walked back to where she was*
○ *standing with her arms crossed.*

○ *"Is something wrong, ma'am?" I asked nicely.*

○ *"Yes there is! I'm trying to get some help, and you just walk away while I'm in mid-sentence. I consider that extremely rude and disrespectful!"*

○ *I struggle to maintain my temper. "Ma'am, I wasn't just walking away. You said you wanted someone else to help you, so I was simply going to get them. I'm sorry if I gave you the wrong idea. I . . ."*

○ *"I bet you're sorry! You're going to be sorry when I call your manager tomorrow and complain. I bet you'll be sorry then, won't you?"*

○ *I couldn't believe her. She was definitely going overboard. I tried to dissuade her from calling my manager. "Ma'am, do you think it's really necessary to call? I'll just go get someone older to help you if you'd like, and you can get your Christmas lights,*
○ *OK?"*

○ *"Oh, so now you don't want to help me yourself! What, are you too good to help me? Do you value your job young man? Judging by your actions, one wouldn't think so, being so rude to customers."*

○ *I was becoming exasperated. I went back and forth with this woman for another five minutes or so. She still was going to call my manager and demand I be dealt with. I told her to have a good day, and she left the store. It wasn't until some time later that I realized what had happened, and that when I thought she wanted me to get someone older, she had actually agreed that I should help her.*

☐ *I continue on my way to the light bulbs, which are more difficult to display than the potting soil. There were only three kinds of potting soil, whereas there are close to*
☐ *twenty kinds of light bulbs. Everything from light floods to reflectors, soft whites to cool whites, night lights to spotlights, bulb fluorescents to halogens, appliance bulbs to energy-efficient bulbs. I don't know where to start. There are so many ways I can*
○ *set them up, and I don't know which one is best.*

○ *I begin with the reflector bulbs and arrange them from biggest to smallest. The 150 watts are on the bottom, all the way to the forty watts on the top. I do the same with the standard lamp bulbs, and then again with the soft whites. Next come the*
✳ *colored bulbs. They are all the same size and wattage, so I arrange them by color: black, red, blue, green, yellow, and pink. After the colored ones come the long fluo-*
✳ *rescents. I stand them up vertically. Finally I set up the specialty bulbs—halogen*

✳ bulbs, energy-efficient bulbs, night lights, and various types of decorative bulbs.
✳ I finish two hours later, satisfied with my job. As I look back again at the fluorescent bulbs, I remember something that happened to me my first day at work
several months ago.

✳ Two other employees were fixing the eight-foot-long fluorescent bulbs on the ceil-
✳ ing, the longest size we sell.

"Hey, you want to do us a favor," one of them called to me, "and bring these two
✳ burned-out bulbs to the back room for us?"

"Sure, no problem," I said, and grabbed the bulbs out of the corner where they
✳ were standing. With one in each hand, I headed towards the back of the store.

✳ The doors that go to the back room are double doors, and they are the type that
swings both ways. The bulbs were too tall for me to walk through the doors with
✳ them standing vertically, so I turned them around so they were horizontal, and
tucked them under my arm, with about the last four feet of each one sticking out
✳ behind me. I approached the doors wondering how I was going to pull this off.
When you push the doors open, they swing right back towards you. My plan was
✳ to kick the doors open hard so they would open all the way, then run through fast
so the bulbs would make it all the way through without getting hit by the doors
✳ that would be swinging back. At the time, it seemed like a perfectly practical
idea. I realize now it was a terribly stupid thing to do.

✳ I kicked the doors as hard as I could, they flew open, and I charged like I was using the light bulbs to joust. I was almost through when the two doors hit the wall,
✳ snapped back, and closed right behind me, shattering the last three feet of each
bulb. It made the most horrible noise, and I knew the whole store could hear it. I
✳ threw the remainders of the bulbs in the trash and swept up the rest off the floor.
It was one of the most humiliating things that ever happened to me at
✳ work.

☐ I decide to take my fifteen minute break. I buy a candy bar and a soda at the
registers, go upstairs, sit down in the break room, and read the paper. After fif-
☐ teen minutes, I throw my wrapper away, toss the bottle into the recycle box, and
go to the bathroom. Then I open my locker, get a piece of gum, and walk back
☐ downstairs.

☐ It is now 7:15. I have another forty-five minutes before I can go home. I notice
the registers each have a line, so I get behind the third register and ring some
✳ people up. Running a register is always a good way to run into some very interesting people. When people ask me about things that happen at work, I remember
✳ something that happened once while I was working a register. One of the customers tried to return a lamp shade.

✳ "Hi. I'd like to return this please," she said. "It's the wrong size for my lamp."

113

* *"Sure. If I could just see your receipt, ma'am."*

* *"I don't have my receipt with me, but I really did buy it here."*

  "I'm sure you did, but without a receipt, I can't give you a refund."

* *The lady started to get defensive and aggravated, as was I.*

* *"I can't believe you don't believe me! You think I'd really come in here and lie?"*

  "Ma'am, it's not that I don't believe you, it's just that I'm required to see a receipt
* *before refunding any merchandise. The best I can do is a merchandise credit."*

  "Well, all right. I guess that's better than nothing. Let's do that."
*

  Happy that we'd resolved the issue, I took the lamp shade and searched for the
* *price sticker so I could get the computer number. I finally found the sticker, but in*
  big red letters was the name of another store. I gave the lady a disappointed glance
* *and showed her the sticker.*

  She blushed and mumbled sheepishly, "Oh, sorry, wrong store. I get you guys mixed
* *up all the time." She grabbed the lamp shade and hurried out.*

☐ *I ring up customers and it stays busy until about 7:45. When it dies down, I go out*
  back and make sure the back gates are locked. A customer comes in and wants five
☐ *gallons of kerosene. The girl on the register calls me to the front so I can get it. I go*
  outside to the kerosene pump, fill the can, and bring it back to the register. It is now
☐
  five minutes of eight. I relax for a bit, standing around with a couple of employees,
☐ *talking. When it is 8:00, I run upstairs, punch my time card, take off my apron, put*
  it in my locker, grab my jacket, and run downstairs and out the door. I am free until
☐ *4:00 tomorrow afternoon.*

REFERENCES

Macrorie, Ken 1984. *Writing to Be Read*. 3rd ed. Portsmouth, NH: Boynton/ Cook/Heinemann.

———. 1985. *Telling Writing*. 4th ed. Upper Montclair, NJ: Boynton/Cook.

Section 3

Okay, But What Now?

Teachers build on what they know

A Cure for Writer's Block: Writing for Real Audiences

Anne Rodier

*Written by Anne Rodier about her teaching experi-
ence with high school students in Louisville, Kentucky, this article was originally published in the
spring 2000 issue of* The Quarterly.

Every August I look over the new faces in my classroom and feel a mixture of frustration at the need to whip a new group of kids into writing shape and excitement at the possibility of watching these students
become proficient writers. Each one has his or her unique instructional
needs, and I know that it is my responsibility to learn what those needs
are.

Years ago, I thought that I could construct a single lesson that would
reach all of my students if only they really paid attention and applied the
wisdom that I shared with them. Then I started writing to publish, writing because I had something to say, not because it was an assignment for
a grade. At first I appreciated the advice from more seasoned writers,
which I knew was graciously offered, but I found that a lot of it didn't
apply. My writing process was different from theirs. What a huge breakthrough that was! If I believed that my writing process was unique to
me, why was I not affording the same understanding that my students'
writing processes were uniquely their own?

As soon as I accepted this concept, my approach to teaching writing changed. I stopped being the expert teacher of writing and started helping my students figure out what they need in order to be expert writers. In the end, I know that if a student and I explore the problem long enough, we'll figure something out. However, even though I understand I must help all students find their own way, a few general questions have helped my students, me, and indeed all writers figure out where they are going. The main question I have learned to ask is, "Who are you writing this for?" This is the wisdom that I applied with Rudy, one of my bigger teaching challenges.

~ *Anne Rodier, 2002*

I work in an inner-city school. Our crumbling walls are set amid the projects, a place where one wouldn't expect to find young people writing much besides graffiti or love letters. Over time I have discovered that the motives that drive my students to write successfully are pretty much like the ones that motivate me to do my best writing. Like me, my students have to believe that what they have to say is important enough to bother writing. They have to experience writing for real audiences before they will know that writing can bring them power.

This year, I've been watching the way one of my seniors, Rudy, approaches writing. I find it amusing that he's a lot like me. He can't settle down to his work. Any distraction interrupts him. He can't use a pencil, needs music, a better chair, a different atmosphere. According to him in his letter to the reviewer of his portfolio,

> *You can't make romantic love at a head banger's ball or tap dance at a Hip-Hop party. I wish I could scribble off hundreds of pages, but if my surroundings aren't right, then I can't work. . . . I'm an artist. I'm committed to the art form. We've been dating, engaged, and married until talent do us part. I love what I do.*

I've been working on *Emily*, my great American novel-in-progress, for years, and I think I'm also at the wrong party. I've probably bought about fifty new pens to try for inspiration, experimented with blue, pink, and yellow legal paper, tried wide ruled and college. I've moved my writing desk to every room in my house and discovered thirty different favorite composers who most inspire my writing. I never write in my loft. My exercise bike is there, and it makes me feel guilty because I'm not using it. I go to my favorite restaurant, the Come Back Inn, try a glass of wine, wear a special shirt, put my hair up, take it down, hold a crystal, put pictures of my last trip around me.

PLAYING WRITER

Like Rudy, I'm in love with being a writer. It doesn't matter that I talk about writing my novel more than I actually write it. Even my daughter caught me at playing writer. We were shopping for lamps. She wanted cheap and functional. She found hers quickly. I turned on each one, traded lamp shades, and tried to sense the mood each might create for my writing. After forty minutes, her patience gave out.

"I know you need the perfect lamp to create your romantic notion of being a writer in your loft. Here, pick the Victorian one." I did.

Why do Rudy and I fidget rather than write? Rudy calls it "writer's block." I think it's something else. We both have a hard time finding exactly why we are writing and to whom.

Rudy and I both write very personal, autobiographical stuff. We both read works by others who do the same. We still get nowhere. Rudy has a deadline; portfolios are due in April. *Emily* has no deadline. Her purpose is to help me keep my romantic image of being a writer. The audience for my novel is nebulous. I can't seem to pin it down. I don't know how to help Rudy.

"What are you trying to say here, Rudy?"

"I don't know. It's a feeling I want to give the reader."

For him, it's always love. For me, it's the wonder of revelation about life.

A few years ago, I published a book. My publisher made me meet deadlines. I procrastinated, but I had a story I wanted to tell and an audience who needed to hear it. A very good friend had just died of AIDS, and I had to navigate my way through the medical and legal issues attached to his long and depressing illness amid an array of attitudes expressed by the people surrounding us. His parents abandoned him completely, while some very welcome and sometimes unexpected support came from friends and AIDS organizations. It was important to me that I let others who were dealing with similar issues know that they weren't alone, that there are many who are caring supporters when family fails to be so. With AIDS at an epidemic level, the need for immediacy hung heavy on my pen, and I pushed myself to get my story into my readers' hands.

HAVING A STORY TO TELL

When our department became embroiled in censorship, my students learned firsthand the power of having a story to tell. One of our teachers was offering an optional novel that dealt with issues of race, religion, and homosexuality. When some members of the community got wind of this book's contents, they objected, and our students' real-life lessons in writing began. Parents wanted the book banned and the teacher fired. Our students felt otherwise. They spoke at hearings, wrote the press, spoke to reporters. We told them to shape all their thoughts in writing first so that they would be better prepared, more organized. After months of turmoil, their efforts were rewarded and the book remained as an optional reading choice with parental permission. The author sent us flowers, and we all felt powerful. The English department finally learned the meaning of real-life writing: it allows one to shape one's life and change one's world.

Louise Rosenblatt talks about the "poem," or the meaning, being the coming together of the writer, text, and reader (1994, 12). What we discovered through our censorship experience is that the "poem" is the coming together of any writer, text, and reader for real purposes, not the student writing for the teacher for a grade.

MOTIVATING STUDENTS

What if part of every student's curricular year included real-life, change-your-world writing? What if every teacher guided students to find the right focus for the right audience? What if they actually expected responses as a result of their writing? The possibilities are endless: papers in science journals, poetry in *Redbook,* changes in local government, financial support for school and personal projects, TV scripts, children's books, grants to fund science projects, fights against censorship.

Students writing for real audiences are motivated in a way that students churning out papers for grades are not. As for Rudy, I knew he did not care much about grades. I approached him after his two-week winter vacation at his family's home in New York.

"How'd your writing go over the break?" Rudy was sprawled in my chair, a bit on guard, wondering about my motives. I am his teacher, after all, and he missed a big deadline. Several totally revised, ready-to-publish pieces had been due before the break. He'd left town planning to work on a delightful, unfinished piece chronicling his love for beautiful women, specifically one who had been unfaithful, causing him to end their relationship. I had hopes that he'd found his muse in the Big Apple.

"Well," he shifted and put on his best student-working-the-teacher attitude. "I went home and I saw three shows!"

This ruse worked for a minute because he knew how much I envied his time at these Broadway shows. I really wanted to hear his story.

"Of course, we did New Year's on Times Square. It was packed, you couldn't move, and someone started shooting right after the ball dropped."

How could I not respond to that? I'd clung to the television coverage of Times Square while he was actually there.

Rudy squirmed again then confessed. "I didn't really write. I just hung out. I was home, in the old neighborhood." He paused. Fidgeted. "I still can't figure out what to write."

NAMING YOUR AUDIENCE

That's when I pounced. "Rudy, I know what your problem is. Who are you telling this story to? Who would you really talk to about your feelings about this girl?"

At first, he just looked at me like I was nuts, but I could see his brain working. He smiled, "Yeah. That's exactly the problem."

"Who's your audience, Rudy?"

"I guess anyone."

"No. You need to find a real audience."

"But who would want to read this?"

"My point exactly! Let's try out some ideas. How about a feature article for the school newspaper offering advice to students about relationships?"

No response.

"Maybe a letter to her telling her what you think about what she did to you?" He shook his head.

"A short story creating the anguish and pain you felt, aimed at teenage readers so they know they aren't alone in their misery?"

He gave me a "duh" kind of look as if to ask why he would care about other teens' problems.

"Come on, help me here. You obviously want to tell this story. Who cares about it?"

Rudy finally lifted his eyebrows. I knew he had an idea. "I have a cousin in Brooklyn. I talk to him a lot. He could be my audience." Pause. Brain action. "But then should I write it like I'd really write to him? I mean, we'd say she had a fat ass, but that doesn't seem right for what I'm writing."

"Hmm." I paused. Brain action. "Sometimes when I write home, I actually employ my craft. My family knows I'm an English teacher and a writer. But every now and then, I write a letter that makes them say, 'I can see *why* Anne's an English teacher and a writer.'"

A grin. "Yeah, kind of like performing, acting through writing, like having a—"

"Persona, a voice, telling the right story to the right person in the right way."

"That's what I'll do then. Yeah! I'll write to my cousin, he'll be my audience. But—well, the girl has tried to get tight with me again. I don't like her anymore. I don't want to see her. Do I add that or what?"

"I don't know. I guess you're going to have to make that choice as a writer."

"Okay, yeah, I think that's what I'll do."

"And, Rudy, about your deadline."

"I know, it's due in March."

"No, it's due next week. A full draft."

I escorted him, late, to class amid protests that he wanted to stay and write. Maybe he'd go home and finish it if I let the tension build.

We really do fail our students when we don't help them find a way to write real stuff, and if I hadn't struggled as a writer as Rudy has struggled, I wouldn't have been able to help him find his audience. What it all comes to is this: if what you are writing has no possibility of making a difference, of reaching a real audience for real purposes, then there will be no investment in the work. When our inner-city students score higher in writing than the East End privileged kids, we know it's because we don't have them write just for a grade. We have them write for real.

That year, Rudy became a professional writer. He learned to identify an audience for the story that he was aching to tell. Now he's in New York with a recording contract, writing song lyrics for—it goes without saying—real audiences.

REFERENCE

Rosenblatt, Louise M. 1994 *The Reader, the Text, the Poem: The Transactional Theory of the Literary Work.* Carbondale, IL: Southern Illinois University Press.

Quoc Tin and Sona: The Story of a Peer Journal Project

Myron Berkman

Written by Myron Berkman about his teaching experience with students at Newcomer High School in San Francisco, California, this article was originally published in the fall 1995 issue of The Quarterly.

During the time the events described in this article took place, I was a teacher at Newcomer High School in San Francisco, the first educational stop for many immigrant children coming into the city.

In looking back at my teaching, during that time I think I can see two problems. Or, perhaps, two significant ones out of many. First, I had a polyglot of students, many of whom knew no one and all of whom were newcomers to America. They came with lots of different baggage: different backgrounds, levels of education, and languages. They had been exposed to a variety of teaching styles or, in some cases, not much teaching at all. From this diverse group, I wanted to create a community. If I could do this, it would make my teaching easier and the lives of the students in my classroom more comfortable.

The second problem was more general. No matter what, I want my classes to be interesting. I guess this need comes from my own student days when I was an extremely squirmy student, easily bored, who had a hard time paying attention. I had little interest in school writing because all my writing had been for the teacher, but now I was the teacher.

Then I had a breakthrough. What if students were to write to someone other than the teacher? And not just any other—a peer. We know how important it is for teenagers to be accepted by others their age. They might even forget that they are writing for an assignment and let go of all their anxieties, or what linguist Stephen Krashen calls their "affective filter," and just write what they think or feel. Especially for these newcomers, I thought, becoming comfortable as writers in a new language was primary. The accuracy and the grammatical principles could come later in other, more structured, venues.

What follows is my account of how this project evolved. I believe that teachers who follow this design and consider the caveats I advance can have success with peer journals in venues less specialized than the English language development environment in which I taught.

$\sim$ *Myron Berkman, 2002*

I'm slowly disengaging myself from being the source of all knowledge in the classroom and inching towards building a community of learners, all learning from each other. Well . . . I might as well jump in and see what happens. . . . (excerpt from my teacher journal)

n o one ever spotted Duong Quoc Tin and Sona Diwa hanging out together in the school lunchroom. Quoc Tin, a Vietnamese immigrant, the perfect student, a voracious learner and constant note taker, found his friends among other Vietnamese boys. Sona, who had studied English in her native India, would have seen herself as too sophisticated in her up-to-the-minute jeans to have much to do with the less savvy Quoc Tin. Yet these two students became friends of a sort, sharing experiences and ideas and helping each other learn. I can take some credit as the matchmaker in this unlikely relationship. Quoc Tin and Sona became acquainted through the peer journals I was using in my classes.

The basic idea of the peer journal is to pair students in two different classes—in my case an intermediate English Language Learners (ELL) class and a World Civilization class—and have them write letters to each other about themselves and about the subject matter they are studying. The expectation is that, uninhibited by a teacher's intrusions, students will begin to feel comfortable with one another and start to take pleasure in sharing their experiences and ideas about the content of their studies.

This technique sometimes works well and sometimes does not. For Quoc Tin and Sona, peer journals were liberating, and in this paper I want to take a close look at this pairing and try to figure out why it clicked.

GETTING STARTED

My experiment with peer journals occurred at Newcomer High School in San Francisco, a school dedicated to teaching recently arrived immigrants and refugee youth from around the world. In any class I could expect to be working with—for starters—Central American, Chinese, Vietnamese, Russian, Arabic, and Filipino students. Our school serves as a port of orientation for these students to both the school system and the United States. There are no native English speakers at

Newcomer, and the majority of students have had six years or less of education in their country.

The goals I set for my peer journal project, then, were intimately connected to the Newcomer environment. First, since our school population consisted solely of immigrants and refugees, I wanted to see if students from different cultures could become comfortable using English by engaging in a written conversation with each other. Fluency, not accuracy, was what interested me. Students must feel at ease with English before they can worry about grammar.

Additionally, I wanted to see if students could use their own experiences and backgrounds as resources for each other. I thought the World Civilization curriculum provided a unique opportunity to tap the richness of my multicultural classroom.

Next, I wanted to see if the students could write about the content they were studying. I didn't want them just memorizing facts. Could they integrate what they were studying into meaningful communication with another student? And finally, as a teaching goal, I wanted to see if I could integrate my curriculum in the two classes, getting more writing into my World Civilization class and more content into my ELL class.

My ninth grade World Civilization class was composed of students from over a dozen countries, including Mexico, India, Vietnam, Russia, El Salvador, Iran, China, and Nicaragua. At our school most of the students study history in bilingual classes, but my class was composed of those students who did not speak one of the major language groups—such as Spanish, Chinese, or Vietnamese—and other students who for special reasons were assigned to my class. Students from ELL I through ELL 5 were placed in this multilevel class, an arrangement that brought with it obvious difficulties. In World Civilization we were expected to study some of the early civilizations such as China, Egypt, and India.

My ELL class, on the other hand, was grouped by level: an intermediate ELL 3 class, which meant that most of the students had studied English perhaps for a couple of years in their country. In the class we focused on communicative competency with lots of opportunities for the students to speak using dialogues, role-plays, and skits. During the second hour of this two-hour class, we usually focused on writing.

To begin my project, I paired up students from the two classes. I tried to match each student with a partner from a different country so as to facilitate as much exchange and learning as possible. Each pair of students shared a note-book, which always remained in the classroom. They wrote two or three times a week for fifteen to twenty minutes. Because I was interested in getting students to write about content, I asked students to write about topics they were study-ing. For example, I asked my World Civilization students to ask their partners if they knew anything about the country we were studying.

Sometimes the topic would spring from the ELL class. During Halloween, we had a discussion about superstitions. I asked the ELL students to write to their partners about a superstition in their country and to find out about one in another country. The students then wrote essays about superstitions around the world.

At the end of the year, the journals contained an abundance of writing. But how could I use this writing to answer my original questions? At first I planned to compare several sets of journals. But the writing was so different that it was hard to compare. Many of the ELL students were writing at a higher level than their World Civilization counterparts. Some students would write two or three paragraphs, while their partners could respond with only one or two lines. In many journals I found little writing about content and much writing about typi-cal adolescent issues such as school, homework, teachers, and boyfriends and girlfriends.

But the biggest problem was continuity. Our school's population was very transient, and students were constantly moving in and out of classes. Very few partnerships remained intact. I often had to change writing partners two or three times. It was difficult to compare the writing in a partnership of five months to a partnership of two to three weeks.

I looked through many journals and found a few pairings that had managed to stay intact throughout the school year. One of these pairs was Duong Quoc and Sona. I decided to look at their journal to see if I could find out why their pairing succeeded.

Duong Quoc Tin was in my ELL 3 class and had been in the United States for about ten months. He was a good student who worked extremely hard and got almost all A's in my class. Prior to coming to America, he had studied for three months in a simulated American high school program in a refugee camp in the Philippines. Sona, one of my World Civilization students, had been in the United States for six months, but Sona had studied English in India so her Eng-lish level was higher than Quoc Tin's.

129

ENCOURAGING THE PERSONAL

Between the two of them, they generated so much writing I didn't know where to start. Taking an idea from Courtney Cazden at the Bread Loaf School of English, I looked for a sustained period of time during which both students had focused on the same topic. At the beginning of the year, their journals lacked continuity. For example, Quoc Tin might write about school, but Sona would respond about a personal matter. However, for about two months in the early spring, both students seemed to be focusing on the topic of India and Southeast Asia. Quoc Tin begins this interchange:

Dear Sona,
February 16

How have you been? I haven't seen you a long time already. I think you don't come to school on these day. Are you sick or you change school. If you sick, I hope you're better now. I heard Mr. Berkman say you're studying about India now in your World Civilization subject. He told me to give you some ideas about India. but I think you're Indian, so you know better than mine. I've been studying about India from Mr. Vu already. I think I've got some of them to tell you. As I've studied, India is located in Asia. Its civilizations was located in the Indus River.

    ~ Quoc Tin

Dear Quoc Tin,
February 23

Hi! How are you? I am sorry I was sick for a long time. First I got chicken pox and then after one day I immediately got flue.

In Mr. Berkman's class we are studying about India. I am myself Indian so it's not so difficult for me to understand. Tomorrow is India day in Mr. Berkman's class. Tomorrow I and my two friends are going to bring food and some Indian song. O.K. See you next time. If you can give me a reply.

    ~ Sona

Quoc Tin's writing is very advanced for a first-year ELL student. Although there are some minor errors with tenses and phrases such as "you know better than mine," his use of the present perfect tense demonstrates good use of language for a first-year ELL student.

But even more important, Quoc Tin weaves both content and personal reference into his letter. He shows concern for his partner by immediately inquiring where she has been. His keen awareness of audience is demonstrated even more when he points out the incongruity of writing about India to an Indian. Even though the period ended before he could finish writing about India, his two sentences summarize a major point of ancient Indian civilization: Indian civilization began along the Indus River.

Sona's writing shows an instant familiarity. She begins with "Hi!" She not only tells him that she was sick but even describes her illness. Then she proudly tells what she and her friends are going to do for India Day. Each month I devote a day to the country we are studying. Students are asked to bring in cultural items such as food, clothes, and music from that country. Sona's admission was quite surprising. For the past week I had been trying to persuade Sona to participate in India Day. It was like pulling teeth! She insisted she had no Indian clothes and couldn't cook. I wasn't sure if India Day was going to take place. Yet, in her letter to Quoc Tin, she breezily tells him all about it. As might be predicted, her writing to her partner is more revealing than her communication to the teacher.

GOING INTO DEPTH

The next few exchanges are dominated by two topics, one related to a question about black and white people and the other related to a definition of a Vietnamese trait. Both were content issues from the World Civilization class. Even though Quoc Tin was in my ELL class, he became actively involved in writing about these topics. It was at this time that both classes watched the movie *Gandhi*.

Dear Sona,
March 1

I just saw a movie about an Indian, Gandhi. He has brown skin, and the white people don't want to do anything together with the brown or black people. Gandhi hates it and he wants to change this system.

　　~ Quoc Tin

131

Dear Quoc Tin,
March 2

Today I also saw a movie Gandhi. *Did you liked him? I already knew the story about Gandhi because I use to study in India. . . . Do you believe in black and brown people?*

~ Sona

Quoc Tin's letter is focused on content. There is no reference to Sona. His observation on the attitudes of white people is an acute one. He made it after watching Gandhi get thrown off a first-class South African train car because he was "colored."

Sona is more focused on communicating with Quoc Tin. Her breezy personable style contrasts with Quoc Tin's more formal writing. Her last question, "Do you believe in black and brown people?" triggers a series of exchanges over the next three letters.

In these next letters, the students reach a new level of communication. Both of them begin referring back to previous letters in order to understand each other. Quoc Tin's writing starts to open up in response to Sona.

Dear Sona
March 15

How are you?. . . Today, I've already finished all the movie about Gandhi. I think Gandhi is a very nice man and sometimes he's very stupid, too. He always thinks for his people. He doesn't care about him. He is also a very stubborn person. He wants to wear his own clothes (make by the Indians). He doesn't want to wear the foreign clothes or anything that's not made by the Indian. . . .

Sona! Last time you ask me, "Do you believe in black and brown people?" I don't understand what you mean. Would you please explain it?

Thank You

~ Tin Duong

Dear Quoc Tin,

How are you? I am sorry I didn't write you for a long time. In previous letter I asked you about black and white. I meant that do you believe that

black and white people are different. What does "tanh hieu hoc" means?
O.K. bye. I will write you next time. Thank you

Yours friend,

∼ Sona

Quoc Tin continues to write very well about the assigned topic, Gandhi. Again he deftly integrates his own opinion into his summary of the movie. He shows a keen understanding of Gandhi's obstinacy in refusing to wear foreign clothes. In the last paragraph, for the first time a direct question is asked about something written in the journal. Quoc Tin asks Sona to clarify her question about black and brown people. The use of the exclamation point after her name shows that this is important to him. He wants to answer her question, but he needs more information. He politely asks her to explain more fully.

Since Sona was absent for several weeks, she probably had to refer back to her letter written a month earlier in order to answer Quoc Tin's question. Even though she changes the colors "black and brown" to "black and white," her intention is clear. She wants to know if Quoc Tin thinks that people with different skin colors are different.

Immediately after explaining the black-white question, Sona introduces a new topic, Southeast Asia. She asks Quoc Tin about "tanh hieu hoc." Sona had come across this term in a handout from her World Civilization class. Sona demonstrates reading comprehension and responsiveness by picking out this one Vietnamese term from a variety of terms she had been studying from Cambodia, Laos, and Vietnam and asking her partner about it.

INCREASING COMFORT, INCREASING FLUENCY

In the next exchange, Quoc Tin's writing style continues to evolve. His formal content-based writing is changing to a more comfortable conversational tone of writing to a friend.

Dear Sona,

April 11

How are you? thanks a lot for your writing. I enjoyed read it very much. I think you're too busy on your work so you don't have time to write letters for me, but it's O.K. . . . I would like to answer your question about black and white people. In my opinion, black and white people are the same. They are all human being and they should have equal rights.

Dear Sona! something you asked me in your letter, is that Vietnamese or English. Would you write a little more clearly please, so I can read it easily.

Thanks.
From your friend

~ Duong Quoc Tin

Quoc Tin is writing to a friend now. The first paragraph is written completely on a personal level. This contrasts sharply with his previous letters. He answers Sona's provocative question about "black and white people" with remarkable succinctness and clarity. "In my opinion, black and white people are the same. They are all human being and they should have equal rights." Then Quoc Tin turns to Sona's latest inquiry, about *tanh hieu hoc*. He wants to answer her question, but Sona's writing of the Vietnamese words is not legible to him.

The next day Sona answers in her longest letter to date. She, too, is feeling more comfortable and is now able to express some of her feelings.

Dear Quoc Tin

April 12

. . . I read your letter. . . . I am glad you wrote me. . . . Actually my problem is I don't finish my homework at home. So I do in classroom. Everyday I get a lot of homework. I am so confused about what should I do. That's the reason I am so busy. I am moody. Most of the times I get tired during last period and I don't write. I think you must be getting a lot of time. You are a intelligent student.

Now a days we are studying about Southeast Asia. It's little hard. All different kinds of names and they are hard to pronounce. . . . In previous letter I wrote you a word, "tanh hieu hoc." It's in Vietnamese. I wanted to know that what does it mean. If you don't know I don't mind just forget it. O.K. Mr. Berkman is telling to stop. So see you in next letter. Bye.

Thanks
Your Friend,

~ Sona

Dear Sona,

April 24

How are you? Did you have a nice weekend? When I read your letter, I knew that you're very busy on your work so you can't write for me. But it's O.K., because it's more important for you to do your work than to write for me. You are even intelligent but diligent too.

In your letter, you asked me what does "Tan hiew hoc" mean. it means that some body likes to study or to learn something news.

　　$\sim$ Duong Quoc Tin

Sona is clearly opening up here. But even more important, finally, two and a half weeks after the initial query, Quoc Tin is able to answer Sona's question about *tanh hieu hoc*. Quoc Tin makes sure to include the correct accent marks. Sona's negligence in writing these marks prevented Quoc Tin from deciphering the words in the first place. In the reading unit, *tanh hieu hoc* was defined as "a Vietnamese trait of showing a great respect or love for education." "But somebody who likes to study" is a reasonable explanation from a beginning-level English student.

CONCLUSION

What stands out in this brief study of a writing exchange is the change in voice by both students. As both Sona and Quoc Tin begin to feel more comfortable in their writing, they are able to express themselves more clearly and become more responsive, taking risks, asking questions, sharing opinions, and expressing inner feelings. Real communication is going on. Both students become more aware of their audience and adjust accordingly. Quoc Tin probably goes the farthest. At first his letters are stiff and very content oriented. But in responding to Sona's more personal, informal way of writing, his writing slowly becomes less formal.

Sona's first few letters are short, almost terse. As she grows more relaxed writing to her "new friend," her letters become not only longer but more revealing. Sona's final letter of this exchange helps explain why her earlier letters were so short. Sona's revealing admissions about herself are more significant in light of what she had to say later about her letter writing. In an interview after this project ended, she said that one of the most remarkable things about this project for her was that it was the first time she had ever really communicated about feelings with a boy. By the end of this writing exchange, both students were writing with an easy familiarity.

Even though not every pairing succeeds as dramatically as did the team of Sona and Quoc Tin, I am convinced that letter writing is a wonderful way to teach writing. Students writing for a real audience are motivated writers. And when that audience is a peer, young writers may blossom in surprising ways.

I would recommend this project to any teacher, regardless of level—but with a few caveats:

At the outset, you'll need to determine how you are going to pair your students. If the writing levels of the two students are vastly different, they will both become frustrated. Other pairing decisions depend on your objective. I try to pair students of different ethnic groups so more cultural learning can take place, but this may not always be possible.

The logistic challenges will loom large. You must have a regular time block. I ask my students to write two or three times a week, usually in the last twenty minutes of the period. A further small but important point: you'll need to make sure that the journal shared by the two students remains in the room at all times.

Even with the best of plans, however, do not expect this activity to run smoothly. In my case students constantly move in and out of my classes. In January, one entire class exited. One of my classes had thirty students, while the other class had twenty-five. I was constantly trying to find new partnerships. Sometimes I asked higher-level students to write to two partners. Or in a few instances, I got students from another class to participate.

Despite these minor aggravations, I will continue to use peer journals. I'll do this because I have watched students like Quoc Tin and Sona connect during these exchanges, becoming more engaged with language as they struggle to communicate their ideas. Focusing on this important communication with a friend, they are thinking not at all about the writing proficiency test, yet with most every exchange they are becoming demonstrably more proficient writers.

Getting Real: Can a Writing Prompt Be Authentic?

Patricia A. Slagle

This article, written by Patricia A. Slagle about her teaching experience with high school students in Louisville, Kentucky, was published in the summer 1997 issue of The Quarterly. *An earlier version of this piece appeared in* The Louisville Writing Project Network News.

As a beginning teacher in 1971, I didn't have a clue about how to teach writing effectively. Somehow I had learned to write but not how to teach others to become writers. Examining my own approach to writing, I helped students as best I could. Then In 1982, things began to change. I became a participant in the Louisville Writing Project summer institute. I learned concrete strategies for helping students develop as writers.

Returning to my high school classroom, I leaped into teaching writing using the writing process, journals, learning logs, peer response, rubrics, and other tactics I had learned from the project. I encouraged my students to write for a clear purpose with a specific audience in mind. Interestingly, this was much more challenging for my students than I had anticipated. The practice of writing essays that only a teacher would read and then mark in red had taken its toll. Attitudes about writing that apparently grew from this decades-old approach had become ingrained, perhaps even passed down from generation to generation. But I knew that if I found ways for students to write for someone other than me, their writing would improve.

At this point I got some help from the state of Kentucky. With the implementation of the state writing portfolio, Kentucky introduced students and teachers to transactive writing, mandated as a portfolio form. Transactive writing required teachers and students to seek ways to direct students to authentic, that is, real audiences and purposes for writing. For all Kentucky teachers this was a challenge.

However, this portfolio requirement also created a world of possibilities for me as a writing teacher. While I had been encouraging students to write with an audience and purpose in mind, in reality, that audience and purpose were usually hypothetical. With the advent of the transactive writing portfolio requirement, I was nudged to take the next step, to move beyond writing for imaginary audience. What a door this opened! Once I got into the momentum of creating prompts for authentic writing activities, my ideas seemed to flow.

This is the story of how I helped my students find readers for their words, folks who were genuinely interested in what these kids had to say.

~ *Patricia Slagle, 2002*

*L*et's say that in the last year, three serious traffic accidents have occurred near your school at the corner of Sycamore and G Streets. Now, in your class it's time for a persuasive essay prompt, and one of your students decides to convince the reader (you) that it is high time to install stop signs at this dangerous intersection. The student does a more than capable job, performing on-the-spot observations at the intersection, interviewing police officers, collecting anecdotes from students who have experienced close calls at this corner. This is "A" work, and when you hand back the papers you make the student aware of your enthusiasm for her arguments. But, alas, there are still no stop signs at Sycamore and G.

The problem, of course, is that you are neither the chief of police nor the mayor, and those are the folks who should be hearing these arguments. The obvious answer, but one that eluded me until fairly recently, is that the student should have communicated directly with these officials; she should have been encouraged to engage in what is these days called authentic writing. Authenticity is a key concept that I have learned to keep in mind when designing writing prompts.

Traditionally trained, I was not introduced to the concepts of audience, purpose, and form as integral components of writing assignments until I participated in a writing project. Previously I made writing assignments that required students to write academic pieces such as essays, themes, or reports. My students knew I was the only person who would read their finished work. They also knew that my primary reason for reading their writing was to assign a grade.

Now I ask students to write pieces for a genuine audience beyond the classroom, using a real-world form such as a letter to the editor. Their purpose is to communicate effectively with that reader, whether to persuade the reader to agree with their position on an issue, share their sentiments in a memoir, present their solution to a mutual problem, or explore many other possibilities determined by the student-writer. Writing for audiences beyond the teacher using publicly recognized forms such as letters to the editor, and writing for real reasons, produces more effective writing.

I want to describe some of the authentic writing prompts I have used. I recognize that the very expression "authentic writing prompt" will strike some readers as an oxymoron. They would argue that "authentic" writing is generated by something the student feels compelled to say and thus cannot be prompted. To them, the strategies I suggest here may seem halfway measures, but I believe that, in teaching, change for the better usually begins with small, realistic steps.

At the outset, I want to make clear what authentic writing, for me, is not. Sometimes we become creative in our lesson planning and ask students to assume the persona of someone else and write a piece from that person's perspective. They may become homeless persons, presidents, or characters in literature. Role-playing of this sort can provide a useful exercise, but it is not authentic writing. Authentic writing implies that the student is writing in his or her voice to a real living person or group about a matter of concern. A role-playing prompt may have valuable writing-to-learn potential, allowing a teacher to see how well a student understands a concept, but it allows little room for developing a personal voice.

When I have asked students to write from a perspective other than their own, I have added yet another challenge to the one they were already facing by asking them to compose, revise, and edit. This is an unnecessary writing burden that can be avoided if I design prompts that allow students to write from their own knowledge and perspective in their own voices.

Consider two writing assignments. The first is: "Imagine you are the drama critic for your local newspaper. Write a review of an imaginary production of the play that we have just finished studying in class." This prompt asks students to assume the contrived role of a professional writer and drama critic. Most students, even if they happen to be familiar with drama reviews, would not be able to assume that persona successfully and therefore would produce a piece that had problems not only with voice but also with meaningful support and development. The result: the piece striving for authenticity would in fact be inauthentic.

I developed a more effective alternative: "Write a letter to the producing director of your local theater company in which you present arguments in an effort to persuade him/her to include a production of the play that we have just finished studying in class in the upcoming season." The student is expected to state and defend a position. Yet this prompt allows the student to write as herself, in her own voice. Writing in her own voice, she builds into her argument concrete references to personal experience. Of course, this prompt would constitute authentic writing only for those students who, in fact, would like to see the play produced. Note the naturalness with which Jeff, who *was* an advocate for Shaw's *Caesar and Cleopatra*, communicates with his audience:

Dear Mr. Jury,

Recently we held an election for President of our country. We saw many examples of fighting, bickering, and debating between the candidates. All of this was intended to convince the American people to choose the "right" candidate for their leader. In George Bernard Shaw's Caesar and Cleopatra, *Ptolemy and Cleopatra are vying for power using verbal sparring and subtle threats in much the same way as today's presidential candidates. Why not show the public that the methods of political competition have not changed in two thousand years? Anyone who has watched the election closely would not only find this parallel intriguing but enlightening.*

Jeff mailed his letter and in fact received a reply from the producing director that gave Jeff and his classmates insight into the director's play selection considerations. The producing director wrote that *Caesar and Cleopatra* was "simply too expensive for Actors' Theatre to perform because of the large number of people in the cast and the stage setting demanded."

The director also invited our class to attend a dress rehearsal at the theater, an example of how a piece of authentic writing helped us build an authentic link to the community.

The basic question for the teacher in developing authentic prompts is, "How can I turn what could be an academic exercise into something real?"

After studying Dickens's *A Tale of Two Cities,* I might once have asked students to respond to a typical prompt, a variation on "Write a literary analysis essay in which you analyze the strengths and weaknesses of Dickens's *A Tale of Two Cities.*"

We English teachers have been giving such assignments for decades and decrying the unimaginative writing that results. But now, as a creator of authentic prompts, I had another idea: I pulled out Brian Ford's February 1993 *English Journal* article, "Choosing the Canon," and asked students to read it. I asked them to write to Ford stating "your position regarding his thesis that *A Tale of Two Cities* should be eliminated from the curriculum. Then defend your position with sound arguments and reasoning." Because I identified a concrete audience and specific purpose in the prompt, students were able to write without trying to figure out what they imagined I wanted them to say, which so often happened when I used nonauthentic analysis prompts. This time, students were clear about how to proceed in developing their pieces and free to write in their own voices rather than trying to emulate some imagined academic tone.

To my pleasant surprise, only a small minority of students agreed with Mr. Ford's thesis that *A Tale of Two Cities* should be eliminated from the high school curriculum. The following representative samples demonstrate the genuineness of the students' voices. This is not the style students adapt when they are writing what they think the teacher wants to hear. Andre's response:

> *You say the book is politically naive, but that is exactly what is needed at the point this book is taught. Most students who read this are also just learning about the history of France, including the Revolution. Many would be completely lost if this book was a complex analysis of French government. This book helps give a basic grasp of what went on during the French Revolution without seeming to be teaching.*

Ryan finds *A Tale of Two Cities* attractive to modern teens in a way Ford has overlooked:

> *When one thinks of teenagers, what are some television shows that come to mind? Perhaps soap operas or "Beverly Hills 90210." Now ask: what are the elements of these programs that make them so appealing to teenagers? The answer is simple: romantic intrigue.* A Tale of Two Cities *has romantic intrigue in abundance.*

Similarly, Jill:

> *How do you propose to get a class full of teenagers, with their minds on dates and zits, rather than Dickens and Shakespeare, to read a novel, if it's boring? If we have to cut short our phone time, and read a book, the book better be entertaining, or else it'll end up in the back pack, unread. For me, that didn't happen with* A Tale of Two Cities. *The book was so full of twists and turns, that it was hard to put down. At the end of each installment was a catch that made me want to read on. All the scandalous excitement in the novel made it very appealing to me and my classmates.*

Very few, if any, of my literary analysis essay prompts have generated such genuine, authentic, natural, and readable responses.

Unlike our local theater director, Brian Ford did not answer my students. One of the real-world messages built into the authentic writing process is that even the sincerest communication may be ignored or otherwise fall through the cracks. On another occasion my students wrote letters to Steve Martin inquiring about his writing process in adapting Rostand's *Cyrano* for his screenplay *Roxanne*. Despite research into probable addresses, letters were returned as undeliverable or else we heard nothing at all.

Providing prompts that identify an authentic audience, purpose, and form for students before they begin composing is certainly not limited to literary response writing assignments. For example, sources abound in the newspaper: "Write a piece for the Bright Ideas column that appears daily in the Features section of our local newspaper." (This feature solicits contributions from readers.) Shannon wrote:

It's been raining all day; therefore you'd rather stay in out of the mud. So much for being a couch potato because only re-runs are showing today. Now you are sitting home alone and bored to death. Here's an idea you may want to try: make a "Things To Do Kit."

Robbie's effort may have had the effect of increasing local sales of a certain soft drink:

Do you ever have trouble cleaning those big dirty windows outside? Well, if you're like me, you do, and I have a tip for you that may be very useful in cleaning them. Take one cup of vinegar and mix it with 1/3 of a cup of baking soda. Even though it may sound weird, it's time to add an odd ingredient which, nevertheless, works. That weird ingredient is Coke, but you must make sure that it's a can of Coca-Cola Classic.

Yet another source of authentic writing has been our own school. My students developed a high school survival guide for freshmen. Carlos told a cautionary tale:

Do you know how to survive high school?? What do you need to know about how to survive? And how can you make surviving it simple for you?

Here's Bob. Bob is very excited about going to high school, but when he got there, things were not as he thought. Bob's grades began to fall,

*because he wouldn't get up early and come to school. During the times
that Bob came to school, he often didn't feel like doing the work he was
assigned. Bob fell a couple of months behind and never got caught up. .
. .*

*School is not as hard as some people think. As you enter high school,
you are going to have butterflies in your stomach. That's natural; don't
panic. Remember your attitude makes all the difference in the world.*

Another school-based prompt asked students to "develop a guide for English language learner (ELL) students in which you explain various English-language idioms." Joe began his entry:

*The English language can be confusing and tough to learn because there
are so many expressions that need to be learned in addition to the basics.
Idioms in particular can be very strange. For instance, the phrase "birds
of a feather flock together" has nothing to do with birds at all. . . .*

The ELL guide and the high school survival guide were not "published" in the traditional sense. However, I believe they both qualify as authentic writing as they were delivered to the intended audience in their classroom as a prelude to class visits. When the classes met together, the ELL students and my students discussed idioms in the various represented languages. The ninth grade students and my older students discussed high school expectations and pitfalls.

The ELL and high school survival guides have been cataloged and placed in the school media center for use by any students who would find them useful or interesting.

I do not intend to make authentic classroom writing sound easy or even always possible. I teach 150 students each day, and it is not possible to direct all student writing to a real audience or publish everything students write. But authenticity stays in the forefront as I have created my prompts, and because it is remains an important goal, my ideas for authentic prompts continue to blossom. My students are writing more effectively, and when I read and respond to their essays I find the experience more interesting than tedious and sometimes, blessedly, even compelling.

Tensing Up: Moving from Fluency to Flair

Suzanne Linebarger

Written by Suzanne Linebarger about her teaching experience with third- and fourth-graders in Chico, California, this article was originally published in the summer 2001 issue of The Quarterly.

My third-graders were fluent writers. They could ramble on, confidently and enthusiastically, about anything. They loved to write and share their writing. Nevertheless, I was frustrated. They were going through all the writing process motions, but there was little motion in their products. The writing often lacked focus, and the students weren't sure why they were writing except to produce a longer piece than the student across the table. I knew that fluency should be a place to start not a place to end. What could I do to get students beyond these tedious one-person marathons? With the help of colleagues and Ralph Fletcher (1993), I discovered an element of writing I had previously ignored: tension. As I introduced the notion of tension into prewrites, modeling, and revising, my students were able to write with far more passion and conviction. The element of tension made their writing more complicated and therefore more engaging. The essay that follows is the story of how my understanding of tension moved my students from fluency to flair.

~ *Suzanne Linebarger, 2002*

*D*eveloping fluency in young writers is easy. I know; I've been doing it for years. Colleagues constantly ask me how I get my third- and fourth-graders to write so much, and while the answers seem pat, there really are only a few simple coaching techniques that lead to fluent writers. No matter how much we may want to bypass developing fluency, there are no shortcuts. Good writers are fluent writers. However, all fluent writers are not good writers. I'm interested not only in developing fluency but also in what it takes to move our writers from just being able to write to being able to write with passion and flair. Nevertheless, we begin always with fluency. The key word here is *begin*. Fluency is a place to start, not the goal itself.

The first step in developing fluency is obvious. Our students need to write daily for a variety of purposes and audiences. The teacher who has the time to read all of her students' writing is simply not asking for enough writing. The purpose of this type of informal writing is to use writing as a support for learning. It is not to assess a student's writing ability. Informal writing includes a wide variety of writing experiences:

- *quick writes, which are motivating and allow for enough student choice to ensure that all students have something to write about*

- *writing in response to reading, including learning logs and response journals*

- *writing to solve problems, from math to social problems*

- *writing to complain*

- *writing to summarize.*

This writing not only increases the student's ability to write but demonstrates multiple uses for writing. At best, these invitations to write eventually include all students—something for everyone.

Next, the classroom environment must be designed to support fluency. Students constantly ask, "How much do we have to write?" The response to that question needs to be, "Don't ask 'how much,' but I *will* tell you how long." Setting a timer allows the teacher to impose a limit on students' writing (even if it's his name over and over). This is one way to discourage the "I'm done" syndrome. In my classroom, being done is not the goal; perseverance is.

Further, behavior expectations must be clear. I expect my students to take risks, make mistakes, and share what they write, but I am not orchestrating a sixties love fest. My expectations are high. However, it is also my job to provide an environment in which all students can succeed. Even my weakest writer can write for ten minutes and manage to say something worthwhile.

I don't expect my students to have great ideas, but they do need to have ideas. We work hard to make sure everyone has something to say, and then it's up to the individual to actually say it. No one gets to choose to not participate.

Another important factor in building fluency is the sharing of writing. Motivation for informal writing remains high when informal writing is paired with informal sharing. My students are required to share what they have written. This sharing time is simple and unstructured. The instructions aren't fancy: "Find someone close to you to share with, and do it. You have ten minutes." The purpose of this sharing is to quickly explore ideas, and I'm not a player in the process. When I get involved, the purpose of sharing immediately becomes evaluative rather than interactive. Interaction is a key to motivation, and it's the interaction that keeps everyone writing.

So, yes, my students are fluent—especially after the two years they spend with me in our third and fourth grade loop. But after they build this fluency, my response must be, "So what?" Really, so what? For years, I've had no trouble getting students to write a lot about a little. In far too many classrooms, that is where writing development stops. Our writing project mantra, "fluency, form, correctness," too often gets mired down in the development of fluency. Year after year, young writers build their self-esteem based on how much they've written, not on how well they've written. I needed to find out how to move from developing confident writers to developing really good writers who knew the difference between getting words down and writing well.

My goal was not only for my own students but also for the students working with other teachers in the Northern California Writing Project. In my role as inservice director for our site, teachers looked to me for ways to improve their students' scores on holistically scored writing samples as well as in writing in the content areas.

As I have thought through how best to help my students and the teachers with whom I work, I have come to the understanding that an increase in writing activities alone does not necessarily lead to improvement in the craft of writing. If writers are to develop more than fluency, writing teachers must coach students in the skills essential to writing with flair. For me this has been an evolving understanding. In fact, I have been coaching writing as long as I have been teaching it. In the early days, I could hear my coaching voice in my third-graders' writing. Ray's writing (below) reflects what his teacher asked him to do. You can almost hear me asking students to limit their "I remember" piece to one incident, to include sensory details, to describe the setting, and to make sure the incident actually has an ending.

Skiing Struggle

I remember the time I went skiing on Mount Shasta on April 18, 1994. I was wearing a coat, turtleneck, fleece sweatpants, wind pants, ski hat, ski goggles, socks, and ski boots.

On my first run, I skied perfect, and it was the first time I skied in 1994! On my second run, I took one harder. It was called "downhill" because it was exactly like a course without the gates. It was really steep.

After that we went back to the van and had lunch. I had tuna and hot chocolate.

Then we went back up. On the chair lift I saw one ski pole and a glove. When we got to the top we took a new run.

We took about ten more runs and went home.

Ray is a competent third grade writer. His spelling and punctuation are perfect. He wants to please his teacher. He is able to check off everything I had asked him to do, from detailing what he saw to listing what he ate, and he even provides a conclusion of sorts: "We took about ten more runs and went home." So what's the problem? The problem is that nothing happens. What's the point? He's writing because he's supposed to, not because he has something that he really wants to say. This is not the gift of writing that I wanted to give to my students.

About the same time as I was struggling with my need to move my writers from fluency to flair, two of my writing project colleagues, Ron Scudder, a middle school teacher, and Kevin Dolan, a high school teacher, were struggling with the same demons. We began to search for current work on the craft of writing that reflected the ability of good writing teachers. We examined our own students' writing and discovered common elements that made their writing sing

149

to us. And then we set about searching for ways to give the gift of the writer's craft to all our students.

My students began keeping writer's notebooks that celebrated the writer's craft—theirs and others'. Ron, Kevin, and I copied Patricia Pollacco's line, "She had a voice like slow thunder and sweet rain," from *Chicken Sunday* and wished we had written it. Kevin coached his students in the use of juxtaposition, placing interesting ideas side by side, and Ron worked with identifying tension in student writing the way Ralph Fletcher describes it in *What a Writer Needs:*

> *Now the story becomes interesting. This is such a fundamental expectation that while we read we are always on edge, slightly tense, awaiting the first signs of calamity. We actually get disappointed when events unfold smoothly: Nothing is happening. (1993, 101)*

All of these approaches are less directly prescriptive than the kind of direct coaching I had engaged in at the time Ray wrote "Skiing Struggle." But it is Fletcher's and, by extension, Ron's notion of tension that now has had the greatest impact on my teaching. By *tension* I do not mean conflict. I don't spend much time discussing conflict with my students. They think conflict means a fight between good guys and bad guys and that's it. But the notion of tension is one that they can really grab onto and actually use as they write.

I explain it with rubber bands. As I hand them out, I tell my students to leave the rubber bands on their desks. "Don't touch them." Of course, they are jittery, waiting to get their hands on the bands and "accidentally" shoot them off. As they wait, I take a large one and just dangle it on my finger. However, when I stretch it out and point it (not at a student), the rubber band suddenly becomes more interesting. It's the tension, the potential energy, that rivets our attention. It's the same in their writing. Too often, students believe humor or fear are the only elements that make writing engaging. I believe that tension is a much better place to start. The difference is illustrated in Derek's "I remember" piece.

Skiing Struggle

I was at the Mount Shasta Ski Resort on a Sunday. Everything was fine. I was having a fun time there, but one run was not very much fun.

I had to start off on steep slope. It might have fun for the rest of the family (including Ray, my dad, and my mom), but it was a struggle for me. The snow was almost as hard as ice. I had to turn and stop and turn and stop all the way down the mountain. Every time I turned, the snow crunched, and finally I had made it down that run.

After we made it down that run, it lead us to a chair lift that was brand new, so we decided to take that chair to see where it went.

When we got to the top, it looked like we were in the clouds. We went on to a run that was just as steep and icy as the one before, but this time it was worse because it took me about an hour to get through that run. One time I fell and slid, but my dad caught me.

I never went on that terrible, no good, icy, sliding run again!

The similarity in the two third grade pieces is not a coincidence. Derek is Ray's little brother. His writing is in no way stronger than his brother's. The difference in the writing clearly reflects the difference in coaching. Derek has a sense of his audience. Even his line, "Everything was fine," let's us know that everything wasn't fine. We understand that the entire family, except for Derek, was confident on the runs, and we get the feeling that they were probably unaware of his tension. His details are included for a purpose. He wants us to know that this was indeed a challenging run, not a wimpy bunny hill. Finally, he demonstrates an ability to work his writer's craft as he closes with his version of Judith Viorst's line from *Alexander and the Terrible, Horrible, No Good, Very Bad Day*.

One way I demonstrate the use of tension to students is through children's literature. I look for tension and develop ways to bring it into our discussion of a piece. There are plenty of wonderful choices. In *Ira Sleeps Over*, by Bernard Waber, Ira wants to bring his teddy bear when he goes to spend the night at Reggie's house. His parents assure him that Reggie won't laugh. His sister says, "He'll laugh." The tension is set, and all young writers get it. The Mercer Mayer classic, *There's a Nightmare in My Closet*, is a natural for any discussion of tension with writers of all ages. *The Wednesday Surprise*, by Eve Bunting, develops a secret between Grandma and Anna. Everyone believes that Grandma is babysitting, but the reality is that Anna is teaching her to read.

Tension is inherent in all learning experiences. I tell my students that it's the tension, in my case terror, that keeps me skiing. I'm scared every time I push off and exultant every time I get to the bottom of the hill alive. My students are enthusiastic about exploring their own struggle to learn and are willing to reflect back on the experience and see how far they've come. Nick writes:

151

Do I Really Want to Water Ski?

It was a hot summer day when we were going to our friend's house. When we got there they said that we were going water skiing. I was really excited. But by the time we got to Lake Oroville, I was having second thoughts. My dad and Paul were putting the boat in the water. It took a long time so my mom, Carol, my sister, and I went down to a little shop to look around.

Finally, my dad and Paul yelled to us to get into the boat. By now I was so scared that I was shivering all over. The skiing order was Paul first, then me, then my sister. We all watched Paul ski. He is an excellent skier! Then it was my turn. I put on my life vest and said to myself, "Relax and concentrate," over and over again. I was ready! My dad held onto the back of my skis to keep me balanced. I said, "Olly!" That tells the driver to go slow. I held onto the rope tight and said, "Hit it!" I was water skiing! But I was only up for about forty seconds. After I skied, I swam up to the boat and shouted, "I want to do that again!"

Now I am an excellent water skier. I love water skiing. Now I am practicing knee boarding!

Writing prompts without tension lead to flat prose that lacks life and sparkle. A third grade writing prompt reads:

PERSONAL NARRATIVE: *"A Special Possession"*

WRITING SITUATION: *Everyone has something in his/her life that is very special or important. This possession may have been received as a gift. It may be a prize or award, or it may be something that has been bought or found.*

DIRECTIONS FOR WRITING: *Write about the special possession you have. Tell what it is and how you got it. Describe what it looks like. Use lots of picture words. Tell why it's special or important to you.*

In my view, this prompt is deadly. First, it assumes that all students have a special possession when in reality many live in environments that don't contain many special possessions. And even if a student can write about her baby blanket, what can she say?

152

"My Noni crocheted it before I was born. I dragged it all over the house. It's faded yellow and white yarn and is now in the cedar chest as a special possession."

The prompt itself leads to flat writing without passion. By design, the writing will be filled with description that is designed to fit the prompt rather than to move the piece along.

A fourth grade prompt was a bit better and, with a little tweaking, actually worked.

PERSONAL NARRATIVE: *"A Special Friend"*

WRITING SITUATION: *Everyone has a friend—or would like to have one—that is special. This may be a friend that you had in the past, have now, or will have in the future. This friend may be the same age as you or younger or older.*

DIRECTIONS FOR WRITING: *Think of a friend who is special to you. Write about something your friend has done for you, you have done for your friend, or you have done together. Tell important details about when and where this happened. Tell how and why this happened. Share why it was memorable.*

At first reading, I was reminded of using a similar prompt when I was teaching at California State University, Chico. The papers were deadly. They all said something like, "My best friend is really good to me. She is always there for me," and so on. I also cringed at the line "everyone has a friend—or would like to have one," envisioning some poor student writing about a fantasy friend because she or he didn't have a real one. Nevertheless, I thought that if we brought some tension into this prompt it would have potential for all my students. So during our prewrite discussion, we talked about how hard it is to stay friends when we're met with a challenge. Students talked about times they had let their friends down and times they had been let down and discussed how they managed to stay friends in spite of their problems. In other words, we talked about some tense situations.

And suddenly, these students had stories they were burning to tell—all of them! These are the openings of a sampling of fourth grade papers:

The Hate-Like Friendship

I used to hate Terra when we were in kindergarten. We never played to-
gether. I was jealous of her. I thought that she was better than me in roll-
erblading and coloring. Then in first grade we became best friends.
I remember one of our most exciting adventures . . .

Stuck!

Me and Chelsea have known each other since birth. But, I didn't say we
liked each other! In fact Chelsea bought a diary so she could write, "I
hate Becca," in it. Even so, now we're inseparable. And sometimes I have
to admit we're pretty good when it comes to mischief-making. One of
our biggest on a summer Saturday was something like this. . . .

My Best Friend Jessy

When I first came to this school it was hard to make friends. I got in
trouble a lot and I was lonely. Then I met Jessy . . .

Many of the incidents they described had to do with spending the night, which for fourth-graders is always a bit tense. These essays were not negative. Our discussion had merely reminded students of incidents that had an edge.

After our discussion of this prompt, a greater percentage of students than ever before managed to produce essays that presented clear, fairly well developed ideas. The difference was not that these students were handpicked or gifted; neither did they all score "sixes." However, more students managed to score in the proficient range than in many of the other classes tested.

In informational writing, tension also plays a role. I have long championed the use of powerful, well-written nonfiction or informational books in primary classrooms. Personal narrative has a role in all writing programs, but for writers to become not only fluent but skilled, they need experiences far beyond the realm of fiction and personal narrative. I struggled with getting my students to interact with information instead of regurgitating it. Young writers love to write information books in which they copy countless facts that they can neither read nor understand. I've managed to avoid some of these problems by asking young writers to record key words instead of "notes" as they read nonfiction and then to use these key words to reconstruct understanding of what they've read, first in a discussion and then in an essay. Darcy Weagant, a Northern California Writing

Project teacher-consultant, developed this concept. I needed to fine-tune it so that it worked for my students.

In experimenting with this idea, I began to understand the connection between tension and surprise. I discovered that if I ask my students to explain what surprised them as a result of listening to an article, reading a piece, or conducting an investigation, I am able to accomplish two things. First, they have to interact with their information in order to respond, and, second, they develop another element of tension. They are tensed as they read or listen and are ready and expecting to be surprised. It's almost a competition between themselves and the writer. They are disappointed if they truly find no surprises. That usually indicates that the material they chose was too simple. When they write about these surprises, their writing comes alive in ways lacking when they write, "What I learned was . . ."

For example, I read my students an article called "Mummies" from the "Pyramids" issue of *Kids Discover* magazine. As I read, they write down key words that strike them as important. Then they discuss the article using their note cards with their key words only. Involved in the process, students are tense, waiting to be surprised. One key word always appears: *brain*. They then explain that the Egyptians used a hook to pull the brain from the body through the nose! While they think they know a great deal about mummies already, this bit of information really surprises them. I extend this notion of surprise throughout their responses to reading and to larger assignments such as their "I Search" papers.

This fourth grade "I Search" paper concludes with a series of surprises:

Star Wars Conclusion

It surprised me that I didn't find answers to lot of the questions that I have. Most of the questions that I didn't answer were the questions about prices and costs of the movie. I did find out more things about the characters and other details about the action in the movie.

I was surprised that it took more than one person to play some parts.

It surprised me that Imperial Walkers stood over 45 feet tall. I was surprised that R2D2 and C3PO had names for the kind of droid they are.

My most interesting discoveries were that Darth Vader's real name was Anakin Skywalker and that blaster pistols were the most used weapons

throughout the galaxy. I didn't even think Darth Vader had a name be-
fore Darth Vader. I knew he was on the light side before he was on the
dark side, but I didn't know that he had that name. When I saw about
the blaster pistols I thought there would be a different [sic] that was used
because you don't see blaster pistols that much in the movies, but a lot
of people do have them if you really think about it.

I was surprised how hard it was to find information. The web site was
always full, and when I finally got in, it didn't have that much informa-
tion. Star Wars is a big thing now and I just thought there would be a lot
of information on it.

If I were to do this again, I could make it better. I would go straight for
a book sooner, and I would go to the internet sooner because once I got
on I did get information, but I did not have enough time to use it all.
I would also interview more people. If I had more interviews it would
be more interesting, because I could find out what people know ad like
about Star Wars.

I really enjoyed this project. It was fun and interesting for me and maybe
for you!

For years, I had been reading conclusions that did not convince me that the writer actually knew what he or she was writing about. They tended to rehash a list of facts mentioned earlier in the paper. By adding the element of surprise (tension), the writer becomes involved in an evaluation of the learning experience and is able to set realistic goals for a future research experience.

It's important, as I conclude, to return to the role of fluency in a writing program. Our students need to develop fluency at all levels. If a student comes into my classroom who is confident, sees himself as a writer, and is capable of writing a great deal, I can coach that writer from fluency to flair. If a writer is fearful and incapable of getting any ideas on paper, I cannot avoid the need to help that writer develop fluency. Our writers must be writing for all sorts of reasons if we are going to find the one topic that will light a spark in each of our students. My goal is not that of a minimalist. I am a maximalist. I don't want my students to merely be able to write. I want them to love to write. I want them to be great writers. I want them to have fluency, form, correctness, and pizzazz!

PICTURE BOOKS THAT MODEL TENSION

Bunting, Eve. 1989. *The Wednesday Surprise*. New York: Clarion Books.

Fox, Mem. 1984. *Wilfrid Gordon McDonald Partridge*. New York: Scholastic.

Giff, Patricia Reilly. 1980. *Today Was a Terrible Day*. New York: Puffin Books.

Gilman, Phoebe. 1992. *Something from Nothing*. New York: Scholastic.

Mayer, Mercer. 1968. *There's a Nightmare in My Closet*. New York: Dial Books for Young Readers.

Polacco, Patricia. 1992. *Chicken Sunday*. New York: Putman & Grosset.

———. 1993. *The Bee Tree*. New York: Philomel Books.

———. 1994. *Pink and Say*. New York: Philomel Books.

———. 1998. *Thank You, Mr. Falker*. New York: Philomel Books.

Viorst, Judith. 1972. *Alexander and the Terrible, Horrible, No Good, Very Bad Day*. New York: Alladin Paperbacks.

Waber, Bernard. 1972. *Ira Sleeps Over*. New York: Scholastic.

REFERENCES

Fletcher, Ralph. 1993. *What a Writer Needs*. Portsmouth, NH: Heinemann.

Harvey, Stephanie. 1998. *Nonfiction Matters*. York, ME: Stenhouse.

Hindley, Joanne. 1996. *In the Company of Children*. York, ME: Stenhouse.

Sound and Sense: Grammar, Poetry, and Creative Language

Ray Skjelbred

This article, written by Ray Skjelbred about his teaching experience with seventh grade students in Corte Madera, California, was originally published in the fall 1997 issue of The Quarterly.

As an English teacher I have often been asked the question, "Do you teach grammar?" I assume that most other English teachers have heard this question—asked with curiosity, innocence, or suspicion—from parents, administrators, and the general public.

Confronted with this query, I used to feel a bit uneasy, not because I didn't teach grammar, but because the public concept of what grammar means or why grammar is "good" for us is usually misguided. First, kids from an early age generally know a huge amount of grammar without being taught. They know what linguist Steven Pinker has called a "mental grammar." They apply rules and they speak correct sentences with infinite variety before they have ever learned any prescriptive grammar laws in school. Also, the notion seems to persist that grammar is an essential body of knowledge that needs to be learned in advance of other language experiences so that writing will be "correct." Of course, the irony in this concept is that if teachers spend a thorough amount of time turning the pages of a traditional grammar text, there won't be any time left for writing that demonstrates how that knowledge is used.

That's how I went to school. Grammar didn't prepare for writing; it took the place of it. How could I help my students avoid this dead end?

For me the solution to the question of teaching grammar lies in the belief that grammar resides in the human system to begin with. A successful practical-creative application in "learning" it, then, proceeds from having a sense of play about how language is used along with writing experiments that fool around with a variety of grammatical and syntactical combinations. If basic terms for parts of speech or syntactical elements become part of our everyday writing vocabulary, then we can have infinite ways of discovering the "how" of writing.

Although all students are not equal in ability, they can all improve their confidence in writing as they move along these grammatical stepping-stones. Many students I know begin organizing an expository idea by thinking of a subordinating conjunction first. Others are able to begin descriptive observations simply because they have established their first thought as a prepositional phrase. Anyone can say "When" or "Over my head," and something's got to follow.

As for me, grammar instruction and writing instruction will always be linked. To paraphrase a remark passed on by Annie Dillard, "When I teach writing, I like the smell of the verbs."

~ *Ray Skjelbred, 2002*

*A*rianna and Jill are working as partners during a writing practice in seventh grade English. One of them is writing a detailed description of a photograph she has been given. The other, who is not looking at the photograph, has been asked to quickly write a list of active verbs, the kind that might provide unexpected energy if they were suddenly dropped into a piece of writing. Now comes the next step. All around the room, partners go on to try out the new verbs in the descriptions of photographs. Many verbs won't work at all. They might be too silly or even too predictable. But within minutes, with a little nudging and bending, a few minor miracles begin to happen.

Arianna and Jill's piece is one such miracle:

> *The chic lady lounges casually on a plush couch. Cigarette in her left hand black gloves and a silver sequined purse in her right she wears a carefree look on her made up face. Her hat saunters over her glowing eyes and her red lipstick shines in the light. Her black and red blouse falls loosely over her toned arms, and her shoulders smile out from underneath it. Her thick ring antagonizes her thin fingers, red nails floating to a perfect point.*

When Arianna and Jill inject into their paragraph surprising verbs like *saunters* and *antagonizes*, they begin to explore language possibilities they might not have considered had they not been asked to try out some alternative verbs. Arianna likes this writing practice, noting,

> *It shows how I incorporated words that are not expected to fit in and made them work. I particularly liked where I wrote "Her hat saunters over her glowing eyes" because you can imagine a hat strutting and showing off, even though it really isn't possible.*

I incorporate a generous dose of grammar into the writing portion of my seventh grade English classes at Marin Country Day School, but not grammar in the traditional sense. Students do not learn to diagram someone else's writing. Instead, students use grammatical and syntactical principles in their own writing to construct more effective sentences, paragraphs, and poems.

BEGINNING WITH VERBS

Verb practices are easy. If I ask students how they entered the room and they say, "We walked," I can always say, "Well, that's one way. Now let's think about other possibilities, some other actions. How else could a person get into this room? Maybe the room is locked up tight. Or perhaps someone is trying to stop you. You'll notice yourself expanding your verb choices, expanding the action of your sentence." Then, to make it a little more fun, we pick someone from the class to be the one trying to get into the room. The class takes a few minutes to write verb possibilities, they read them aloud, and I gather the choices together to make a composite action sentence.

Leanne pounded, dissolved, seeped, threw herself, butted the wall with her head, chopped her way with a hacksaw, smashed, rocketed, chainsawed, oozed, bit through the lock, shrank into an atom . . .

Michael hammered, sifted, waltzed, screamed and the building caved in, bashed, vaporized, used a can opener, dug his way, morphed into, used a library pass, clicked the heels of his red slippers three times . . .

Not every practice leads to "serious" writing, but when the habits are established, I think serious writing comes more easily.

ADDING SOUND

We also study phonology, the sounds language makes, listening as we read for overlapping sounds and repeating rhythms. By combining the study of the structure and the sound of language with creative writing, we practice skills and discover infinite writing possibilities all in the same pen stroke.

Then what about *saunter?* Arianna and Jill knew it was an active verb, a surprising one that made a new kind of sense in relation to its context. But this word is full of listening as well as seeing. Listen more closely to the repeating *er* sounds in their sentence: "Her hat saunters over her glowing eyes." Are the girls conscious of the rolling *r*s in their sentence? I hope so. I want to train them to hear these patterns. I give examples, we practice, we read aloud, we listen and learn from each other. Then listening, as well as seeing, becomes habit.

One way I begin to train their ears is by asking students to make lists of wonderful-sounding words. This is strictly a listening game; they shouldn't write *lunch* just because they're hungry. Students usually fly into this sort of thing, and a few minutes later, when I ask for words, almost everyone (including me) wants to contribute. I rapidly write these words all over the blackboard. There are lumpy words, silly words, long, flowing vowel-filled words, and short, hard lumps of consonants. Students have fun saying them aloud, and generally some words elicit laughs. I then tell them to use their own words, borrow from other contributors if they wish, add other words as necessary, change forms when logical, and put together a good line or good lines or a poem or a serious thought or whatever else might happen, this time making use of sense and ideas but concentrating on the sound possibilities in the original words.

Lisa wrote this list: *cauliflower, syllable, sifted, chickadee, volcano, sloth,* and *detergent.* Then she quickly assembled this piece:

> *She stumbles home carrying groceries with the cauliflower peeking out.*
> *On the other side of the street a man loads his laundry into the tumbling*
> *washer and his detergent sifts into the bubbling water.*
> *Outside, the homeless dog spots a chickadee. Leaving his master he darts*
> *through the traffic like a determined sloth.*
> *Just as the syllables creep through her teeth the fog erupts like a volcano*
> *in the dust.*

She was surprised by what she had written, but she was beginning to see that the possibilities of writing are much larger than what she'd imagined. Unexpected words can go together, creating amazing images —like syllables creeping through teeth—and unique sound relationships can provide a poetic energy.

AND MORE PARTS OF SPEECH

A mixing of sounds, syllables, and parts of speech suggests a wide set of possible mix-and-match writing practices. On one occasion we made separate adjective-noun lists and blended them together. They first made random lists of nouns and adjectives and then paired the nouns and adjectives on the basis of various vowel sounds: *I* as in *thin, eh* as in *rent, ou* as in *loud, oo* as in *moose, e* as in *key.* The phrases they came up with appeal to the ear: depressed bed, messy letter, jittery clip, eccentric ticket, idiotic pillow, dumbfounded empress dowager.

Then I had them practice matching a particular adjective suffix ending, such as *-ous, -ing, -able, -ible,* and *-ful,* with any noun that sounds good, resulting in: vicious pillow, victorious lipstick, faithful eraser, rentable desert, tiring eyeball, plentiful mildew.

Writing models are easy to find. If I ask for nouns, I can show them Mona Van Duyn's "A Small Excursion," which is full of the physical weight of names and places as she takes us on a journey through America. The opening reads:

Take a trip with me
through the towns in Missouri.
Feel naming in all its joy
as we go through Braggadocio, Barks, Kidder, Fair
Play,
Bourbon, Bean Lake
and Loose Creek.
If we should get lost
we could spend the night at
Lutesville, Brinktown, Excello, Nodaway,
Humansville, or Kinderpost.

Claire wrote a noun poem after looking at a forestry service poster:

What strange names we come up with
Trees called
Ginkgo,
Ash,
Magnolia,
Pine.
Come sit with me under a Sycamore tree.
Come walk with me under American Elms
Hickory,
Oak,
Dogwood,
Holly,
Maple,
Spruce,
Juniper,
Fir.
Come stand with me in the shade of a Tulip tree
Come walk in a grove of Redwood.
Come rest on the trunk of a Cottonwood.
Come enter the forest with me.

If I ask them to exploit prepositional phrases, I can show them James Wright's "Lying in a Hammock at William Duffy's Farm in Pine Island, Minnesota" to demonstrate the particular creative and grammatical force of prepositions. It is a wonderful poem and often used by writing and poetry teachers, and his observations—"Over my head," "Down the ravine," "Into the distances," "In a field of sunlight between two pines"—not only show how he is seeing but how language works. Student practices grow easily from the language concepts in this poem, and I often have students write prepositional phrase observations as they quietly sit outside and write about what they see in specific locations. Ben's poem is an observation full of the rhythm of prepositional phrases:

Below me the brown sugar sand clumps in the indentation of my foot.
Up the hill I hear the sound of a jackhammer smashing the smooth, gray
  concrete.
The trees down by the creek are mostly leafless,
After years of constantly taking the burden of watching six year old chil-
  dren.
Off in the distance the bay is throwing itself up on to the shore
  as it has always done.
In the trees by the office a few lingering leaves struggle to cling to their
  branches.
Silently a gray seagull swoops by from overhead.
The once orange pole which holds the basketball hoop is now gray
  from many years of missed shots.
Across the creek, behind the rings,
  a lonely sweater waits patiently for its owner to come and get it.

CONSIDERING SYLLABLES

If I ask for writing that emphasizes one-syllable words, I often present Gary Snyder's "Yase: September," which begins:

Old Mrs. Kawabata
cuts down the tall spike weeds—
more in two hours
than I can get done in a day.

Of course there is much to say about the "how" or "why" of this poem, but the force, perhaps even the dignity, of the characterization comes from the simplicity of sound, especially in contrast to the long, flowing sound of *Kawabata*. The practices and possibilities seem obvious.

Nick was inspired by a Galway Kinnell poem about blackberries and tried his own, with an emphasis on one-syllable words:

The bushes grow thick around the swings,
curving up the red, rusted metal,
the forest green, punctuated with the punctual growth
of black, blackberries
every winter, with the frost, they come.
My hands reach for the fruit, and grab hold of a black one,
red juice spurts out and it leaks down my hand,
down my arm, to my shirt
where every year a new stain shows,
marking the beginning of the time,
when black nights,
lead to bright, red days.

INFINITIVES, PREPOSITIONAL PHRASES, CLAUSES, AND OTHER POSSIBILITIES

We have also had some success with an infinitive–prepositional phrase exercise that seemed to stimulate some solid writing and thinking. Every student had learned the infinitive verb form, and we considered infinitives and imperatives in writing and the general force of beginning lines with verbs. We looked at the use of verbs in Gary Snyder's poem "Things to Do Around a Lookout," which begins:

Wrap up in a blanket in cold weather and just read.
Practise writing Chinese characters with a brush
Paint pictures of the mountains
Put out salt for deer

Students also discovered that in contrast to the potentially short, blunt impact of opening verbs, prepositional phrases were long, flowing, and visual, like rocks skipping across water. They all wrote separate infinitive-preposition lists, and we made random connections. I called one student to supply an infinitive, then another to produce a prepositional phrase, then an infinitive, then a prepositional phrase, and short lines of grammar and poetry took shape in the air.

Helena looked at the process carefully, took the concept, and fashioned this poem:

Things To Do

To saunter through anger
And laugh out loud
To swim through fear
And still breathe under water
To flip over hate
And land on my feet
To sing through despair
And hear my voice echo
To gasp close to sickness
And breathe in sweet air
To dance through chaos
And find my own rhythm
To ignore disaster
And find someone to celebrate with

Although this poem is based simply on connecting infinitives with prepositional phrases, the central connecting theme takes it far beyond simple formula writing. Using ordinary parts, Helena made unforeseen discoveries.

The use of clauses in teaching syntax is particularly exciting, since dependent clauses, especially adjective clauses (linked by relative pronouns) and adverb clauses (linked by subordinating conjunctions) not only connect at least two ideas in an instant but also give a rhythmic "shove" to any idea that spins out from a writer's mind. Whitman's "When lilacs last in the door-yard bloom'd" is great poetry not just because he begins with *When* (subordinating conjunction), but also because of the extension of this idea, which is made possible because of the grammatical "shove." Emily Dickinson can allow an abstract idea to unfold when she writes, "Because I could not stop for Death." Galway Kinnell even wrote a three-page, one-sentence fishing poem ("Angling, a Day"), which hangs together by his use of *though,* until he jars to a halt with his independent clause: "we have caught nothing." And, naturally, Shakespeare's sonnets are full of opening *When*s.

A couple of years ago, I bumped into a William Stafford notebook entry in which he wrote something like, "If goats liked my poetry I would have to start over again," and I thought what a wonderful opportunity for students to see how abstraction works and at the same time exploit the power of the dependent clause. I proposed that everyone write "if" poems that would consider what might happen if certain kinds of animals liked a student's writing. The blending of the abstract and the concrete and the grammatical force of the construction created a strong set of poems that had enough in common that our class was able to give a poetry reading and present the whole thing as if it were a single poem.

Here are some that demonstrate the process and can easily be read together as a single idea:

If birds liked my poetry
the words would soar through the
air and glide onto the page, flapping their vowels.

　　~ Toby

If condors liked my poetry they
Would live in the comfort
Of my words shredded for their nest
They would tie my poetry together
So when their baby birds
Learned how to fly
They would
Have
A
Parachute
To help them

　　　~ Arianna

If fish liked my poetry
they would share it in all their schools

And if they really liked my poetry,
they would propel across the writing,
keeping their eyes open at all times.

~ Oliver

If lions liked my poetry
They might stalk it
And kill it
And guard it all the time
And I would have to start over
Another little rhyme

~ Joe S.

If squids liked my poetry,
they would leave what is good bare,
but they would black out the bad parts,
leaving nothing there.

~ Spencer C.

Listen to Spencer's use of one-syllable words, his natural, comfortable use of rhyme, and his overlapping sounds, even though the exercise was specifically about "if"-generated dependent clauses. The results of practicing language play are cumulative. Once young writers learn to manipulate language, they keep using the techniques because the effects are powerful.

How do I measure the success of this kind of approach to language? Well, if ideas and grammar and accents and syllables and so on all exist together, I can observe and discover success by seeing these elements mixed in the overall writing of students, and if their responses to this process are generally strong and positive, I feel we are on the right track. Of course, I can test skills, too. For example, I often give individual photographs to every student (*Arizona Highways* is my favorite source), then I ask them to observe well and try out certain practices. In one instance, I asked them to begin with a subordinating conjunction then told them to focus on accurate adjectives that give small, specific, seeing details, and to use active verbs that give life to the descriptions and sentences whenever possible. This is what I believe is a grammar test, and here are some samples.

169

Danika wrote:

Although the large and jagged rocks are gray, when the sun shines upon them a golden color seems to appear. On these rocks a messy type of plant grows, covering and protecting the rock's skin. Far off in the distance, through a crevice in the rocks, a desolate town can be seen.

Perry leaned on *when* to lead him in:

When the sun glimmers off the craggy rock, the sunlight makes a reflection and part of the lake turns a golden color. The shadow line is bumpy as is the hill that shadows it. The moon shines dimly above the age old rock. In the water lay rocks with their heads poking out as if to get a first glimpse of the world.

Jesse looked hard, chose *although,* and felt the rhythm of one-syllable words:

Although this cliff is hard, solid rock, it also looks like soft clay about to lose its structure and collapse, making the small houses crumble. The houses are almost snuck into the only opening on the plateau.

Remember, this is seventh grade writing. They had about thirty minutes, and they didn't know in advance what they would be called upon to say. They did well, but they were practiced in the craft.

Creativity and basics grow together. Grammar rules are useless if we don't know how language functions. Knowing that one word is better than another in a specific situation is important. Knowing a vocabulary of grammar and talking thoughtfully about ideas and sentence possibilities is important. We should not have to make a choice between the wild poem and the subordinating conjunction. They know each other.

During this last year, Jonathan had success with poetry that grew from an adjective-noun combining process where he came up with "empty/chair" and "grim-faced/optimism," and in response to his work he wrote,

Was this practice useful? Definitely. Randomly combining types of words always creates something interesting. With this random combining, unlikely phrases can be thought up, leading to original ideas that one could never come up with in consciousness. That is what makes a good poem: an idea so different that one could never see it coming.

Jonathan, Arianna, and the others have discovered new approaches to writing that mix ideas, sounds, grammar, and rhythm to create texts that surprise the reader and even the author. If the goal of grammar instruction is better student writing, then these kinds of grammar lessons really work.

REFERENCES

Snyder, Gary. 1992. "Yase: September." In *No Nature: New and Selected Poems*. New York and San Francisco: Pantheon Books.

Snyder, Gary. 1996. "Three Worlds, Three Realms, Six Road." In *Mountains and Rivers Without End*. Washington, D.C.: Counterpoint Press.

Wright, James. *Collected Poems*. Middletown, CT: Wesleyan University Press, 1971.

The Field Trip Within

Peter Trenouth

Written by Peter Trenouth about his teaching experience with high school students in Whitman, Massachusetts, this article was originally published in the summer 2002 issue of The Quarterly.

Whenever I make a writing assignment that yields student work mired in hollow thought or stilted prose, I am reminded once again of how artificial academic activities can be—how disconnected they often are from the sinews of life. But I cannot blame all my failures—and the failures of my students—on the fact that we are required to immerse ourselves in academic thought, form, and language. The truth is that even the "creative" assignments I offer too often generate work that is weak, either mechanistic or formless. The descriptive paper often provided the vehicle for these failings. Publishers of writing texts often include chapters about this mode of discourse, offering many strategies that have merit. However, one question these books seem not to ask is why anyone should write a vivid description of anything in the first place. Too often these days the answer to this question, as well as the answer to many other questions about what we teach, is defined by the demands of statewide, mandated assessments, or similar extrinsic tests. We are told that students need to learn to write vivid descriptions because they will be tested on their ability to write vivid descriptions. This is the kind of thinking that stands education reform on its head.

So I've developed my own answer. If descriptive writing is to have a point, it must be linked to the significance of things. Meaning is not adrift. It is anchored in experiences. And when we experience sights, sounds, textures, odors, and flavors—and translate these into language—we establish in the objects that project these sensations and in ourselves significances otherwise unnoticed. We give additional meaning to life. One step along the way is to create a list of what is perceived, a helpful prewriting activity provided it leads to something other than a queue of superficial details passively waiting for a topic sentence—another exercise in disconnection and ambiguity.

But my breakthrough experience came with my increased understanding that lists need a nurturing context to make meaning. Descriptive writing must be about something. I provided my students with models that demonstrated how the best description advances meaning through the use of action verbs, vivid modifiers, and lively figurative language, models that depended on insight and audacity, not mere cataloging. In their writing, I wanted self-expression that resists simplemindedness. I wanted them to understand that in the best writing, observation, feeling, insight, and order are all part of the mix. And in my class descriptive writing became a tool for developing this awareness.

~ *Peter Trenouth, 2002*

*R*alph Fletcher writes about "a kind of food chain," a hierarchy of thought ranging from the lofty and abstract down to the ordinary and concrete. "Writing," he asserts, "needs to be grounded in plenty of physical details. Without them the whole food chain falls apart" (Fletcher 1992, 45). Central to Fletcher's theory is a concept all teachers of writing and their students need to grasp: good writing embraces interpretations and conclusions together with the specifics from which they evolve—what Ann E. Berthoff in her books calls "the generalities and the particulars." Although the proportions between the two can vary, no matter the subject matter or genre, in composing, the little stuff must get first attention.

With "Stopping by Woods on a Snowy Evening," we are touched when Robert Frost's speaker senses he is in "the darkest evening of the year" and decides sleep should only come after his "miles to go," but without the "woods," "snow," "frozen lake," "little horse," "harness bells," "easy wind and downy flake," the poem would not have its loveliness and depth. Attentive readers devour a great work's entire chain, sometimes unconscious of the interdependence that gives it wholeness. Writers, however, are not mere table setters. They must become forces of nature who discover various elements and forge them into something unified and essential, maybe even mystical and wise, often unsure at the outset of the generalities and purpose their composing will create. Like the speaker in Frost's poem, writers are first drawn to the details and the arresting implications they suggest.

To achieve this level of detail in their work, writers must first employ what Scott Peterson calls "the writer's eye," which is the same close, patient examination all careful artists employ. A teacher and writer with his notebook always handy, Peterson jots away, focusing his lens: "When I view things through the eyes of a photographer, I am more aware of the world around me" (Peterson 2000, 27). Often in a Sherlock Holmes mystery, a bumbler from the local police force gives the crime scene a cursory look and dashes off to catch the wrong man, while Holmes, down on all fours with magnifying glass in hand, examines what no one else stops to see. The observant detective discovers novelty in the familiar. With so much emphasis in education these days on accountability, we could easily push our students into formulaic practices that reduce observation to quick glances neatly arranged, as though this were good writing. It is not. Before students can synthesize their perceptions or even arrange them, they first must perceive. One way to initiate this habit is through descriptive writing. The subject matter is always nearby. We need only open the classroom door, step outside, and go for a walk.

The walk can provide students with an opportunity to observe and record. Such an opportunity, however, will yield little more than a collection of details reorganized into sentences. Preceding the listing must come a sense of what constitutes specific sense stimuli and how those can inspire lively, perceptive writing. In other words, a model is needed. Many anthologies provide such examples; a few include samples written by students. The best samples demonstrate another quality—the author's willingness to feel as well as think. "Bright Light" by Casey Braun, an eight-paragraph essay about a day at the beach, became an excellent model for my freshman class. Working in cooperative groups, each with a separate paragraph, students were asked to find action verbs, vivid expressions, figures of speech, and excellent uses of vocabulary in a passage like this:

> *I couldn't taste the sun, but as I walked back to my blanket, I licked the salt off my lips which had dried quickly in the heat. Salt, I decided, must be the taste of light, at least this morning. The salt on my skin made it feel like stretched leather, tight across my cheekbones and shoulders and stiffing at my joints. I walked across the glinting sand, through mid-day air heated to luminous, shimmering waves to the outdoor shower.*
> (Braun 1995, 367)

Each group quickly found examples to fit the categories and presented their findings to the class. Although two of the criteria—action verbs and figures of speech—were objective, two others called for subjective assessments. After all, just what is a "vivid expression" or "excellent use of vocabulary"? Is, for example, "the taste of light" a fascinating, sensuous image, or is it silly? When students respond to questions like this, they tend either to limit their imaginations or to liberate words and experience from conventional situations. Fortunately, most would rather do the latter and thereby invite themselves to merge their recordings of whatever is out there with frank, personal responses. That is how perception works. A good model, especially one written in a voice like their own, can encourage students to combine some risk taking and fun with their close observations. Eventually, the dynamic will produce a conclusion, if only implied, about something not previously or recently considered. For Casey Braun, it is this: "I realized once again the power of light to change everything."

As architectural splendors, school buildings almost always fail, often looking like factories—a telltale sign of what some people think schools should be.

Inside, despite the steady progression of rigid, pale rectangles, one can also find myriad softer shapes, brighter colors, and evidence of spontaneous energy. My previous school, a suburban high school, is fifty years old and looks it, but it is still a vibrant place. Last winter, I tried an "in-school field trip" as a way to generate descriptive writing. With the freshmen, my goal was primarily to get each to use the "close, patient observation" that is the writer's eye

In earlier classes, they had written sentence- and paragraph-length exercises in descriptive writing and read lengthy samples like "Bright Light." They had become aware of technique in its most objective sense: action verbs, figures of speech, and images based on adjectives and nouns. But technique can still deliver lifeless prose when tethered to the editing process. Students need more than familiarity with linguistic devices. They need license to use these in their own natural ways whenever they endeavor to translate experience into language. Therefore, the original listing should draw on close observations recorded with immediate, subjective impressions, which almost automatically will beckon action verbs, figures of speech, and workable images for completion. So, with notebooks and pens in hand one January morning, we darted down the back stairway, hurried outside and around to the school's main entrance, and from there we walked, stopped, and recorded. I told them to delay writing complete sentences, unless impulsively compelled, and to keep looking and writing about anything they saw, heard, touched, or smelled. Give no thought to how "lame" or "fancy" an observation seemed, I told them, and feel free to overrecord. Decisions about what to keep and what to trash would come later.

Once inside the main lobby, the students shook off the winter chill and busily recorded. Patrick's notes later became sentences describing the field trip's first stops:

> In the lobby there was a warm glass trophy case in which I could see my
> dulled reflection. I could hear squeaks from people in gym class slipping
> on the floor. There was a trash barrel in the corner of the room that was
> half way full. On the ceiling there was a painting of a globe and a sen-
> tence that read: "Through these halls walk the greatest people on earth."
> As we left the lobby, we passed a crimson colored coke machine and
> a man with brown eyes, brown hair, a flannel shirt, a beard, a brown
> leather belt, and jeans. . . . We walked down the main hallway of the
> building, passing the office, guidance office, library, and a disgusting

177

trash barrel which left an odor chasing us through the hall. There were
ancient rusty lockers on both sides of the hall and different shades of
dusty green tiles on the floor.

Patrick began with a pile of loose observations, yet most were colored with
personal interpretation from the beginning: "warm trophy case," "dulled reflection," and "dusty green tiles." His composing process deleted details about some
spaces we visited during this stretch. What became important to him were gym
noises, athletic trophies, a slogan, and a workman or visitor he had never seen
before. Because he owned these decisions, his paper gained a genuine tone. He
can be a playful writer who likes "crimson" (and alliteration) and deems fifty-
year-old lockers "ancient," yet his voice remained authentic. His writer's eye
joined with his artist's sensibilities to personify an unpleasant odor. An adult
observer might conclude Patrick tends towards hyperbole (what high school
freshman does not?); nevertheless, he stayed within bounds and blended accuracy with personal authenticity and style very well. The editing process alone
did not impose these qualities. Patrick began developing them at the outset,
having given himself permission to "taste the light" of his observations. Since
our field trip took in nearly the entire campus, his "topic" became only those observations that most provoked his sensibilities. The other students made similar
choices. Since there wasn't an assigned topic, each case depended on a defined
mode of discourse, an ordinary subject matter, and a huge resource of specific
details requiring selected observation and response. Later would come further
selection, development, and revision.

At one point, we exited the building again, the morning sun now warm
enough to keep us outdoors for a while. A circular driveway around a patch of
lawn affected Jenna's imagination in a way that prompted her to be especially
vivid:

As I take a step outside, the glaring sun shines in my eyes as if it was
trying to blind me. Our bodies and many other objects make imprinting
shadows on the rough pavement. The road has a curving look with a
center of grace in the middle. The grass . . . is wilting to a shade of brown
in the cold, misty air.

The sunshine was quite bright, making shadows sharp and dark, forceful
enough to justify "imprinting," although such conditions meant the day had
ceased to be "misty," reminding me how vulnerable to inaccuracies writers

become when translating experience into language. Nevertheless, her overall sense of contrast drove Jenna's attempts to capture what she saw and what she felt, both physically and emotionally. Her original list contained her key nouns, verbs, and participles and her touching image, "a center of grace." For Patrick and Jenna, writing about something else became in part self-defining because there truly was something to write about. Their depth of thought emerged from the abundance of observations and its metamorphosis into words. Whatever physics and chemistry go into the making of a photograph, a similarly complex human dynamic needed to be involved with these students. Without the dualism of objective and personal responses, the observations would have been less intense and the compositions less worthwhile. Essential to the process are three criteria: plentiful available details, the students' familiarity with successful technique, and the students' willingness to chance self-revelation and verbal extravagance. These young writers implied more than stated their conclusions about what they saw, but, given the minimum length of their assignment—three well-developed paragraphs—they discovered and expressed much more than mere listing and sentence combining would have accomplished.

About two months later, my senior advanced placement students were reading essays by E. B. White, Joan Didion, and others. With such works, we saw quite clearly how writers can take their close observations and use them to form grand concepts loaded with emotional power. These models demonstrated Fletcher's food chain with lively style. Rather than have my seniors write analyses of these works, the usual kind of paper in this course, I opted for a version of the assignment the freshmen completed. With both groups, I wanted students to observe physical details with the writer's eye, record as much as they could, and compose an essay about what they encountered, maintaining an authentic voice. The seniors could go to another level of thought, as their models did, and develop explicit interpretations. In other words, the seniors would demonstrate their understanding of essay writing through imitation, but this would be a replication of a presumed process rather than of a precise form. In a very real sense, this became an assessment of all their literary studies this past year and previously, because literary studies devoid of personal responses do a grave disservice and leave students no better off than Clevinger in *Catch-22*: "He knew everything about literature except how to enjoy it" (Heller 1994, 78). The issue became whether they could approach the eloquence and insights the assigned essays in their anthology had achieved. In "Ring of Time," for example, White describes a teenage girl who is rehearsing her circus acrobatics on a horse without the gaudy glare of the performance setting:

> *Under the bright lights of the finished show, a performer need only reflect the electric candle power that is directed upon him; but in the dark and dirty old training rings and in the makeshift cages, whatever light is generated, whatever excitement, whatever beauty, must come from original sources—from internal fires of professional hunger and delight, from the exuberance and gravity of youth.* (White 1986, 1416)

What to some observers might have seemed bland compared to the lavishness we expect to find at a circus, White saw the profound in a "dark and dirty" barn. It is this openness to such possibilities that we want students to practice. A similar shift from the particulars to a generality happens in Didion's "Los Angeles Notebook" when she describes the hot, dry Santa Ana winds of southern California and their effects on the atmosphere and people there:

> *I have never heard nor read that a Santa Ana is due, but I know it, and almost everyone I have seen today knows it too. We know it because we feel it. The baby frets. The maid sulks. I rekindle a waning argument with the electric company, then cut my losses and lie down, given over to whatever it is in the air. To live with the Santa Ana is to accept, consciously or unconsciously, a deeply mechanistic view of humanity.* (Didion 1986, 1433)

These writers exhibit how observed details generate personal responses leading to a literary form in which the author's voice should be prominent. As with the freshmen, I urged the seniors to be "personal and daring" with their first impressions. It is difficult to imagine White and Didion, both highly disciplined writers, being self-censuring in their note taking; rather, we sense how the details and the writers' reactions formed the topics instead of the other way around. Because the assignment for the seniors required lengthier and more mature insights, they had to categorize their lists into whatever clusters they deemed appropriate as a way of forming associations leading to complex thought, but this transformation came only after the initial listing was complete, and it needed no precise form. Almost any variety of relisting or webbing would do. The key was first to generate a mess of detailed observations, the bigger the better. Judgments about similarities and differences among the items would follow when the writer developed the clusters, one of which might well be a trash bin for all the stuff deemed weak or irrelevant. Such prewriting begins the evolution toward sentences and paragraphs, especially when the writer notes the reasons for these new associations. As the seniors decided the hows and whys that transform lists into cohesive concepts, they somewhat reversed the formalist approach we employed when analyzing prose passages and poems. Instead of discerning, they were forging the parts that make up a whole, this time encouraged to use personal more than academic perceptions. Notice, for example, how Julie observed much about the building's exterior as we headed toward the main entrance and how what she saw could yield judgments:

> *Bits of trash and bags adorning the parking lot, having drifted out of the nearby dumpster, circulate in small tight circles as the current of the wind takes them in several directions, tugging and pulling at them all at once without ever really getting them anywhere. The bags and wrappers, though never still for more than a moment, do not travel more than a few feet from their original location, and no one pays much attention to them or cares enough to pick them up.*

Here we see a more mature writer at work, and her point about the lack of attention became a central thesis in her essay: indifference breeds neglect, and evidence of disrepair generates disrespect, a condition she found difficult because in many other ways the school has functioned very well.

Ryan noticed how measured time regulates school activity. Places once still became busy at the sound of a bell. As he moved from the observable to the interpretive, his imagination constructed a simile to complete the connection in the same way that Patrick, Jenna, and Julie quite naturally used poetic expressions:

> *Doors open, lockers slam, and the pattern of chalky white dust on the floor begins taking on a new intricate design. Time seems to have started again in the hall. The school is like a water-smoothed pebble. The students wash over the school after every bell like the tide and give it new shape.*

Ryan's classmate Alexis can spot details and use her gift for language to reproduce them beautifully, though her ruminations about time took a different turn than Ryan's. Perhaps the "Time Passes" section of Virginia Woolf's *To the Lighthouse*, which we had read the previous term, influenced her, or finding herself three-quarters through her senior year prompted thoughts of life's progression. Whatever her motivation, the point is that when we form generalities from particulars, we should draw not only from the subject matter but also from very personal and perhaps unknown wells. Of course, bogus profundity sometimes gets imposed in the transition from fragments to sentences and paragraphs. That is why the personal and objective should be joined from the beginning, and this combination will likely yield thoughtful editing, which should be a process of cutting and tempering prose, not expanding and decorating it. This is when decisions about diction and style come in. No matter the grade level, teacher-made handouts for editing, carefully structured peer editing, teacher corrections and subsequent revisions, and other activities can join the editing procedures we would employ under any circumstances. The best editing retains authenticity. We can see the genuine in Alexis's responses:

> *Now the mismatching lockers are blotchy and dented. The walls are*
> *dingy yellow and green, and the paint is chipping and peeling away. . . .*
> *The floors have unsightly gouges in them, like little craters formed by*
> *tiny meteorites. There are cracks running up the wall with gnarled spi-*
> *der-like fingers branching out. The old furnaces are beaten and decrepit*
> *yet still manage to wearily crank out heat. The dim fluorescent lights*
> *create a buzzing that echoes eerily through the otherwise silent hallways.*
> *The speckled white ceiling tiles are sagging with age and yellowing with*
> *spreading water stains. Time continues, and the school deteriorates with*
> *it. Its fate cannot be avoided. Time will win the battle overall. For time is*
> *immortal and tireless, and nothing can outlast time.*

Anyone who can so skillfully weave details and conclusions has a potential for great learning. Alexis would inspire any teacher. She demonstrated Berthoff's central maxim: "We can best help students develop their own powers by assuring that they have occasions to discover that composing is itself a process of discovery and interpretation, of naming and stating, of seeing relationships and making meanings" (Berthoff 1981, 20). All the seniors submitted final papers at least a thousand words long. They examined other details within the school. The passages cited here capture the controlling idea of the compositions. Each paper sometimes veered from an exact focus on the details and offered reflections about the issues their descriptions had revealed, yet the best compositions avoided lengthy, vague contemplations because the broad concepts, through process, evolved from the specific and remained inseparable from it.

In all our endeavors to make students better writers, we must remember that the purpose of education is engagement with, not exposure to, life. Writing often combines spontaneity with patience as it works toward something as wonderful and comprehensive as a literary food chain. The emotional connection with the precisely observed makes descriptive writing forceful. "Writing is about learning to pay attention," writes Anne Lamott, "and to communicate what is going on" (Lamott 1995, 97). Woven between the paying attention and the communicating are the writer's words, knowledge, and desires—the emanation of self when language and stimuli collide. Even an old building worn by age and use can be the arena for such essential activities. Another senior, Callie, discovered this during her in-school field trip:

> . . . We cannot judge the quality of the school by the warped and stained floors or the chipping paint, because life can be hard on us in the same way. Our experiences with others, with business, with careers, with co-workers will leave stains on us, will do a little chipping of our paint as well. Life is education.

Callie demonstrates how the writer's eye can perceive beyond the stars and into the soul. Whether the resulting composition occupies many pages or just enough space to answer a mandated assessment question, the composing process must begin with the little things. Within them, and within our students, waits the profound.

REFERENCES

Berthoff, Ann E. 1981. *The Making of Meaning*. Montclair, N.J: Boynton/Cook.

Braun, Casey. 1995. "Bright Light." In *Decker's Patterns of Exposition* 14, ed. Randall E. Decker and Robert A. Schwegler. New York: HarperCollins.

Didion, Joan. 1986. "Los Angeles Notebook." In *Literature: Reading Fiction, Poetry, Drama, and the Essay*, ed. Robert DiYanni. New York: Random House. First published 1968.

Fletcher, Ralph. 1992. *What a Writer Needs*. Portsmouth, NH: Heinemann.

Heller, Joseph. 1994. *Catch-22*. New York: Scribner.

Lamott, Anne. 1995. *Bird by Bird*. New York: Anchor.

Peterson, Scott. 2000. "The Writer's Eye: Using the Writer's Notebook as a Lens to View the World." *The Quarterly of the National Writing Project* 22 (2): 27–30.

White, E. B. 1986. "The Ring of Time." In *Literature: Reading Fiction, Poetry, Drama, and the Essay*, ed. Robert DiYanni. New York: Random House. First published 1956.

Section 4

I Was Doing the Laundry When . . .

Teachers find inspiration in daily life

Everything I Know About Teaching Language Arts, I Learned at the Office Supply Store

Kathleen O'Shaughnessy

Kathleen O'Shaughnessy's article about her teaching experience with middle school students in Louisiana was originally published in the spring 2001 issue of The Quarterly.

I am often viewed by co-workers as a laid-back teacher, one with a high tolerance for disorder—chaos, some would call it. They derive their impressions from the fact that I teach writing workshop in a way that looks nothing like the textbook-centered language arts class with its weekly spelling tests, grammar worksheets, and book reports. They see paperbacks and beanbag chairs and assume I'm one of those artsy types who can sit happily amid a swirl of disorganized activity. They haven't seen my closet.

People who see my closet don't use words like *laid-back*. They use terms they learned in psychology class, terms for people who, according to Freud anyway, clearly had traumatic toilet training experiences. All my clothes face the same direction on identical hangers—plastic, never wire. Long-sleeved, short-sleeved, and sleeveless blouses hang in discreet sections; skirts are sorted by length, pants by color, shoes by heel height. Chaos and disorder have never seen the inside of my closet.

How can a person like me—someone who enjoys unloading the dishwasher because seeing neat stacks of plates on shelves and forks in compartments gives me pleasure—exist in an unstructured, unorganized mess like writing workshop? There are two answers.

One is that writing workshop is not unstructured at all; it's just not the kind of structure that most people expect in a well-managed classroom. For years, I experimented with the design of my writing workshop, searching for just the right combination of routines and strategies. I changed supply lists, daily schedules, and furniture arrangements every year looking for *the right way* to organize a workshop. After many years of tinkering, I've come to realize that writing workshop is not like building a skyscraper; it's like building a house of cards. The joy is not in the finished, static structure but in the act of building itself. The process is the thing. The challenge of adding a new layer, letting it fall, and starting all over again is what keeps workshop teachers awake and alive. In *A Teacher's Sketch Journal*, Karen Ernst says that what observers may see in her artists' workshop as lack of structure is really "teaching choice—its lessons and responsibilities; I . . . constantly create structures by which to resolve the tensions and challenges I observe and experience."

The second answer is that the "chaos" of my writing workshop is partly mitigated by drawing on the inspiration that has come as I've pursued my life outside the classroom. In particular, while browsing the tidy and orderly shelves at Office Depot, I've found new ways to create and recreate structure. Post-its become more than Post-its. They help me make visible and understandable to students the invisible and abstract processes I want them to learn. They help me find order when the "tensions and challenges" of a rough day make me think back wistfully to the days of straight rows of desks and everyone on the same page of the same book at the same time. In writing workshop, order, like beauty, is in the eye of the beholder.

~ *Kathleen O'Shaughnessy, 2002*

*O*kay, not everything I know about teaching came from Office Depot. I did pick up a few pointers along the way from the likes of Linda Rief, Regie Routman, and Nancie Atwell. Those have been the big ideas, the theoretical frameworks I've internalized, ideas that shape my teaching in ways I'm hardly aware of anymore. But in the chaotic real world of the classroom, the tiny things matter. Tiny things make the difference between feeling scattered and lost or competent and in control. And many of the tiny things that prop me up in my classroom have come from the aisles of my local office supply store, where I can be found on many Sunday afternoons discovering some gizmo I never knew existed but now can't live without.

DON'T YOU WISH YOU'D INVENTED POST-IT NOTES?

Every year, I ask each section of middle school students I teach to bring in one supply to add to the community pile that all classes will share throughout the year. These treasures may include the usual project-making supplies like markers, glue, and construction paper, but I always ask the largest class to bring in packs of three-by-three-inch Post-it notes. We use them almost daily.

Powerlines. We use Post-it notes to tag short passages of effective description. A colleague of mine has coined the word *powerlines* for these. They may be similes, metaphors, or just good writing that is chock-full of vivid images. During whole-class minilessons, I train students to spot these lines, stopping while reading aloud to point them out and reread them. A powerline is more easily illustrated than defined. Christopher Paul Curtis is one author who provides plenty of powerlines, like these from *The Watsons Go to Birmingham*, which I read to the class.

The "official juvenile delinquent," Byron, has just thrown a cookie at a bird on a telephone wire and Kenny, the narrator, says, "The cookie popped the bird smack-jab in the chest! The bird's wings both stuck out to the side and for a hot second with its tail hanging down and its wings stuck out like that it looked like a perfect small letter stuck up on the telephone wire." At these words, most of the boys in my class laughed and most of the girls squirmed, one protesting, "Aw, that's mean." I pointed out that we must have here a powerline because a characteristic of a powerline is the ability to move a reader with a clear mental image. All admitted they had been moved by this image. I read on: "When I got to Byron he'd picked up the bird and was holding it in his hands. The bird's head drooped backward and

189

was rolling from side to side. Dead as a donut." More laughs, more protests, and at least one, "Hey, that's another powerline!"

Once students begin to recognize powerlines in our shared reading, I send them searching in their independent reading material for samples of their own. When they find one, they mark it with a Post-it note and keep reading. Later they copy the powerline, the source, and the page number onto an index card (Office Depot again) to turn in for a grade. These are posted on a bulletin board for a while where students can borrow them for inspiration. Students' writing improves as they become aware of the tricks that authors use to add engaging detail and imagery to their work. I've seen my students using powerlines in their own writing after turning in just one or two cards. In one set of personal narratives from early in the school year, I found dozens. Some sounded very much like eighth-graders:

You could feel the hot wind blowing against your face like a hair dryer blowing on medium.

You could hear the waves crashing against the beach like a car crash.

But others were startling to me in their originality and in the strength of the language:

My line zoomed out like a dog chasing a mailman.

From around the corner came a nondescript white truck like a huge beast lumbering out of its cave.

I saw [my brother's] spider monkey body fly into the air and hit the ground with a thump.

She was curled up like a rosebud, her back to me.

I was so delighted with my harvest of student-generated powerlines that I typed them up and attached each to a separate index card. For our next writing workshop, I had students sort through the cards and choose a powerline to use as a first sentence in a piece of fiction. This gave me the pleasure of reading an entire set of students' stories without a single "Hi my name is . . . and this is a story about . . ." first sentence, and the momentum of a powerful first sentence seemed to energize their pieces. The stories they produced were much more lively and detailed than previous attempts, and they yielded a fresh crop of powerlines to read aloud and celebrate.

VOCABULARY. My students also use Post-its to mark new or interesting vocabulary words as they read independently. There's nothing new about asking students to fish out new vocabulary in their reading. But the Post-it allows them to forge ahead in the text without committing the sin of marking up a book. Later they copy from the text the sentence in which they encountered the word, the title of the source, and the page number, adding a definition in their own words and an illustration or example when appropriate. For *disheveled*, Jenna wrote, "When Coach doesn't give us enough time to dress in, I end up disheveled because I can't get dressed and do my hair in two minutes!" Brian made a card for *dog-eared*: "Don't dog-ear your class novel because Ms. O. doesn't like it when you mess up her books." This was accompanied by a drawing of an open book with arrows pointing to the turned-down corners of the pages. Vocabulary cards are also posted on a bulletin board for a while; then the students who wrote them get their cards back to add to personal word banks in their binders.

PEER RESPONSE. Post-it notes also make it easier to put into action Peter Elbow's reflective feedback technique, "telling." Telling requires responders to describe their reactions as they read. Telling and other Elbow strategies tend to make students' feedback more useful than the usual "I liked it; it was good" that I heard regularly back in the days when I didn't direct student responses. I've found that when I require a written response on a Post-it instead of merely allowing students to respond verbally, the responders take their duties more seriously, and with practice, the quality of their remarks improves. So, for instance, Sean demonstrates the telling technique with this:

> While I was reading your piece, I felt like I was riding a rollercoaster. It started out kinda slow, but you could tell there was something exciting coming up. But then it moved real fast and stopped all of a sudden. I almost needed to read it again the way you ride a rollercoaster over again because it goes by too fast.

This response is certainly more useful to the writer than the usual "I think you could, like, add some more details, you know?" that I often overheard in response meetings.

Writers as well as responders make use of Post-its. I often ask the author of a piece to attach specific questions about the draft. We do this to prepare for a "blind conference" in which students use pseudonyms to identify their drafts. I give the piece to a responder in a different class. This is my attempt to remedy the circumstances in which students who work together every day are sometimes uncomfortable giving what might be seen by the author as negative feedback or in other cases giving, because of personal feelings about the author, nothing but negative feedback. Blind conferences create a level of objectivity that might not exist in face-to-face meetings and provide a more genuine experience of writing for an audience, since most of us don't know all of our readers personally.

Typically, a draft will get handed around to several readers, and the author will get more than one answer to each Post-it note question. One writer, working under the pseudonym Orange Banana, asked, "Do I have a good attention grabber here?" and got four responses. Three were generic: "It's okay," "No. Be more specific," and "Yeah, it was good." But one was calculated to get the writer thinking in new directions: "Say how nervous you were before the game." Now Orange Banana has something specific to consider.

Responders are only required to answer the author's questions on the same Post-it note, but they often attach new ones to add further, unsolicited advice. G.I. Joe's story about a baseball game came back with a yellow note with this advice: "The story doesn't feel over. What did you gain from the experience? What did you lose? Learn? Did you get a moral? What happens next?" Responders are encouraged to critique the critiques. On a hot pink Post-it, four different students responded. The first student wrote, "Explode the moment when you were running at him." Others added, "I agree," "I agree also," and "Whoever wrote this was right. What did you feel?" The final draft that G.I. Joe later turned in, under his real name, was quite different from the draft he'd submitted to his unknown responders.

Sometimes, I orchestrate whole-class swaps, requiring everyone to give me a draft with two or three questions attached that I will then hand out to a different class later in the day or the next day. Or I'll make this activity voluntary. I keep stacking trays (also from the office supply store) labeled with the different class hours. Students who want feedback put their drafts in their class's tray. Usually, within two days, an early finisher in another class will wander over to the trays, take out a draft, and respond to it. Waiting authors will enter class each day asking, "Did I get a response yet?" Any gimmick that has kids begging for revision strategies is, in my book, a keeper.

ACTIVE READER STRATEGIES. Post-its also provide a tool to help create proficient readers who interact with the text, predicting, evaluating, questioning, clarifying, and connecting. I model these strategies, one at a time, reading aloud to the whole class, but I depend on Post-its to help monitor whether or not students are catching on. After I've introduced a strategy, I give students three Post-it notes and some text and have them apply the strategy, noting their thoughts on the Post-its in three different sections of the text. Later, when they know more strategies and are becoming fluent in their use, students will keep a pack of Post-its on their desks as they read and use them to record their thoughts about the text. When they're done, they peel off the Post-its, recording page numbers as they go, and attach them to a piece of paper in their reader's notebooks. These notes serve as valuable review material if students are required to write a response to the literature or take a test on it, and they allow me to assess students' mastery of the metacognitive strategies.

Ashley read "Stop the Sun" by Gary Paulsen, a short story about a boy struggling to connect with his emotionally distant father, who suffers from post-traumatic stress after the Vietnam War. She employs several of the categories of interacting with the text that I have demonstrated. She connects: "My dad was in the Vietnam war. But he doesn't have Vietnam syndrome." She predicts: "He's going to talk to his dad! I just know it!" She visualizes and evaluates: when the father says, "So I crawled to the side and found Jackson, only he wasn't there, just part of his body, the top part, and I hid under it and waited, and waited, and waited," Ashley wrote, "AHHII! The top part!?! Hid under it!?! Gross!" Near the end of the story, she clarifies her understanding of what the story means to her: "Poor thing! His poor dad! Man, Vietnam really messed him up." Not all students are as spontaneous and genuine as Ashley in their Post-it responses, but I can determine from their notes whether or not a student has attended to and comprehended a piece of text.

SOME USES FOR HIGHLIGHTERS OTHER THAN DRAWING ON NOTEBOOK COVERS

My students love highlighters. They love the bright fluorescent colors; they love the snap of the cap. During the first week of school, when best intentions are rampant, or right after report cards have been issued, when middle school students get really serious, I see dozens of students industriously underlining whole paragraphs at a time in their class notes. The rest of the time, I see dozens of enraptured students drawing and doodling and recording the latest loves of their lives on the covers of their notebooks or sometimes on their hands in orange, pink, and lime green highlighter. Rather than ban highlighters from my room, I decided to take advantage of my students' fascination with them and use it to my advantage, so I set out to find some uses, other than decorative, for highlighters.

HOT SPOTS. I give students a hot-colored highlighter while they're drafting. Anytime they have to pause to guess how to spell *believe* or *fascinating* or to wonder if they need a comma or if they should use *I* or *me*, they highlight that spot in the draft and keep writing. Later, when they're ready to consider mechanics, they go back to the "hot spots" and double-check their guesses with a dictionary, grammar handbook, or proofreading partner.

SENTENCE STRUCTURE. I don't know why so many students still write sentence fragments and run-ons in spite of all the red ink their English teachers have spilled in the cause of eradicating them. The following two highlighter tricks are not guaranteed to succeed where all that red ink has failed, but they do make visual a concept that seems too abstract for many students to grasp.

I ask students to highlight the ending punctuation marks in a draft, then put an index finger on the first highlighted spot and put the other index finger on the next highlighted spot. If their fingers are two or three words apart, they may have a fragment. If their fingers are waving to each other from across a vast expanse of ink, they may have a run-on. When Joey saw the gap between the first and last words of "It was a sunny day in October and everyone at school was at lunch outside playing soccer or talking about what they were doing for Halloween, me, on the other hand, I was at the soccer field watching everyone play," he recognized for himself that he had a run-on, and I didn't even have to try explaining to him what's wrong with the "me, on the other hand, I . . . " part of his sentence.

In another test for run-ons, I ask students to highlight all the verbs in a draft then check each sentence for highlighted spots. A sentence with more than two verbs may be a run-on, or it may need careful punctuation, as in a compound sentence. When Patrick counted six verbs in this sentence, he knew he needed to edit it: "Someone all of a sudden *threw* me the ball and when I *looked* up I *saw* the four eighth graders *chasing* me and all I could do was *run* so I *ran*."

DIALOGUE. Here is a query high on my list of life's unanswerable questions: why is it so difficult to remember that a change of speaker requires a new paragraph? Rather than repeatedly asking my students this question, I give these directions: highlight each character's name the first time it's mentioned in a draft, using a different color for each character. Then, throughout the draft, highlight each character's speeches in his/her assigned color. When it's time for a final draft, don't mix colors in a single paragraph. When the color changes, start a new paragraph.

THE FIVE-HIGHLIGHTER EXERCISE. I ask students to assign a different color of highlighter to each of the five senses and then create a key at the top of a draft so they can remember which is which. As students read their own or a partner's draft, they mark sensory details with the corresponding color. After the draft is marked, students hold it up and look at it as if it were an abstract painting. If there's very little color, the draft needs more sensory detail. If one color predominates, the student should try to incorporate more of the other senses. If it looks like an undiscovered Jackson Pollock, perhaps the student has gone overboard with description.

Jesse's story of a fight on the playground was a masterpiece of blue, his sense-of-sight color, but the other senses were scarcely represented. So to his original sentence, "All I can remember was me getting on top of him and punching him in his face," he added a pink, hearing detail, "and hearing the kids yell, 'hit him in his face' and his heavy breathing and groaning." Challenged by his peer editors to use senses other than vision, and handed a green and orange highlighter, Ian enhanced his description of football practice: "We were having our first practice in full gear on the hottest day of the summer. The heat made us dizzy." He added, "The adrenalin built up inside me like a bottle. I got set and my senses were at their highest level. My hearing alerted me to Coach inhaling to blow on the whistle."

NOT TO BE. Highlighters can help students ferret out dull words. Vivid verbs are a hallmark of engaging writing, but students are more likely to use the first words that come to their minds, often the overused and uninteresting forms of "to be." I provide students with a list of these "to be" verb forms and send them searching through a draft, highlighting every "to be" verb. Most drafts end up polka-dotted. I challenge students to eliminate five or more, or every third one of the dots by rewriting sentences with more active, vivid verbs.

RECENT DISCOVERIES FOR WHICH THERE MUST BE USES

Most people go to an office supply store when they have a need and buy the thing that will fulfill the need. But if you're an office supply junkie, you find the thing and then you figure out what you need it for.

ARTIST MOUNT SPRAY ADHESIVE. This comes in an aerosol can and is just sticky enough to hold paper or cardboard to a wall but not sticky enough to be permanent or to remove paint. When you spray it on a sheet of paper, poster board, construction paper, or card stock, you get, in effect, a giant Post-it note. Here are some ways I use this adhesive:

1. Environmental poetry. Georgia Heard calls this "the Living Anthology Project." Students write short poems, illustrate them, and stick them, with the spray adhesive, to spots around the campus where kids stand and wait in line, places such as at the water fountain or on the serving line in the cafeteria. The poems last for a few days, although I'm never certain if the adhesive gives up first or if some fellow middle-schooler has had a hand in the poem's disappearance. But, since all we have invested is a piece of paper and a couple of spurts from the magic can, we don't get upset about the missing poem. In fact, it's sort of a point of honor if some unknown poetry thief liked your poem enough to take it off the wall and keep it. For the line at the Coke machine, Matt wrote "Wait Your Turn."

When you're standing in line
You feel like you're dying of thirst
You push and shove
To get your Coke first
All the little kids try to cut in front of you
When they do, you don't know what to do
After you've done whatever you can
They cry and tell a teacher
And you think, "Aw, man!"

Ian's "What's on the Spout" graced the wall above a water fountain for a short while:

I'm going to warn you before you drink
What's on the spout
What do you think?
After I've told you
I hope you'll be upset
As you drink that nice water, all cool and wet
What do roaches do when they crawl in the bowl?
They crawl and swim around, black as coal
Silent and swift they take a quick drink
Now that you're almost done sipping, what do you think?

Are you upset now because of your haste?
Is it worth the risk for one little taste?
Oh, and I should tell you about that mouse who calls the bowl a pool
I don't think he minds swimming in the water you drink to get cool
Should you really drink from the fountain at school?

2. Poor person's magnetic poetry. I write words on small, blank flash cards or index cards, then spray the cards or a blank sheet of paper so students can move the words around, resticking them several times as they try out new arrangements to create a poem. They could be a random assortment of evocative words or the words from a published poem.

Using the words from Langston Hughes's "Dream Variations," Erin wrote two poems:

Variations of Me
dream beneath the dark night
dance in the pale sun
whirl tenderly in the evening
rest till day is done

While the Day Is Gone
dream of a place like the cool evening
and fling the sun gently at night
wide like a tall tree
coming to rest in my arms
Black to some
white to me

Or students can play around with a sticky collection of roots and affixes and see how many actual words they can put together, or make up some that don't exist and define them according to the meaning of the word parts. One class put to use a collection of roots and affixes related to parts to create prefix monsters for an illustrated class book. Each page included a creature's name composed of word parts, the definitions of each part, and a picture of the creature. One page, for example, featured the macro-encephalo-bi-cardio-octo-ped, which is, of course, a creature with a large head, two hearts, and eight feet.

PRESENTATION BINDERS. These look like regular small vinyl binders except that plastic sheet protectors are permanently bound into the place where the rings

197

would normally be. They come with varying numbers of page protectors. Here's how I use them:

1. Day to day. I keep a presentation binder with ten sheets on each of the student tables in my room. Inside are directions for projects in progress in each class, along with successful samples from previous students, reminders of classroom rules, calendars of upcoming events and deadlines, and anything else I get tired of saying a dozen times a day. Students still ask, "How long does this have to be again?" as often as ever, but now I have an automatic answer: "Look in your table book." Now that students are starting to say "Look in the table book" to each other, I know I'm on to a good thing.

2. Special occasions. For open house night or parent conference day, I clean out the mundane material and, with the help of each student, put in the book a sure-to-please-Mom piece of work from each student who sits at the table. It could be an illustrated poem or, since each page is two sided, it could be a before-and-after display in each sleeve with, for instance, a page of a piece of writing from early in the year in front and a page from a later revision or a later piece of work in the back. Parents appreciate the chance to see their child's progress, and the exercise of requiring students to select what to put in their table book provides an excellent form of self-evaluation.

If you have any money left, stop at your favorite superstore on the way home from Office Depot. For under eight dollars, you can buy a hanging shoe organizer with a dozen plastic pockets just the right size to hold highlighters, Post-its, and all the other tiny and essential things needed to make real and practical the big ideas inspired by Linda and Regie and Nancie.

REFERENCES

Atwell, Nancie. 1998. *In the Middle: New Understandings About Writing, Reading, and Learning*. Portsmouth, NH: Boynton/Cook.

Curtis, Christopher Paul. 1995. *The Watsons Go to Birmingham—1963*. New York: Bantam Doubleday Dell.

Elbow, Peter. 1998. *Writing Without Teachers*. New York: Oxford University Press.

Ernst, Karen. 1997. *A Teacher's Sketch Journal: Observations on Learning and Teaching*. Portsmouth, NH: Heinemann.

Heard, Georgia. 1998. *Awakening the Heart: Exploring Poetry in Elementary and Middle School*. Portsmouth, NH: Heinemann.

Rief, Linda. 1991. *Seeking Diversity: Language Arts with Adolescents*. Portsmouth, NH: Heinemann.

Routman, Regie. 1995. *Invitations: Changing as Teachers and Learners K–12*. Portsmouth, NH: Heinemann.

■

Special thanks to Nancy Romero for the term *powerline*.

Cat Watching: Six Easy Steps to Classroom Poetry

Scott Peterson

This article, written by Scott Peterson about inspiring his grade school students toward poetry, was originally published in the Third Coast Writing Project Newsletter *and later reprinted in the spring 1999 issue of* The Quarterly.

My classroom window looks out on an open field in the middle of the village where I teach. As fields go, it is a little on the small side, but a busy creek lined by leafy trees cuts through the middle of it, and there is enough room for kids to do things. Remaining in my room at the end of the school day, I expect to see some of my students who live in the area playing a little ball, hunting for crayfish and crawdads, indulging in some creative play along the banks of the little creek.

Rarely, though, do I see anyone in this patch of green space. Occasionally, a teenage couple, seeking a little privacy, wanders in and disappears between the trees, but pretty much my little park is vacant of human activity. Almost the only sign that the area is occupied by people comes when the sky darkens. Then I can see the blue light from television and computer screens glow through the windows of the houses that surround this space.

For me, this empty space has come to illustrate a social trend. Our children spend less time participating in and observing the "real" world and more time being passively entertained by television, radio, movies, and computer games. My personal challenge has been to get kids off the couch, away from the screen, and into a place where they take a deeper and richer look at the real world.

The teaching ideas expressed in this piece were in part generated while I looked out on that empty field. These strategies are my effort to foster careful observation among my students and to turn these perceptions into language. I have approached this through the genre of poetry because poetry helps students drink in the details of life while also giving voice to vital ingredients in their experience. My goal is to convince students that by writing poems that grow from close observation of the real world, they will find that words can be as powerful, worthy, and relevant to their lives as anything that floats across a screen.

~ *Scott Peterson, 2002*

$\mathcal{O}$ ne day I was sitting in the window of a downtown café savoring my morning coffee when I realized that a cat in the upstairs window of the house across the street was staring at me.

It was an orange-and-white tabby, stretched out flat in the windowsill, its fluffy head taking in the street scene below. Relaxed yet observant, it would gaze placidly at the world and then jerk around quickly to catch an interesting movement or respond to an unusual sound.

While I continued to sip my coffee, the cat and I continued our leisurely surveillance of the world as it unfolded before our eyes. Occasionally, our eyes would lock into a stare until one of us broke off contact and we would once again continue our meditations. It didn't take me long to realize that the cat and I had a lot in common.

We were doing the same thing. Both of us were taking in our world, drinking in every detail around us. We had opened every pore to the world so that every sound, every noise, every smell, every taste entered our consciousness. I was as contented and satisfied as that cat in the windowsill, and rarely have I ever felt more alive or aware of the world than I did at that particular moment.

It was poetry that put me in that catlike state of mind. I had been studying poetry, reading poetry, writing poetry, listening to poetry presentations during the Third Coast Writing Project Summer Institute. Immersing my soul in poetry opens up my senses. I see more, smell more, feel more when under the influence of poetry. The grass is a little greener, the sky a little bluer, the rain a little sweeter when I make room for poetry in my life. I notice things that normally would slip out of my life unobserved, like that fat tabby cat staring at me in the window across the street.

We need to make room for poetry in our schools, to bring this same heightened sense of awareness that is induced by heavy doses of poetry into our classrooms. Most of us are intimidated by poetry, frightened by its form and rhyme schemes. We feel that the rules are locked behind closed doors, and only those select few who have the keys can play the poetry game.

Not true. Anyone who loves to mess around with words can write poetry. Poet Michael Carey points out that anyone is capable of being a good poet, provided that she or he loves words and is willing to work at it.

For those of us who need an additional nudge, activities such as the following, adapted from Barry Lane's *After the End*, are well suited to poetry. The words generated from these exercises tend to fit naturally into poetic form. Try these steps yourself to see what I mean.

1. First, think of a subject you know well. It can be a living thing such as a pet, family member, or best friend. It can also be an inanimate object such as a stuffed animal or your bedroom. The only requirement is that it is something you know and care about deeply. I chose to write about another cat, my pet cat Poco.

2. Next, list five general characteristics about your subject. My quick list looks like this: soft fur, friendly, playful, silly, little.

3. Pair up with a partner. The partners take turns asking questions that bring out concrete details and images about the subject. I had no partner but generated these questions based on my general descriptions:

soft fur	*What color fur? Is it a short hair or long hair?*
	What does the fur feel like?
friendly	*How does it show it has a friendly personality?*
playful	*What playful things does your cat do?*
little	*Is it a kitten or a full-grown cat? How old?*
silly	*Tell me something silly about your cat.*

4. While the partner is asking questions, the author is immediately responding in writing with concrete, specific answers to the questions. Here are my answers to my own questions:

fur	*orange, black, and white. Short hair. Fuzzy like a dandelion*
friendly	*It follows me around and weaves in between my feet. Purrs loudly. Jumps in my lap whenever I sit down.*
playful	*Darts around like a streak of lightning, hides under papers and in baskets.*
silly	*Chases its own tail.*

5. Write a prose piece about your subject, incorporating all the concrete details and images generated by the question-and-answer period in step 4.

My prose piece came out like this:

I open the door and my new little kitten Poco pops out like a cork from a champagne bottle. She circles and weaves between my feet as we move into the family room, barely missing death by being smooched by my size 11 feet. I sit at my computer to begin my day's work and she is in my lap before I can settle my fanny into the chair. She is a calico and her orange and black fur tickle my bare legs while I work at the word processor. She pushes her head against my fingers as I rub the space between her ears and she breaks into a ferocious fit of purring. She shakes and rattles so much that you can see the vibration rings in the coffee cup that is sitting on my desk.

Out of the corner of her eye she sees her long tail flip into the air and she is on it like a hunk of raw fish. She attacks it violently, batting it around and chomping on its tip until she slowly and painfully realizes, with a look of surprise in her eyes, that she has been chewing on a piece of her own body. Not exactly the smartest cat in the world, but I think I'll keep her anyway.

6. The concrete details and images generated by this activity make the writing that comes out of it an ideal candidate for a poem. When you experiment with line breaks, the prose can easily evolve into a poem. My prose piece turned into this:

Kitten

I open the door to the basement and
my new little kitten pops out
like a cork off a champagne bottle.

She circles and weaves between my ankles,
defying death from being flattened by
my size 11 feet and
attaches herself to my toes
like a pair of furry slippers as
we move into the kitchen.

She is in my lap before
my fanny settles into any chair and

her orange and black fur tickles my
bare legs while I sip my morning coffee.

She pushes her head against my fingers
as I stroke the space between her ears,
breaking into a ferocious fit of purring,
rattling and shaking
and stirring up little rings of vibrations
in the cup on the kitchen table.

Out of the corner of her eye
she sees her long, black tail
flip up in the air and
is in like a hunk of raw fish.
She attacks violently,
batting it around and
chomping on its tip
until, with a look of surprise in her eyes,
she realizes she is chewing
on a piece
of her own body.

Using my process as a model, my students jumped into the poem-writing business themselves. Tom, a fourth-grader in my class, wanted to write about his new baby sister, Josie. He began by listing five general characteristics about Josie: smart, sweet, loving, funny, and little. Tom's partner then asked the questions about Josie's characteristics; responding to his partner's questions brought some powerful images to the surface and into Tom's prose draft:

Baby Josie is smart because she can smile already and she is only one
week old and it normally takes a baby six weeks to smile. And when I
put a toy bus on her lap she pushes it of. She is sweet because she stares
at you for about 5 minutes. She is loving because when I stick my finger
in her hand she clutches it tight and sometimes it hurts. She is so little
that she could fit in Robyn's doll clothes. And she is funny because she
doesn't cry properly. It sounds like a car running out of gas. And she is
also funny because her eyes dart around, and she is taking everything in.
And she is also funny because she sticks her tongue out at me.

As Tom and I conferenced about his paragraph, we highlighted the best lines and boiled down the prose so that only the most powerful details and images remained. Out of these details, Tom set up line breaks and came up with his poem:

Baby Josie by Tom Crane
Only one week old and
can already smile.
She clutches my finger so hard
sometimes it hurts.
Her eyes dart around
taking everything in.
She is so small she could
fit in a doll's clothes.
When she cries it sounds like a car
running out of gas.

I love my new sister as much as a lion
loves its cubs.

Poetry is far too important to leave outside our classroom doors. Our students are loaded with the images, ideas, and concrete details needed to produce poetry. We need only allow a little inspiration, supplemented by a touch of technique, and soon our students will be producing poems faster than we can read them.

REFERENCES

Lane, Barry. 1993. *After the End: Teaching and Learning Creative Revision.* Portsmouth, NH: Heinemann.

Skeletons Out of the Closet: The Case of the Missing 162 Percent

Bob Pressnall

*Written by Bob Pressnall about his teaching experi-
ence with eighth grade students in Albany, California, this article was originally published in the
summer 1995 issue of* The Quarterly.

It's a given that teachers think on their feet, sometimes in front of their
classrooms, sometimes while thinking about their classrooms, as they
do the dishes or mow the lawn. But I'm a little different. I do most of
my serious brainstorming at night. Even then I need a problem student I
can't ignore, the realization of my own ineptitude, and the jumbled whis-
pers of every teacher I have ever listened to offering advice.

Unfortunately, this auspicious convergence usually happens between the
hours of 2 and 4 A.M. when all in their right minds are dreaming. In the
case at hand, from which the "skeleton revision exercise" sprang, there
was Gina, the kind of student who complained when she got a B+; there
was me, a third-year teacher who knew enough to stir up trouble but
not enough to get out of it; and, thankfully, there was the echo of writing project teacher consultants whose workshops I had attended. On
this particular night as I lay there in bed, staring at the ceiling, suddenly
I heard the creaking of a closet door, the rattling of bones, and Aha! the
case of the missing 162 percent began to unravel. . . .

~ *Bob Pressnall, 2002*

*N*ATURE'S WAY . . .

One morning several years ago, after my back-to-school night presentation, the parents of an eighth-grader sent me a comic strip. In the first frame, a marshmallow-headed figure enthusiastically pecked at a word processor. In the second frame, he stared motionless at the monitor, his trash basket full. In the third frame he sat on a couch next to his desk, the floor littered with paper. He held his head in his hands. The caption read: "Writing is nature's way of showing us how sloppy our thinking is."

I tacked the cartoon up in my classroom on the wall over the assignment checkoff sheet. I'd been teaching the "joy of discovery" in the process of revision, but the cartoon suggested that one must run a gauntlet of drafts and endure a certain amount of pain before one experienced this success. My students had progressed as writers. Most of them were no longer paralyzed by sheer terror when they faced a blank sheet of white paper. They could get something down. Many were eager to share their writing with a partner or group. I had trained them to respond in an author's-chair format, in a series of pair response exercises, and in response groups of three or four. We compiled a Dictionary of Response under the subheadings of "what you like," "what you don't understand," and "where you want more." We made class books Furthermore, they were able to write about their writing, to reflect on their process of prewriting, drafting, responding, and so on.

Unfortunately, for all their skill and willingness to communicate through and about their writing, very few students were actually using the responses they received. In other words, no one was revising in any substantive way—a word or two changed, a sentence or phrase added, a page recopied in ink and they were out the door; no new vision was happening.

"It is possible," I preached, "to experience joy in the act of revision." Everybody groaned.

"Okay," I said, "let me tell you a story." Everybody cheered.

REVISION AND REALITY

I tried one of my little instructive analogies. I hoped to convince them that writers must be brave enough to examine their drafts and make changes and that, in fact, revision had everything to do with their everyday lives.

I said, "I want to tell you the story of a time an old, old friend confided to me that he'd fallen in love for the eighth time. This was no surprise since he'd told me about his seventh and his sixth, and, in fact, I recall his very first numero uno back in junior high school. But there was something very different about number eight: my old buddy had a long face.

"'Doug,' I said. 'Why so sad? You love to fall in love. You've virtually made a career of it. What's the problem?'

"'I think I see a pattern,' Doug said.

"'No kidding,' I said. 'Great insight; time for a change.'

"'No,' he said, his eyes dimming. 'There's nothing I can do. I've kicked the ball, it's gonna roll and bounce around like it always does and then drop. . . . No.'

"Doug's chin fell to his chest. Then he said the thing that made me really sad: 'Wake me when it's over,' he mumbled."

A few students laughed nervously at this punch line, so I dredged: "Why did Doug say, 'Wake me when it's over?'"

A smattering of students spoke out: "He was tired. He didn't want the dream to end. He was sorry. He was stupid. Number eight was ugly. Number eight was too beautiful. He didn't know what to do next." Then they started coming closer: "He didn't want to change. He wanted to change, but he didn't know how. He knew how, maybe, but he was afraid."

"Afraid of what?"

"It's hard to change. Things might get worse."

"Good," I agreed. "In the area of relationships, Doug was writing the same draft over and over again. He didn't know how to revise, and now he was afraid." I stared at the class and they stared back.

"So what happened next?" they wanted to know.

"Well, he married number eight, but that's not the point."

"Do they have kids?"

"Two, but . . ."

"Are they happy?"

"Sorta, but let's talk about what this story has to do with your writing."

"Huh?"

The bell rang, and everybody dashed for the door.

"Change is inevitable!" I shouted.

CULTIVATING DISSATISFACTION

I do not give up that easily.

"Okay," I said the next day, "let's try again. Imagine this is an art class on a field trip. We carry our sketch pads down to the bay or up to the mountain or out to the mall. We stop in ten locations and make ten quick sketches. The next day we return to our studio and choose one sketch to turn into a more full blown piece—a sculpture or an oil painting, whatever you want."

"You mean we get to go on field trips in this class?"

"Of the imagination . . . of the memory . . ."

"Oh."

"That's what writing is all about. Or drawing. You whip out a bunch of sketches and choose a few to develop into longer pieces. You'll choose a sketch because you're passionate about it and because you want to work on it some more. You'll also choose it because there is a tinge of dissatisfaction—that's important, to recognize and appreciate your dissatisfaction. At the point you're unhappy with your writing, if you can let yourself see it, there is the possibility of envisioning more than you have put down on the page. It is because of your dissatisfaction that you see greater, more defined shape and color. You generate new vision. You have somewhere to go. You look for a way to get there. Maybe. But first of all you have to cultivate some dissatisfaction with your writing and thinking, like that guy in the cartoon over there by the assignment checkoff sheet. Cultivating dissatisfaction is something you're not used to."

"You're not making sense, Teacher."

The next day, I decided to forget the analogies and try a visual aid.

THE MISSING 162 PERCENT

"Look at this cartoon," I said. "Everybody has a story in their head. Everybody has a memory or an opinion, everybody has something to say. And when they think about it, they experience it about 212 percent—like this marshmallow-headed guy here—because our minds exaggerate. Now, if you try to put it on paper and you have time, motivation, skill, and luck, you'll at best get only 50 percent onto the page because language is limited. Okay, here's the crucial part: if you reread your own paper, you still reexperience it 212 percent because we tend to fill in the gaps.

"Then, along comes your response partner"—I draw another head on the board—"who might be a fellow student, friend, parent, teacher, girlfriend, or whoever, and if she's a good reader, has time, concentrates, isn't too mad at or madly in love with you, and is not overly concerned with what's for lunch, when the bus leaves for the basketball game, who's going with whom, or even with her own paper, she might help. Under these circumstances, she might get 25 percent of what you've written down on the page."

Response and Revision by Bob Pressnall

FRAME IT OR FLUSH IT

"You know you'll be expected to revise, so you ask for some help. You ask her, 'What do you think of my paper?' Generally, she'll lean in one of two directions:

"She'll either say, 'What do I think of your paper? You wrote this? It's okay, I guess. It's not bad, it's pretty good, actually it's great, fantastic, I love it! Wow! You wrote this! Just copy it over in ink and fix this spelling word and put in this apostrophe, run down to the store and buy one of those gold frames and give it to your grandma for her birthday; she'll love it! You're a great writer!'

"Or she'll say, 'What do I think of your paper? You wrote this? It's okay, I guess, well, I don't know. Actually, it really sucks but don't worry, I promise not to tell anyone. Just crumble it up and drop it in the nearest toilet. You've got a great idea, though. It's not a problem, really, just start over. You're a great writer!'"

COMPASSION AND PRECISION

"But neither 'frame it' nor 'flush it' is likely to help you with revision. The ideal response," I announce, "has two qualities. Whoever can name these two qualities gets to go to lunch five minutes early. Here's a hint: One of these qualities allows you to feel dissatisfied with your writing without flushing it. The other quality points a path toward satisfaction without handing you a gold frame. One starts with a *c,* the other starts with a *p.*'"

Hands flew up around the room. "Cut . . . paste . . . cram . . . put . . . push . . . pull . . . progress . . ." But at four minutes to lunch they were still guessing.

"Compassion and precision are the two qualities," I said. "If a response is not compassionate, or kind, it will never be heard. But if it is not precise, or specific, it does not deliver useful information."

"And what if there's nothing I like in my partner's paper?" one kid drawled.

"Then identify what you hate the least," I said.

A HARD LESSON

I thought I had made my point, and I worked for results. And although my students' ability to communicate about writing continued to improve, their drafts were still not moving; nobody was changing much of anything. Response, I was learning, did not guarantee revision. I ranted and raved about the relationship between talking and doing, communication and change, language and action, and they claimed that they were trying their best. When one student insisted that I was trying to revise him, not his writing, I almost gave up.

Then one day I returned a batch of second drafts, and Gina, the kind of student who complained if she got a B+, stormed up to my desk. "How could you?" she demanded.

"You didn't revise," I said. "You recopied in ink, corrected your spelling, and added two words."

"I don't get D's," she said. "Change it! This is the best paper in my response group."

"I'm grading a process," I explained. "You got wonderful suggestions, and you didn't move your paper."

Meanwhile, the rest of the class, equally outraged, grumbled behind her. Gina leaned over my desk, flapping her paper in one hand, and fixed me with an accusing stare. "Oh, yeah?" she said. "Well, you never taught us to revise."

215

SKELETONS AFTER MIDNIGHT

I didn't think about Gina's comment until 2 A.M. the next morning. I glared at the red digital display on my bedside clock. I began to brood about my students' grumblings. They are too easily satisfied with the sloppiness of their own thinking, I told myself. They say it once, and they think they're done; like pigs rooting around for truffles, they're onto the next thing. They are lazy. They don't care. They're too young. They watch too much video. Maybe next year . . .

At 2:30, I was still lying there. Gina was wrong. I *had* taught her to revise. I'd taught them the "footnote method" of revision, for one. Another time, we'd gotten out the scissors and paste and made a huge mess. We'd examined models of drafts and constructed rubrics. What more did the girl want?

About 3 A.M., I rolled over. An insight! It occurred to me that there are at least two steps to revision. One involves getting more of the 212 percent onto the page; the other involves organizing it so that it makes sense. Why not, I asked myself, start with the first step? Their papers were skeletal and the bones didn't hang together in any recognizable shape. They needed an exercise in which they could practice hanging meat on the bones, maybe, a warm-up before they revised their own papers.

The next morning I wrote the following paragraph on butcher paper:

I walked into class late. The teacher looked at me. I sat down and opened my book. I heard footsteps approach. The teacher cleared her throat. I looked the teacher in the eye.

"That is a skeleton," I said, pointing. "Each sentence is a bone. Your job is to bring the skeleton to life with muscle, blood, fur, claws, guts, and a beating heart. Literally, I want you to write between one and three sentences or phrases between each of the bones. You may extend sentences or change vocabulary or point of view, if you wish. For example, 'The girl sauntered into class late, chomping her gum.' Any questions?"

They got down to work. It was quiet for fifteen minutes. Pencils wagged.

When I asked for volunteers, Darryl raised his hand, a first for him, and read his piece:

I sat down. And I started to eat. The Teacher stared at me. I hid the things I was eating. I opened my book. Then I started to whisper to my friends. I heard his footsteps approaching. I acted like I wasn't doing

216

anything. He cleared his throat. I started to think about what I was go-
ing to do today. I looked him in the eye. While I was opening a bag of
potato chips. They spilled all over the floor under my desk. He started the
class. I listened a little bit. I looked to see what I had missing in home-
work. He told everyone to sit down. I looked at the time like I always do.
He started to talk about the assignments. I just started to think what bus
should I catch home. Last it was time for break.

The class applauded. It was the longest piece Darryl had written that semester. Gina raised her hand. "Uh, Mr. P., did you notice that Darryl amputated the first two bones of your precious skeleton? Did he cut off the head, or what?"

"Did he bring it to life?" I asked.

"I gave it a longer tail," Darryl said.

WHO'S THERE?

The next day, I hung this skeleton:

The tide crept in, erasing the footprints in the sand. The beach curved
away into darkness. How long till the moon rose? Another wave crashed
against the nearby rocks.

"Add a person or two to the scene," I suggested. They did. Romance, suicide, sea lions, murder, slapstick, and serenity spilled from different pens. There was no single right way to do it. Their writing was interesting. They seemed to enjoy it.

WHAT ARE THEY SAYING?

After a brief review on the correct forms for writing dialogue, I hung this skeleton:

Kids streamed into the courtyard for lunch. Jake watched Daisy close
her locker. She turned and faced him. She had that look in her eye. They
headed toward the snack bar. The yard supervisor intercepted them.

"When bringing this one to life," I said, "get the characters to talk to each other." They did.

WHAT ARE THEY THINKING?

When, eventually, everyone seemed to be writing nothing but dialogue, I brought in this one:

"You're not old enough."
"Come on, give me a chance!"
"Not now. Maybe next year."
"I'm not gonna mess up."
"I said, 'No!'"

"Show what these characters are thinking and feeling," I said, "and show their status and mood through dress and gesture." Five minutes into it a student approached my desk.

"I can't think of a single word to go between these two bones. Is that all right?"

I shrugged.

Five more minutes and another student came up: "I accidentally wrote three paragraphs between these two bones."

"Do you like them?" I asked. He nodded. "Then keep them."

WHY ARE THEY DOING IT?

The speedometer showed 70 miles per hour. Jason floored the accelerator.
He didn't care. A curve approached in the road.

"Okay," I told the class. "Show Jason's motivation. Show the significance of this event in his life. Put someone in the passenger seat if you want. And by the way, you must use at least three base clauses with adverbial or noun phrase extensions, like I introduced yesterday, when you bring this one to life."

"They're more like ladders," Darryl said to Gina at the end of class. "I pull myself rung by rung through the scene. I don't know what they're for, but they're fun."

"Oh, they're just a gimmick Teacher made up to kill time at the end of the period," Gina responded. "Personally, I'm sick of skeletons! Now we have social studies skeletons and essay skeletons, skeletons almost every day. It's like a graveyard around here. Why can't we just write?"

"I am writing," said Darryl.

TRAINING WHEELS

I showed my skeletons to other teachers. "Story starters," one commented. "Not bad."

"Yeah," I said, "but all I ever got from 'It was a dark and stormy night' was stuff like 'The monster jumped out of the bushes and strangled me. The end.' With skeletons they're not taking single steps, they're learning how to walk. Call them training wheels, but look at how much they're writing! It's great stuff and they love it!"

"A variation on 'show, not tell,'" said another teacher. "May I borrow?"

"Why not?" I said, and I returned to my classroom and wrote another skeleton.

SKULLS, VERTEBRAE, AND LIMBS

I had demonstrated to myself, my colleagues, and my students that when writers construct narratives, skeletons help them get down more of the 212 percent. But can skeletons also help writers of exposition?

On the history side of my core class, we'd been wading through primary documents, speeches, and writings from the Civil Rights Movement. On test review day, I hung the following skeleton:

In the 1960s Dr. King, Rosa Parks, Malcolm X, Thurgood Marshall, and others tried to change a few things. They had many goals. They tried many tactics. They met resistance. They met success.

As the semester advanced, I asked students to flesh out other expository skeletons, adding to the bare bones of everything from interpretive essays to problem solution pieces.

CUTTING TO THE BONE

I read three pages of Gina's ten-page essay and stopped. It was overwritten, padded, and flaccid. I was used to trimming the fat from student papers just so they could recopy my edits. Then I thought of turning the skeleton exercise on its head. The next day, I called Gina to my desk. "You've got some great ideas here," I said. "But they're buried. I want you to reread your paper and underline the thirteen most indispensable lines, or bones. Then show me."

Gina nodded.

When she brought her paper back to me, I said, "Good. Now you have a skeleton. Start from there. Build it up. Remember, you may write between one and three sentences between each of the bones. . . ."

WRITING SHOWS US . . .

That first year "skeletons" took over my classroom. Of course I overdid it. A single strategy does not constitute a writing program. Too much of a good thing finally prompted one student to say, "Mr. P., I wish you would just stuff all your skeletons back into your closet."

When faced with the sloppiness of our own thinking, we often feel embarrassed or defensive. Then, if the reviews are mixed—frame it or flush it—we wonder who we are writing this for, anyway? With each successive draft, we want to feel finished, even satisfyingly so. We turn the printer on, cross our arms, and tell ourselves that if the rest of the world is so stupid that they can't get our message, who needs them! We turn our papers in to the editor or the teacher and hold our breath.

The nature of writing is that it leaves a record. Two hours, two days, or two years later, we may see that draft X does not match our original vision—whether it was published or not—or that our thinking has changed since we last read draft X. Maybe our vision has changed simply because we wrote draft X or because somebody else read it or is about to. We smile. We grit our teeth. Now we know what we wanted to say. We pick up the pen, turn on the PC, open the file.

If we have been doing this for years, we will see dozens, maybe hundreds, of ways to resee a piece of writing. And among the first questions we ask are the same ones my students have learned to ask. "Where are the skeletons? Where are the bones? How can I flesh them out?"

Obviously, the solution to all student revision problems isn't skeletons. Skeletons don't take the place of student-generated topics, for instance, but they do teach a structure for one type of revision. They help define what revision is. Of course, for most teachers, constantly observing, changing, rearranging, and fine-tuning their practice, revision goes beyond what students do with their writing.

Revision is a teacher's life. I used to think one day I would master the craft of teaching. Then I found out I was really a student. Learning is endless. Learning is hard work. Learning is joyful.

Bring this skeleton to life.

Pruning Too Early: The Thorny Issue of Grading Student Writing

Stephanie Wilder

This article, written by Stephanie Wilder about her teaching experience with high school students in North Carolina, was originally published in the fall 1997 issue of The Quarterly.

It seems that the closer I get to something, the more difficult it becomes to see it clearly. I study my face in a small compact mirror. My nose isn't really that big, is it? And those pores must be visible from across the room! Similarly, a project into which I pour my energy becomes an extension of me, and any sort of criticism feels crushing. Especially as I write and struggle to clarify my thoughts, I find myself falling in love with my words, and I growl at anyone who suggests that maybe I'm a trifle wordy.

As an English teacher, I have watched my tender students recoil at well-intentioned suggestions about their writing and throw down their pens the minute they see a grade on their papers. To the better writers even a B is proof that their teacher is a buffoon and certainly lacks good judgment about writing. Most of my students, however, already have so many fears about writing that whatever grade they see is a welcome signal to them that they can quit.

Frustrated by the results I was getting in class, I would come home and find satisfaction in working in my garden. My students were not growing as writers, but my flowers looked great. Daydreaming among the azaleas, I began to conceive another approach to the teaching of writing. I would be more the loving gardener, nurturing young writers as they struggle to survive in the red clay of North Carolina. Now, I pile on the loamy compost and prune only when the time is right. My students are much more willing to take risks and to keep at their drafts as I offer praise and positive suggestions and resist grading until the student and I agree the draft is ready.

~ *Stephanie Wilder, 2002*

*T*he tiny garden I have planted around my house grows larger in my mind as I order from winter seed catalogs, unable to resist Easter Egg Radishes and Green Envy Zinnias. In spring I squeeze new seedlings into the small space left among the herbs and perennials. All summer I tend my garden lovingly, watering and weeding, and then stepping back to admire it. Sometimes I fantasize that I am a pedestrian coming upon my garden with delight on a hot North Carolina afternoon. It is usually bursting with color, and I love it.

Imagine my horror when I receive a notice from the city one July, saying that if I don't "remove the overgrown weeds" from my yard, the city will do it and charge me for the job. My garden is "an eyesore." I rage to all my friends about the stupidity of the city inspector who can't distinguish a garden from a mess of weeds.

Before I changed my approach to grading student writing, my high school English students regarded me the same way I saw the city inspector. When papers they thought were just fine earned only a C- or worse, my students considered me some kind of idiot not to recognize the value of their work. After all, my students had spent a lot of time completing their assignments, and they thought their pieces sounded great. To my students, the grade at the end was as demoralizing as the letter from the city was to me. Many girls wiped tears from their eyes, and boys launched their balled-up papers into the trash, flashing their eyes at me. If looks could kill, I would have been a dead woman years ago.

It appeared that they did not even read my carefully phrased comments but simply scanned for the grade and reacted emotionally. I didn't think I was giving unreasonable grades, either. I'd spend hours agonizing over the grades, taking into account the rubric we had established for the assignment, the individual student's progress, and the student's effort as I perceived it. Sometimes I'd put two grades on a paper, content and mechanics, but the disappointment in the students' eyes was the same. Myopically confronted by a B+ over a C-, my students only saw the C-. I would justify their bruised feelings to myself. I'd reason that the students would not get better at writing unless I was honest about their grades. But in the cold light of dawn, I'd realize that they were not showing much progress.

My students at a competitive independent day school have a history of poor grades in English class. Some carry labels like learning disabled and ADD, and most have little interest in English for whatever reason. They come to my class with bags loaded with past failures and feelings of inadequacy. To encourage my students, I would offer them the opportunity to revise their papers at any time for a higher grade, but I would feel discouraged when few papers would be resubmitted and fewer yet significantly improved.

The few changes made would often be limited to corrections of the mechanical problems I had already pointed out and halfway corrected myself. Even though I had written many suggestions for ways to restructure the papers or even suggested starting in a different place or on a different topic, the revised papers hardly differed at all from the earlier drafts. Conferences with me might have led to substantive revision, but students were often "too busy" to show up, and as a result I got to read miserable papers several times each.

When the revised paper still did not receive the coveted A, students would often turn belligerent. "But I corrected what you said to correct! What else am I supposed to do?" My suggestion that they reread my comments didn't mollify them. I had just confirmed for them what they already "knew": they couldn't write, so why bother trying?

I was asking the same question: "Why bother trying?" I did not want to spend the rest of my teaching career meeting anger and tears every time I returned a set of papers, particularly when those emotions seemed to block student progress. I was looking for a way out. I decided to implement a portfolio assessment, an idea I had acquired several years before in the writing project. I still graded papers, but now students saved them in a folder, noting strengths and weaknesses, finding patterns, and finally choosing work to be polished for portfolio submission. I was pleased with their improved commitment to the writing and the enthusiasm the portfolio seemed to create. Their choices, however, were dictated by the grades they had seen on the drafts as they worked on them. Students would say, "You gave the paper a pretty good grade, so I chose it for my portfolio."

It seemed to me that the grades were standing in the way of students' progress with their writing. Not only were the weaker students discouraged to the point where they stopped trying, but also many students relied on my grades as the standard by which they judged their own work. I knew I had to think harder about how to overcome these problems. So two years ago I tried an experiment: I decided to postpone my grading until the portfolio was completed. I continued to comment on papers, encourage revision, and urge students to meet with me for conferences. I would simply wait to grade the papers until the portfolio was complete.

When I started school that August, I bounced my idea off several colleagues and got back worried looks and cautions. Ours is a school where grades matter a great deal, and students are accustomed to knowing where they stand. Some colleagues said that students and their families would panic if they didn't see a grade at the bottom of each paper. Others wondered how much effort students would put into writing if there was no grade. We know that the only way to make sure that students do their reading is to quiz almost daily. Would they see writing as less important if it was not graded along the way?

It took time for the students to stop leafing to the ends of their papers looking for the grade. Gradually they stopped saying, "You forgot to put a grade on my paper!" The students who grumbled the longest and loudest about not seeing a grade were predictably those who had always seen excellent grades on their work. One boy wrote on his reflective letter that he did not like the new grading system at all because "Even though I got an A in English, I was nervous about my grade all year. I wasn't sure you liked my writing and didn't know which papers to choose for my portfolio because none were graded." I guess he didn't know it, but his discomfort was my satisfaction.

The majority of the students seemed to flourish. The first change I noticed was that they actually started to read my comments and make the changes that I suggested. The kinds of comments I wrote were more global than those in the past. Instead of marking every little mechanical problem and flaw I saw (to justify the grade?), I wrote my reactions as I read. I emphasized those places where the paper really worked for me, wrote in the margin "Do you really need this part?" beside extraneous passages, and suggested ways to totally restructure a paper: "Why not start with this last paragraph and see what happens?" Often I would rave about a paragraph that contained a good but undeveloped thought and suggest that the writer develop that idea more or add more information about that idea.

The story of Andy illustrates that now that drafts were going ungraded, students were putting more effort into their work than ever before. Andy, a ninth grade student, built a sketchy glimpse of a character into a vivid story. The first draft of the piece was inspired by a man he had seen the previous summer in Taos, New Mexico. He read it to his writing group and was pleased that they responded with laughter and enjoyment. I instructed him to go back to the group and ask for their help in selecting those parts of his draft that they could visualize most clearly and then to work those details into a first draft of a narrative featuring this character, who came to be known as Rico. He wrote a lively but rambling draft. I advised him to highlight those parts of the story that he and his group seemed to like best, cut the rest, and start the narrative with one of the most vivid passages.

The cutting was difficult. Like most writers, he had fallen in love with the entire work. Each time he thought he was finished, I urged him to trim just a little more. Finally, we sat together and looked at the construction of the paper. Since he has strong mechanical skills, we focused instead on varying his sentence patterns. Many of his sentences were long, compound sentences, and I reminded him of other possibilities. We practiced a few sentence-combining activities, and he went back to work.

Andy's final draft now jumped off the page. It began:

Rico awoke, as usual, late in the morning and alone. The sun shone through the bed sheets hanging over the window. Thick smog from the street below had already begun to drift into his apartment. Rico lay in his bed, a mattress on the floor, eyes half open. With a groan he opened his eyes wider and stared at the ceiling wondering what he was going to do that day.

It was a struggle for him to build up the strength to swing his stubby legs around and off the mattress. Finally, though, he was ready to start the day, and as he stood the rolls of fat around his gut straightened out to reveal his tattoos, and the beads of sweat that had accumulated in the folds of skin evaporated.

Placing his hands on top of his head, Rico could feel stubble. He ran to the bathroom to inspect his scalp, and saw that after the few days he had stayed in bed, his hair and perfectly groomed goatee had given way to tangled whiskers and facial stubble.

Taking out his dull razor, Rico frantically tried to remedy his image. The blade couldn't slice hot butter, though, much less hair, so Rico resorted to using his switchblade. He repeatedly nicked his face and the top of his head, and he placed corners of toilet paper over the raw flesh to stop the bleeding. He looked like a honey baked ham. . . .

On Sunday afternoons I usually sit down with a stack of papers. In the past I would dread this activity, procrastinating with chores that seemed pressing and more desirable, like stripping the wax off my kitchen floor and applying a fresh surface or cleaning out the basement. When I was no longer confronted with the responsibility of coming up with a grade for the papers, a load seemed to be lifted from my shoulders. I still read with a pen in hand, but I wrote thoughts as they occurred to me in the margins.

My remarks became more like those an editor might make to a reporter: "Refocus this paper. You're going in too many directions," or "Your thesis just doesn't work. Try again with this interesting idea in the third paragraph." In the past I had bled red ink all over the papers, but instead of helping students revise, my marks had the opposite effect. The corrections seemed to signal to the student that if he or she just fixed what I marked, the paper would be great. They didn't attempt more sweeping changes.

Once grades were postponed, students began looking at the bigger picture instead of getting stuck too soon in editing. Now I downplay the mechanical problems of early drafts, commenting instead on content, organization, and development of papers. Later, when that work has been done, we can focus on remaining mechanical problems.

Students have reacted positively to the comments they have found on their papers. I find, though, that they can still feel a bit wounded when the comments are not gushing with praise. Ashley, a ninth-grader, expresses this ambivalence in her reflective letter.

> I was always frustrated when I got my papers back because you had always written so many suggestions, especially, "Put more details in this part." This past week as I looked them over, though, I realized you were right. My stories had great potential, but I got tired of writing them and put on a lame ending. When you are a procrastinator like me, a good ending is not as important as finishing a paper. In fourth grade I always ended my stories, 'To be continued . . .' I feel that most of the work in my writing folder needed 'to be continued.' I'm glad I had the chance to be able to do that.

Without the specter of a grade to scare them, shy and weak students felt liberated to write longer pieces and to take more risks. One such student was Juliet, a Korean-speaking student with limited English. At the beginning of the year, Juliet was so shy that even her writing group couldn't hear her when she spoke. I put her in a group of very kind girls, however, and they encouraged her by listening carefully, helping her think of words when she couldn't think of them, and teaching her when to use articles. On one occasion, Juliet wrote a personal essay about her love of music. Her group pointed to places that were very clear to them, and they asked her to explain herself more thoroughly in other places. She showed me her revision and mentioned that she was thinking about putting it in her portfolio. I was impressed by the power of her images, so I suggested she rework the piece as a poem. She did so and brought me a piece that was good but had problems with structure. I reminded her that the first and last words of each line are most important, and that short lines carry more weight than long ones. She restructured her work, we reviewed it together for mechanics, and it was ready:

My friend
He doesn't speak a word
In any language of this world
Yet he makes
His presence known
When we are together.
He speaks of passion
Love
and
Hate
He suffers
It is his fate
To come to me
When I am lonely.
He makes me
Be with power crowned
Which disappears like a mist
When I leave him.

I speak through him
We combine in melody.

Graham was a senior who had given up on English years before. His work was so hard to read and understand that teachers couldn't give it a decent grade. Most of the time he didn't even bother handing a paper in, although sometimes he started a draft. It seems he would rather fail because he hadn't tried than get a D after spending time working on papers. He had a million excuses for why papers early in the year were not handed in, but when he realized I was not grading draft writing, he started showing me his work. As we sifted through his papers together, we found glorious passages. I was delighted, and he started showing me more.

Graham is a talented artist with an eye for detail and, as a result, an unusual and fresh view of the world. Once he gained confidence in himself as a writer and began to internalize some ideas about how to tell when a sentence or a paragraph should end, he was on his way. By the end of the first semester, one of his essays was chosen for the school literary magazine.

In "A Room Square as a Tissue Box," he writes about the day his family went to the funeral home to view the body of his dead grandfather, and "memories started flashing through my head like an out of control slide projector." Using his artist's eye, he sees the family

flock to the adjoining room like ducks. My family became a living smoke screen which let me catch only glimpses of the other room through the negative space their bodies did not shield. I could see a piece of wallpaper here and a picture on the wall there, but no whole images. . . . When I saw the crest of my grandfather's big nose and his eyebrow and a little bit of his mouth, I turned away.

I shared in Graham's pleasure as he found his voice and gained the self-confidence to try new ways of expressing himself. He gained a sense of when his writing worked and when it did not and continued to write in college. In his reflective letter at the end of his senior year, Graham explained why he made progress.

In the past I was discouraged about my writing. I knew I wasn't stupid, but seeing all those C minuses and worse on my papers made me feel like a moron. I knew I should try harder and revise my papers, But I just didn't have the heart to look at them again after they had gotten such low grades.

Bryan, another senior, echoed Graham's sentiments.

I got to the place with my writing that I would rather get an F than look at the papers again after the teacher had given them low grades. I simply believed that I was a lousy writer, so I didn't think it was worth my time

to even try to revise the papers. When I didn't have my face rubbed in a
low grade, I was more willing to try again with a paper.

Now that I had relinquished the power to judge early drafts, the students' writing groups became more important to them. They began to see for themselves, and to help others see, when the writing worked and when it didn't. My grade was no longer a factor in whether or not they included a piece in their portfolios, but instead they made their own assessment of the value of each piece.

I see the change even in the quality and content of their reflective letters. When I was still grading every draft, the reflective letters were defensive. They were of the "I think you'll see that even though my paper is not as good as some people's, it's pretty good. I worked hard on it, even though you might not be able to tell that. I have been really busy this week, and really didn't have a chance to work on it." Here in North Carolina we call this kind of defensive introduction "Southern Biscuiting."

Early in the year I get letters like this one from Gary:

It was hard for me to start this paper. Every idea I had sounded stupid
once it was written down on the page. I filled my trash can with crum-
pled papers and finally wrote this one. You'll probably hate it.

Now that I wait to grade the writing, students write more introspectively and show growing confidence in their work. They talk about what they know they do well and what they still must work on. They see writing as a process, and they see themselves as writers.

Grading student work too early stifles their growth as writers. It seems to give students a false sense of closure. The work has been graded; the teacher thinks it is either good or bad; the teacher has marked the mistakes in red ink. At this point the highly motivated student corrects the mistakes and resubmits the paper, believing that the paper is now perfect. The discouraged student feels like a failure and stows the paper in a bulging backpack if he keeps it at all. They have learned to distrust their sense of when their writing works, relying on the teacher to judge.

Because I wait to assign a grade until the revision process is complete, students consider more thoughtfully what their strengths and weaknesses are, when to get help, and what they must do themselves to polish and improve their work. I ran into two of my recent seniors this summer, both of whom took writing tests for waiver of freshman writing classes in college. One said, "I kept telling myself, 'Be brief, get to the point.' And guess what? I'm exempt from Freshman Comp!" The other was less enthusiastic. He said, "You know how I can get carried away with details? Well, I ran out of time and couldn't go back and choose the most effective ones. I haven't heard from college yet, but I'm worried that they'll think my work rambled. I certainly do." Both boys approach writing with confidence and maturity. I believe that because I have not been so quick to judge their work, they were now better able to judge it for themselves.

I am as proud of my students as I am of my beautiful garden. They have blossomed as writers as brightly as my red azaleas on a summer afternoon now that I have learned to wait until the time for pruning is right.

It's a Frame-Up: Helping Students Devise Beginnings and Endings

Romana Hillebrand

Written by Romana Hillebrand about her teaching experience with college students in Pullman, Washington, this article was originally published in the winter 2001 issue of The Quarterly.

When I began teaching composition thirty years ago, the five-paragraph essay was such a standard part of the curriculum that it was virtually inviolable. I came to call this formulaic pattern the "Dummy Model" because, in a sense, what it says to its reader is "Dummy, listen up. This is precisely what this essay is about. Now, Dummy, if you cannot remember what already has been explained twice in the previous four paragraphs, here is a third explanation." Readers who do not qualify as dummies are often bored and insulted by this structure. Granted, teaching students form gives them a sense of confidence as they confront writing assignments, but I was looking for ways to help them experiment with style, breaking away from the five-paragraph form in large and small ways.

One morning, reading Jack Smith's column in the *Los Angeles Times*, as I did each morning, I began to think about a form that Smith used on most days: the framing device. Smith's informal articles about life in Los Angeles always began with an interesting specific and ended with a reference to it, giving the commentary a firm sense of closure.

I was struck by the fact that I, as well as my students, could learn something from Smith. When I had attended the summer institute of the UCLA Writing Project I had given a colleague a one-page draft to review. She quickly read it and then looked on the back for more. Clearly, my conclusion did not satisfy the reader. What my writing needed was a Jack Smith frame.

The following essay describes strategies I use to demonstrate my conviction that linking the introduction and the conclusion helps unify a paper and satisfy the reader.

~ *Romana Hillebrand, 2002*

*O*ftentimes, getting an essay started and getting it concluded can trouble my college sophomores and juniors more than finding something to say in between. They can always rely, of course, on the old standbys: the traditional introduction and the traditional conclusion to the traditional essay, telling the audience what will be said and concluding with what has been said. Granted, this approach works well in speeches or with lengthy writings, but in shorter essays, these crusty techniques come off as predictable and boring.

WHAT IS A FRAMING DEVICE?

I encourage my students to find instead a single word, a literary or historical reference, or a personal narrative that can provide a fresh way into and out of their writing, surrounding it much like a window frame surrounds a glass pane or a decorative frame surrounds a picture or mirror. Just as the right picture frame becomes one with the painting, the right rhetorical frame becomes one with the composition, enhancing as well as complementing. This frame not only starts and concludes the writing but can also reinforce the main idea, offer a broader perspective, or even interject a bit of humor. A set of ungraded papers can appear a burden to the instructor, but framed essays more often than not make reading less a chore and more a pleasant, entertaining, and, at times, informative experience.

Last year, a student in my research class wrote a lengthy paper on the relationship between humans and plants, beginning her rather serious topic with a reference to a well-known nursery rhyme: "Ring around the roses, a pocket full of posies . . ." She explains that the pocket full of flowers masked the stench of death during the time of the black plague, only one of the many useful purposes of plants that have benefited us throughout the ages. The paper ends with a reinforcement of the warning that we depend on plant life to add quality to our own lives: "Without plants, life on Earth would cease to exist as we know it: 'ashes, ashes, we all fall down.'"

On a much different note, a student in my rhetorical conventions class wrote a short paper that manipulates his memories of a particular odor into a framing device. Students were assigned reflective memoirs, which for this student was an opportunity to describe his first car-purchasing experience. He opens the piece by detailing the musty smell of the used car and the Blue Bouquet air freshener that made it his. He ends with a description of his strongest memory: "Regardless of where I am or what I am doing, whenever I smell the scent of a Blue Bouquet air freshener, I can hear the rumble of the exhaust behind me, feel the air rustling my hair, and sense the urge to slam the pedal to the floor so I can feel the sheer bone-crunching power of acceleration."

A good place to find rhetorical frames commonly used by professional writers is in newspapers that run feature articles and columnists. I was originally inspired by the work of *Los Angeles Times* columnist Jack Smith, who in most of his articles connects the first and last sentences after taking readers on a journey of other ideas.

THE SINGLE-WORD, SINGLE-IMAGE FRAME

Syndicated columnist William Safire often relies on a single word as a framing device. In a 1994 article, he calls on *tsunami*, the Japanese word for a "great wave caused by underwater seismic shock," to frame an article on the shock that caused the conservative wave of that year. His introduction connects the definition of *tsunami* with the main idea of his article: the majority of voters "shook up" legislators to express their lack of faith in an ever-growing government. The column ends with a second mention of the tsunami, identifying it as a shock that does indeed change everything and that leads to exciting days politically, an analogy that reinforces his (but not everyone's) opinion.

A writer can seduce a reader into considering relatively abstract ideas by creating a framing device that links these ideas to everyday images and experience. In another column, Safire decries the "new disloyalty" that seemingly affects our culture at every level of business and politics. He has his teeth into a large concept, but he introduces his thoughts about a fickle public, fickle corporate world, and fickle government by making a down-to-earth confession: over the years, Safire says, he has been a toothpaste hopper. He writes that the avuncular tones of Harry Von Zell got him to switch to long-forgotten Ipana from even more forgotten Kolynos. Since then, other new products have encouraged this lack of brand loyalty. Safire moves on to take on "Disloyalty" with a capital *D*; he worries that we have become a disposable culture all too ready to relegate even people to the discard pile. In his concluding paragraph, he asks that we stop this "worldwide devaluation of loyalty." He ends, however, with a mundane image echoing his opening: "Pick a brand of toothpaste and stick with it." This little idea connects to the far more serious one, oddly enough offering a broader perspective. The smallness of his framing device may seem incongruous, but this very element awakens us to the exigency of our everyday actions.

ALLUSIONS AS FRAMING DEVICES

Literary references also make effective framing devices. In our local newspaper, a letter to the editor from an angry professor responds to an editorial in which the editorial writer is accusing the university teachers of "salary whining." The professor puts to work Edgar Allen Poe's "The Cask of Amontillado" as a literary framing device, quoting Poe's opening sentence as his opening sentence: "The thousand injuries of Fortunato I had borne as best I could; but when he ventured upon insult I vowed revenge." The writer uses the words of Poe's narrator to convey his own indignation at being flagrantly wronged. The body of the letter details the professor's resentment at what he considers to be the editorial writer's insults, but the final sentence refers again to Poe's story: "Ah, for a fresh batch of cement, a stack of bricks, and a good trowel," the very tools, readers of Poe will recognize, that the story's narrator uses to work his revenge on Fortunato. By humorously framing hostile feelings, the professor gently emphasizes his point: overworked and underpaid, he and his colleagues do not appreciate editorials claiming otherwise.

Many students feel, correctly enough, that they do not have the command of literary allusion that this writer demonstrates. However, almost all have an intimate knowledge of some folk and fairy tales that may serve them as they create framing devices. One student, writing about her struggle with obesity, puts to use the question that opens *Snow White*: "Mirror, mirror on the wall, who is the fairest of them all?" The student quickly explains that in her world *fairest* is changed to *fattest*. She further connects the device by describing her despair each time she stands before that cruel mirror. After revealing her struggle and her growing awareness of others who, for various reasons, do not "fit in," the paper ends with a new version of the mirror question: "Who is the healthiest of them all?" While the framing device gives an added dimension of poignancy to the narrative, the newly recast, final question concludes it on an uplifting note.

PERSONAL EXPERIENCE AS A FRAMING DEVICE

Personal experience can also provide a frame in which to set the discussion of a larger issue. *Boston Globe* columnist Ellen Goodman provides a personal experience to frame an opinion piece calling for labels in clothing to guarantee consumers that child labor had not produced newly purchased garments. Standing at a checkout counter, she looks at the various tags and labels affixed to a pair of shorts she has decided to purchase. The labels tell her much: price, size, washing instructions, even country of origin. Left unasked is the question "Who has produced this pair of tennis shorts?" As she ponders the origin of these shorts, she creates a transition from the frame to the article's purpose—asking consumers to make a connection "between what we wear and the people who make it." Goodman concludes her argument by referring once again to her own purchase, calling herself an "uneasy consumer of one pair of tennis shorts who would like to initiate change by asking one simple question: How about labels for labor?"

Students often use personal experience narratives similar to Goodman's as a way into and out of papers on such topics as racism, the environment, or political and school concerns. By calling on an incident or event from his or her life, the writer adds an extra dimension to the topic as well as an authenticity. When the concluding sentence refers to this opening experience, the reader is left with a satisfying sense of closure. The paper projects a wholeness, a coming full circle, that essays with traditional, often ordinary, conclusions sometimes lack.

In a particularly effective paper on the negative impact television violence can have on children, one of my students begins with a description of his family's extended Thanksgiving dinner. The student explains that the peacefulness he felt as the family members gathered to give thanks for all their blessings vanished once he entered the family room, where his younger cousins were mobilized in front of the television for the *Power Rangers* program. After watching intensely physical confrontations, the normally docile three- to twelve-year-olds turned into "miniature fighting machines." They eagerly kicked and punched any interloper, forcing the narrator to leave and causing him to seriously question the laissez-faire child-rearing attitudes of the children's parents. This incident acts as a segue connecting the family experience with his topic: the growing problem of children's viewing of television violence and possible solutions to this problem. The writer concludes by offering a plan for handling the situation at the next Thanksgiving dinner: "I may not be the most popular cousin for turning off the *Power Rangers*, but what is popular is not always right, and what is right is not always popular. I can live with not being popular."

For many students, the personal experience that becomes the framing device for an essay triggers the piece's central idea rather than the other way around. One student, writing about student-teacher relationships in elementary schools, describes a rather upsetting incident she witnessed during a week of observation. A crying second grader who had been teased beyond endurance ran to his teacher's arms for comfort, only to be shoved away by the teacher. This observation begins the student's essay and, in fact, inspires the central idea of the piece: when teachers touch students they have reason to fear the consequences. The paper ends with the writer once again referring to the incident of the spurned second-grader. She mentions how troubled she was at the time, but after doing research on the subject, she explains, "I clearly understand her reasons for not offering comfort and for not hugging him back."

SOME FRAMING TRAPS

When I first introduce the framing device lesson, I caution students against a couple of traps I have seen former students fall into when they used this technique. Sometimes a framing device can take on a life of its own, becoming more developed than the content. This I call the "runaway frame." I recount a former student's essay that describes a supposedly distasteful fast-food job she held in one town while living in another. For her introduction and conclusion, she gives a hair-raising account of her forty-minute commute to work over black ice. Although the purpose of her paper was to dissuade readers from taking a position at the particular restaurant where she worked, the overly long framing device was far more compelling. No reader would want to live down that hill after reading about the slippery road, the traffic, the delays, and the danger.

There's another trap that students fall into. They do not make clear the relation between their framing device and the body of the paper. One student began and ended a paper on the Cuban missile crisis with quotes from Hamlet. "To be or not to be," the paper begins, ending with the lines "whether 'tis nobler in the mind to suffer slings and arrows of outrageous fortune, or to take arms against a sea of trouble, and by opposing them die. . . ." One may imagine many connections between these words from Shakespeare and the events of the Cuban missile crisis, but the writer did not articulate any of them. As we help students revise, we need to be on the lookout for these connections that have not yet made it from the student's mind to the paper.

When we keep these caveats in mind, however, a carefully crafted frame can make satisfying metaphorical connections for both reader and writer, giving the paper a deeper sense of meaning and a way into and out of the assignment that escapes the traditional pattern and quandary of old hat.

Section 5

I Had to Do Something!

Necessity inspires teaching invention

I Was a
Journal-Topic Junkie

Anna Collins Trest

*This article was written by Anna Collins Trest
about her teaching experience with elementary
school students. It was originally published in the
fall 1999 issue of* The Quarterly.

About a dozen or so years ago, before I started teaching, I thought I was
pretty smart. The truth was that I didn't know much; I just thought I did.
As an experienced teacher, I still suffer occasionally from that same kind
of delusion, but I'm coming around. My high horse has shrunk to the size
of a step stool, and I'm not so quick to climb up even on that. When I'm
tempted to think I have the definitive answer for anything, I remind myself of the time I was a journal-topic junkie. That remembrance and its
accompanying plate of crow keep me grounded. I learned a valuable lesson then that wasn't so much about writing or about students as it was
about the business of teaching. I learned that this is a tricky business, and
success requires acknowledging when something's not working, even if
it is the latest educational innovation. Success also requires finding a way
to fix the problem—often recognizing that there is more than one right
way.

After teaching elementary students for a number of years and using the
freewriting/reflection ideas successfully many, many times (as described
here), I next tried my hand at teaching high school. I inherited students
who, for the most part, were not eager to engage in writing of any sort,

mainly because it happened in English class, and anything that happened in English class was anathema to them. I did my best to persuade them otherwise. Mirrors—as well as artwork, music, and other real objects—continued to be more successful in getting students to write than a journal topic ever could have been. Still I had to make changes for the older students. Beautiful art and music gave way to strange, quirky stuff. I went from Monet and Renoir to Escher and Magritte, from Strauss and Grieg to pop songs and rap. These students weren't moved by a bird's nest in a shoe, but a squashed beer can they could write about. I adjusted.

These days I teach elementary education majors how to teach reading and writing, and I use this article at some point in the semester, not as an example of the definitive method, but more as a cautionary tale: beware the one-method wonder, especially when it doesn't elicit significant response. I want these soon-to-be teachers to think for themselves. I want them to learn how to recognize when a thing is not working in the classroom, give it up, and find a better way.

~ *Anna Collins Trest, 2002*

*W*hen I came through the university education program eight years ago, journal writing was hot. The notion I gleaned from all I was taught was this: any teacher worth half a peck of pencils required students to keep daily journals, and the best way to get them to write in those journals was to assign a journal topic each day. Clutching that little nugget of information, I began categorizing teachers according to their classroom writing practices. To my way of thinking, they could be divided neatly into five groups:

1. DUDS: Those who never gave students creative writing opportunities at all.

2. HAS-BEENS: Those who used the old, mundane, hackneyed topics such as "What I Did on My Summer Vacation" and "What School Means to Me."

3. SEMIPROGRESSIVE. Those who used journal topics from store-bought books in the exact order listed.

4. PROGRESSIVE: Those who carefully scavenged only the best topics from the store-bought books and rejected others.

5. EXTREMELY CREATIVE: Those who used store-bought lists as a springboard for developing their own clever topics for journal writing.

I fell somewhere between progressive and extremely creative depending on the day of the week and my state of mind. I had my routine: pick a topic from my list, date it so I wouldn't reuse it, write it on the board, hand out the journals, and give the command to write. Then I would wait fifteen minutes, ask for volunteers to read, take up the journals, write a personal response in each one praising those who wrote and threatening or cajoling those who didn't. It was a tidy little process that we could all accomplish in our sleep—and often did.

I arrived at the South Mississippi Writing Project Summer Institute with four years of teaching under my belt and the confident assurance that my advanced approach to journal writing made me an upwardly mobile instructor. I perceived myself as being on the cutting edge of teaching classroom writing. After all, I had by that time a closely guarded, highly coveted list of story starters gleaned from umpteen sources and including such gems as "A Dragon Lives in My Closet," "I Was a Wart on a Witch's Nose," "and "My Bed Is a Cloud."

Imagine my dismay when no one asked to see my list. When I casually draped it over my book bag, no one even noticed. Everyone was busy with a couple of new strategies, one called freewriting and the other reflection. After a couple of days, I began to pick up on derisive comments made about journal topics. I got huffy.

"What's wrong with journal topics?" I asked.

"I never could get very good response," said one teacher.

"I wouldn't want to have to write about anything as stupid as 'My Life as a Comb' or 'You've Been Captured by a Band of Pirates on the Way to School Today,'" said another.

Moving from huffy to indignant, I replied, "If I asked you to pretend you were a watermelon seed, couldn't you just think of gobs to write? Imagine— you're surrounded by moist squish. Your whole world is crimson red. Suddenly, there's a blinding light and an earthquakelike crack. You're out! But before you've even tasted freedom, a tongue laps you up, wallows you around, and swallows you. You pass by an esophageal hernia, through a spastic colon, and down to the nether regions. You're searching . . . seeking . . . yearning . . . for a way out. . . ." My enthusiasm peaked and then waned as I realized the group was staring at me as though I had brought new meaning to the word *lunacy*.

"Did you ever get that kind of response from a journal topic?" one woman drawled laconically.

That was the $64,000 question. Had I ever gotten really good writing using journal topics? A time or two but not consistently. "Of course I have. Often," I told the woman. She just rolled her eyes and changed the subject.

This conversation caused a new wrinkle on my brain: Could I eliminate journal topics? The idea seemed almost blasphemous. Give up my list of story starters? But I'd worked so long and hard gathering them, and they were so darn clever! One of my all-time favorites was "I Was an Elf in the Christmas Parade." What could be cuter? Granted, the results were mediocre, as in this piece:

I am an elf named Happy. I am in a parade in Laurel. I say Merry Christ- mas and throw out candy. It is fun. Bye bye now.

   ~ Heather, fourth grade

I chalked up the mediocrity to apathy or sheer laziness on the part of my students. These kids just didn't *want* to write; they'd rather whine about the assignment. A story starter like "Today I Planted an Egg, and This Is What Happened" really fanned my creative flames. I truly believed that any student who made half an effort could produce a fabulous something from that premise. Not so. Some could; most couldn't.

Today, I planted an egg and guess what? An egg tree came up!!! Then I planted peas and butter beans. Then I went home. I hope our team wins tonight. GO BRAVES!!!!!

~ Courtney, fifth grade

I checked with the other thirteen teachers at our school and discovered their experience was similar, with one notable difference. The pieces their students wrote from journal topics were considerably longer than those of my students. Granted, it was still drivel, but it was lengthy drivel. "How do you get them to write so much?" I asked. All the teachers, without exception, told me that they required students to write at least one page before they could go out to recess. I couldn't do that. Two things I strongly believed: no one should tell a writer how long a piece had to be, and everybody's piece certainly didn't have to be the same length.

Hardheaded soul that I am, I muddled along into spring without altering my journal writing plan. Along the way, I read whatever I could find on the issue, talked to anyone I thought could help me, and fumed over the meaningless junk my students wrote. I continued to badger them with cries of, "You're not *trying* to be creative. Just think . . . you've opened a jar of Jif, and there in the peanut butter is written the word *Help*. How could that have gotten there? What does it mean? Use your imagination!"

Edward, a third-grader, wrote this response, typical of what most students wrote:

It was a big jar of peanut butter. I like peanut butter very much. Somebody wrote in it, but I don't know why. That's all I have to say.

Toward the end of the school year, I was so frustrated that I resorted to giving no topic at all. "You may write about whatever is on your mind," I said. Just as I thought—they had *nothing* on their minds. By the time the school year was over, an Alexander Pope couplet kept repeating in my brain: "Be not the first by whom the new is tried / Nor yet the last to lay the old aside." While I hadn't come by my methods haphazardly and certainly wasn't going to give them up nonchalantly, I had to admit that cutesy journal topics did not produce good writing. It was time not only to "lay the old aside" but also to try the new. The problem was how to go about it.

All summer long, I thought about my problem. I considered the unique situation in which I teach. Our school serves a different grade of "gifted" student each day. On Monday, all of the sixth grade gifted students from the ten elementary schools in the district travel by bus to our school for the entire day. On Tuesday, fifth-graders come, and so on through second grade on Friday. My classes are small—about ten or twelve students—but with a total of fourteen teachers, we serve about 150 students each day. So many potential writers! How could I make their potentiality a reality?

By the time the new school year began, I had a plan, and it included my perception of what reflective writing could be for children. I had completed the writing project too embarrassed to ask the definition of reflective writing. I was fairly certain it involved contemplation, but beyond that I wasn't sure. Was it like metacognition—thinking about thinking? Could one only reflect on issues and actions? Maybe "one" could, but I didn't think that was practical for my elementary students. However, I felt confident that I could teach them to reflect on a concrete object.

I decided to begin by using real mirrors to teach the reflective process. I borrowed enough for each student to have one. As the students gazed at their own reflections, I asked this question: "What can you think about while looking in a mirror at your own reflection?" As they answered, I categorized each response and wrote the categories on the board.

Student Response Categories:

"I think I'm a queen."
    Pretending/Imagining

"I look at my cavities."
    Examining/Observing

"I think I'm having a bad hair day."
    Forming Opinions

"What will I look like when I am old?"
    Questioning

"My hair is parted in the middle."
    Describing

"I'm thinking about when I broke my nose."
Remembering

"I look better than my brother."
Comparing

"Everything on my face looks sad today."
Expressing Emotions

We talked at length about the various categories, and I invited the students to give personal examples of each. Then I asked them to look in the mirrors again, reflect on their images, and then write about what came to mind.

When I see myself in the mirror, I think about many things.

Sometimes I look in the mirror, and I see my grandmother's reflection. It reminds me of how she used to call us when she wanted us. I sometimes cry because missing her makes me so sad. I look in the mirror, and I say to myself, "Boy, why did it have to be this way?"

I look in the mirror and think about bad things that might happen.

I think I'm going to fail a test and I won't be allowed to go on a field trip. I look, and I say to myself, "Why am I so discouraged?"

Sometimes I look in the mirror and think about my future, like where I want to live. I even think about what I want to be when I grow up. My younger sister Mandolin tells me I will never do the things I want to do. My older sister Zandra tells me that things will work out if I have confidence in myself. I believe my older sister.

~ William, sixth grade

Another day, I asked the students to choose anything from my desk for me to use to model reflective thinking. I asked them specifically to select something very ordinary that they thought would be difficult for me to reflect on. My fifth grade group picked a stapler. As I reflected aloud, I asked them to categorize my reflections.

My Response Categories:

"This stapler has seen better days."
Forming Opinions

249

"I wonder who invented this thing."
Questioning

"Last year, a student stapled her finger, and I had to do some first aid."
Remembering

"It's bright blue and slightly lopsided."
Describing

"Paper clips are more useful than this."
Comparing

One student challenged me to *imagine* something about the stapler. "There's no way to pretend about a stapler," she said.

"Sure there is," I said. "How about this?" And I related the following: "Mrs. T. was sitting at her desk quietly reading journals when she heard a tiny voice chirp, 'Good grief, it's crowded in here.' She looked up, but no one else was in the room. Being the curious sort and a firm believer in listening to tiny voices, Mrs. T. waited patiently. There it was again! 'Hey, out there. I could use a little help! One of us is jammed, and the rest of us are crammed!' There was no doubt about it. Mrs. T. had heard that small, metallic voice, and it was coming from her stapler."

For the next three or four times I met with each grade, we continued to practice reflecting aloud on a number of very simple objects in the room until I felt like the students understood the technique. Finally one day, I held up a toothbrush, and we brainstormed writing ideas. After the discussion I asked them to write a reflection about the toothbrush. I wrote while they wrote, and I was amazed when the time came to read aloud. Almost every student was able to write something significant. The responses were meaty and varied. From second grade to sixth grade, students had something remarkable to write about that toothbrush. There were great remembrances about lost teeth and braces, opinions about which toothbrushes are best and why, comparisons of people teeth and animal teeth, and wild tales about wicked dentists.

The day after my birthday I woke up and gave myself a good stare in my reflecting glass. I noticed one of my teeth was leaning like the Tower of Pisa. I thought to myself, "I'll give it a little wiggle and see if it's loose." But my mom said, "Don't touch it. Leave it for Dr. Drillo. He'll get it out for you."

I remembered Dr. Drillo, the man who pulls teeth. I didn't trust him. He always got this funny gleam in his eye every time I sat in his chair, and he would lie and say, "Now this won't hurt a bit."

I decided to pull the tooth out myself. I got a piece of paper towel and pushed and pulled. After so much agony, I finally zipped it out. I ran into the kitchen screaming, "Yahoooo!" or in other words, "Thank you, Lord!"

~ Monique, fourth grade

Over time, productivity ceased to be a problem. Journaling was no longer the hair-pulling ordeal it had once been, and *reflection* became a buzzword for us. Slowly the students and I were able to move away from simply trying to grind out some writing and move on to other parts of the writing process, such as making interesting word choices. As the year progressed, we made a giant leap toward reflecting on famous artwork, classical music, and fine literature. I was always careful to make selections that I believed had meaning for my students.

I got an idea when I looked at a painting called "The Piano Lesson" by Romare Bearden. I imagined I was walking down a sidewalk, and I heard an angry sound. It was coming from the instrument store. I went inside. There was a woman trying out the instruments. She was playing the piano. I said to the piano player, "That was very good. Will you play it again?"

Edwin, a second-grader, responded differently, "The music sounded like elephants stomping their huge feet on the ground because they were mad that a leopard came and got their baby."

We reflected on paintings by Claude Monet and Pieter the Elder:

The rosie, red poppies surround and swallow
The resting family like a small child
Devouring his first meal since yesterweek.

~ Susannah, sixth grade

I imagine Pieter the Elder's painting "Peasant Dancers" shows poor country people dancing at dawn to celebrate the king's birthday. They are happy. I know because their lips are not in a straight line. Their lips look like a "u" with their smiles so big and wide showing their white teeth.

I imagine that later that day the king dies, and his son becomes king. Three months later a secret agent is in town, and he hears a servant

251

telling a friend how he poisoned the king. The secret agent tells the new king, and new King James hangs the servant and his friend. No servant ever tries to poison the king again. All the people live happily in my imagination.

    ∼ Allen, fourth grade

We reflected on poetry:

When I hear Longfellow's "Arrow and Song" I think about my fort in the woods covered with trees. The sun shines through them like a river of light going in so many different directions I can't keep track of it. Before I know it, I am standing in that river of sunlight and millions of thoughts run through my mind like cars on a busy highway. I sit and for once enjoy nature's sweet sounds.

    ∼ Fredrick, sixth grade

and we reflected on music:

I am listening to "The Gypsy Baron" by Johann Strauss. The music is pretty and exciting. Part of it sounds slow, and part is fast. It makes me feel good and happy like the time I went to Pep's Point. When I went to Pep's Point, I got a mat. We had to wait in line for our turn. When it was our turn, Mom and my brother and me put our mats together and went down. Around the curves we slipped up and then back down. The mat felt wet, and it went zoom like wheels on a skate board. I was going so fast, and I was so full of excitement that I felt like it was my birthday.

    ∼ Joshua, second grade

Looking back, I see several reasons this strategy worked so well. First of all, when the students wrote, I wrote using the same reflection item they used. This was a new experience for me. Initially, I didn't write with students because I was a new teacher and didn't have time to use the bathroom, much less write with my students. Over the years, I read their responses, and I simply didn't want to show them up and make them feel bad about their feeble efforts. My writing with my students made a tremendous difference in their perception of journal writing. They began to believe that it *must* be important—the teacher did it.

Now when we shared our writing, they asked me to read out loud what I had written. They especially liked the times when I would tell them, "I wrote garbage today. I just couldn't think of anything creative." Through that little confession, they came to see that *all* writers have days when they cannot produce something wonderful.

Second, we succeeded because we spent so much time discussing before we wrote. In the past, I have been guilty of severely limiting prewriting conversation because I thought too much talk would give away too many ideas. Now I see that's the point—to make available plenty of ideas, to crank the creative motor, and to be certain there is something familiar about the road the students will travel. I think that the discussions and subsequent writings convinced many of a "Trest Truism": "If you can say it with your mouth, you can write it with a pencil." Extended, meaningful conversation also resulted in one other unexpected dividend. Students began asking if they had to write about the discussion topic or if they could write about something else that came to mind while we were talking. I was pleased to acquiesce.

Another reason this plan was successful was because I chose starting points that were relevant to the students. Elementary students are extremely concrete and literal in their thinking, but that doesn't keep them from being creative. They just can't be creative about elves and peanut butter messages and other things with which they have had no experience. When I stopped relying on goofy subjects, I was able to tap into the students' prior knowledge, which included love of the outdoors and things of nature. When I gave up the eggs and the elves and offered a branch instead, Edward was able to give me the following:

> *A leaf is a remarkable thing. It helps ants when there is a flood. They can get under it like an umbrella so they won't get washed away. A leaf helps caterpillars stay alive because the caterpillar can eat a healthy leaf lunch. A leaf is also like a big cup for a wasp. He gulps down the water . . . glug, glug, glug.*

Puny Poetry Meets Its Match

Gerri Ruckel and Jim Horrell

Gerri Ruckel and Jim Horrell wrote this article about their teaching experiences in the Lower Moreland Township School District in Pennsylvania. It was originally published in the fall 1999 issue of The Quarterly.

This article was really the result of colossal frustration. We knew we were good teachers, we knew our students had poetry in them, but we just couldn't seem to find the missing step to our sequence of lessons. What we had missed, as it turns out, was something that in hindsight was painfully obvious. In this article, we call it scaffolding and handover. More basically, it's called guided practice.

But how do you do guided practice for poetry? This isn't as clear as doing a few long division problems on the chalkboard while randomly calling on students to ensure understanding. Because writing poetry is a very personal thing, we wanted to provide several levels of safe guided practice, providing less support gradually, as one does when teaching someone to ride a bike.

Since writing this article a few years ago, we have continued to be amazed by watching poetry go from puny to powerful. In addition to blanketing the walls and halls with poetry, we culminate our poetry study with a poetry café and class anthologies. Original poetry has crept into end-of-year scrapbooks and punctuated landmark school trips.

Some of our sixth-graders have even taken the odd piece they've written in prose and found it works better as a poem. All of this seems a world away from where we were at the start of the article.

~ *Jim Horrell and Gerri Ruckel, 2002*

Puny Boy

Puny boy is puny,
He looks just like George Clooney,
He's yeller and green
if you know what I mean
Puny boy is looney and oh so puny
He gets bugged by the goonies
And they are all so puny
and they'll beat him up soonie

$\sim$ Zeke

t seems that when it comes to writing poetry, students decide to take the plunge when they don't know what else to write or there's some sort of deadline approaching. Then it's time to produce, as quickly as possible, a short, silly rhyming poem devoid of meaning.

Zeke, a new student to our school, came from Israel by way of a public school in nearby Philadelphia. He had plenty of things to write about, including a new school, a new home, new friends, fears of not fitting in, and the experience of having lived in another country. Why, then, did he refuse the opportunity to write about any of those things? He chose to write "Puny Boy." Why?

Consider Bill. A very intelligent young man, Bill seemed bent on proving to his classmates that he was clever. He has many interests, including baseball, HTML programming, and world affairs, since his father works for the military. Bill unveiled his poetry prowess with a little ditty about our class mascot, Bubba the giant plush green frog, a few stanzas of which are printed here:

Bubba in Da Tubba

Bubba's in da tubba.
He needs a good rubba.
He's really awfully sad.
He broke his lily pad.
He needs a bite to eat.
He needs something sweet.
Morris Moose came over to say hi.
He brought a cherry pie.

He also sang a song.
It took him rather long . . .

     ~ Bill

When we conference with students about poems like this, it can be hard to know where to start. Equally difficult is the challenge of trying to figure out what you'd like the outcome of the conference to be. Bill's conference went something like this:

"Bill, I see you've written a poem here," the teacher says. "Tell me about it."

Bill smiles. "It's about Bubba. He smells bad."

"So you're telling me that Bubba, the plush frog, smells bad. I see."

"Yeah. So I figured he could use a bath."

"Hence, 'Bubba in Da Tubba'?"

"Yeah."

"He looks hungry to you?"

"Well, I needed it to rhyme."

"Uh-huh. What is it that you really want to say about all of this? Bubba is important to you as our class mascot? You enjoy seeing him every morning? You remember winning him in the magazine drive contest?"

"No. I just thought it was funny."

"So, you're happy with 'Bubba in Da Tubba' as is?"

"Yeah."

Root canal is a simple, painless process compared to cajoling these students to rewrite or revise these pieces. To them, the poem is done, and no amount of educated teacher prodding is going to make a difference. We began wondering why we were pushing students to revise. Whatever they were trying to say, they had said it. There was no meaning, no message, nothing expressed here beyond simple wordplay.

But what about those times students had real feelings to express and no other poetry voice to use?

WHEN THERE'S A POETRY ITCH, HOW CAN ONE BEST SCRATCH?

When Jeff, a classmate, died suddenly in an accident, Ken worked secretly on this poem for a month. Ken was a new student, and Jeff had taken him under his wing. They shared many interests, such as skateboarding, music, and clothes. Ken intended to write a tribute to his friend, some of which is printed here.

Jeff

Jeff loved to skate
And even stay up late
Jeff loved to surf
And even mark his turf
Jeff loved to play soccer
And was a very good blocker
Jeff loved to roller blade
And even make a card trade
Jeff made me a friend
And even let me lend
Jeff made me apart of the school
And was very cool
Jeff always made me laugh
And lead me through the path . . .

　　　　~ Ken

Ken obviously had a poetry itch that he needed to scratch, but he was frustrated at not being able to say what he needed to say. During his writing process, Ken had been advised that he might be better able to express his thoughts about Jeff if he didn't worry about rhyming. In the end, after several revisions, Ken felt as if he had worked long enough on this piece and was satisfied with this poem. He said, "It's good. I like it. It rhymes."

Ken and everyone else had read Dr. Seuss, Jack Prelutsky, and Shel Silverstein, and each had formed a file in his or her mind called "This Is Poetry;" where rhyming and language play rule. Any linguistic ambiguity could be cleared up with an accompanying illustration. Unfortunately for Ken, there was no illustration to make his message clear. As Donald Graves put it in *A Fresh Look at Writing:*

> *At first, children are often caught up in the "form" of poetry. This is especially true of children who insist on rhyming. Unfortunately, the form of the poem, the straining for rhyme, can push meaning to the sidelines.*
> (1994, 335)

MOVING STUDENTS BEYOND "PUNY POETRY"

Ken was not alone in this poetry wasteland, not by a long shot. What was going wrong? As teacher-consultants of the Pennsylvania Writing and Literature Project (PAWLP), we decided it was our duty to move our student writers beyond puny poetry. In writers' workshop, we shifted all focus onto poetry. Our new poetry unit was supposed to go very smoothly, a slick combination of strategies gleaned from two different PAWLP summer writing institutes. It was time to get out the shovels and dig through the writing gurus.

We wanted to inspire our students. Georgia Heard said, "Every writer of poetry is first a reader of poetry" (1989, 1). Following Heard's suggestion, we placed all kinds of poetry books in the classroom. We cleaned the library out of all the old forlorn books of poetry that hadn't been checked out in years. We raided our closets and bookshelves, and we encouraged our students to do the same. The children were given several class periods to pour over the poetry anthologies, selecting and sharing their favorites. Ultimately, they copied their favorite selections into their writers' notebooks. Some students carried these notebooks everywhere.

We decided to follow Heard's suggestion to hang poetry all around the school. Suddenly, our students were eager to locate and recopy the perfect microscope poem to decorate the science teacher's door. Poetry about windows appeared on the glass in the hallways. Even the cafeteria and bathrooms weren't safe.

The principal's well-known distaste for cats prompted the students to blanket his office with cat poetry. But since there were only so many poems about cats in our collected anthologies, the students pitched in, adding some original cat poetry. Polly, eager to please, created "Three Fat Cats" to add to the collection. It illustrated how far we still had to go.

Three Fat Cats

three fat cats wobbling & balancing on a high sky wire
juggling & jumping higher & higher
the first fat cat with a bat
went & crashed into another fat cat
when wham bam
down went those fat cats.
fat cat three said, "Hey what about me?"

Three fat cats moaning & groaning
but when they were done
they were very mad at fat cat one
    ~ Polly

The students were enjoying poetry. They were developing a sense for which poetry they liked and which they didn't. Bill loved Edgar Allen Poe's "The Raven" so much that he committed it to memory. It was fun to get him started by saying aloud in the hallway, "As I wandered, weak and weary . . ."

"I never knew poetry could be so neat and spooky," Bill said.

Another student, Maria, noted, "I thought poems were just about flowers. It's cool that they can be about everyday things."

Each student's "This Is Poetry" file was expanding, filling up with many different styles and types of poetry. Randy Bomer in *Time for Meaning* (1995) calls this "creating a sense of genre." We couldn't wait to see how their original poetry would show this growth. We realized, however, that this wouldn't be enough, by itself, to strengthen puny poetry. They were developing an appreciation for poetry, but there was no transfer into their writing. It was unrealistic to expect the kids to grow in poetic voice by merely reading, selecting, and sharing poems. We were only building to that moment. As Graves said, "Children need to hear the voices of many poets when they are writing poetry, to discover how they shape words and sounds to meaning" (1994, 337).

We asked the students to examine some of their newfound favorite poetry and ask themselves, "What did the writer do to help me understand and enjoy this poem?" Now that there was a heightened awareness of writer's craft, we began, as Nancie Atwell would say, "to tease out" the elements of poetry. These included: line breaks, organization, use of white space, sensory images, figurative language, rhyming, alliteration, repetition, word choice, rhythm, and descriptive detail.

Then, the words of Ralph Fletcher from *What a Writer Needs* surfaced: "It turns out that many writers actually discover what they have to say in the process of writing it. The writer's challenge is to keep this sense of discovery intact; this keeps writing fresh and vibrant" (1993, 21). Fletcher also recounts a tale that illustrates this concept beautifully:

A little girl watches a sculptor at work. He begins carving into a large
wooden cube and works hard all day. By late afternoon, the shape of a

lion has begun to emerge. Absolutely dumbfounded, the little girl looks at the sculptor and sputters, "But how did you know there was a lion inside that wood?" (23)

So our next step was clear. It was time to write. Maybe all of the yucky—for lack of a better word—poetry that our writers had been churning out had a purpose after all. Perhaps it was just their way of trying to find that lion.

BRIDGING THE GAP

In this fairly typical piece of poetry, Katie tries to recount her memory of a recent day at the beach. Through the sometimes-forced rhyme, some sensory images and personification stand out. Perhaps this piece is not an emerging lion, but certainly something worthwhile is emerging.

The Beach

The wind brushes my hair
A kite flies in the air
The water is cold
Hot sand I hold
The sun goes down
Without a sound
The sun is down, so
We have to go

Like May Belle in the Katherine Paterson novel, the students needed a *Bridge to Terabithia*. To be able to apply what they were being taught, students needed to be ready to learn it. According to Lev Vygotsky, some tasks are too difficult for students, even when clearly explained. He goes on to say in his theory of the "zone of proximal development" that while learning, the child at times "cannot solve a problem alone but can be successful under adult guidance or in collaboration with a more advanced peer." Jerome Bruner called it scaffolding. Scaffolding is where a teacher provides the needed support by supplying "clues, reminders, encouragement, breaking the problem down into steps, providing an example, or anything else that allows the student to grow in independence as a learner." Our student writers needed help taking the first steps into writing meaningful poetry.

Poet Julia Blumenreich, a PAWLP Summer Institute presenter, offered us our first step, an approach she called "parallel poetry." Students write parallel poetry by imitating the form of a published poem. She also emphasized the importance of working on whole-class or large-group poems of this type before turning kids loose to try it on their own. After consulting Kenneth Koch's *Rose, Where Did You Get That Red?* (1973), it seemed that William Carlos Williams's poetry would provide the perfect stepping-stone. His poems are simple; they are about ordinary things, and they're short. It's entry-level meaningful poetry. Williams's "This Is Just to Say" became our first model:

This Is Just to Say

I have eaten
the plums
that were in
the icebox
and which
you were probably
saving
for breakfast

Forgive me
they were delicious
so sweet
and so cold

~ William Carlos Williams

We read aloud to the students then gave each a copy to examine. Next, each accepted the challenge of writing "parallel poems." Parallel poems borrow the pattern and spirit of the original poem, but the students supply their own words and ideas. We wrote several group poems of this type, then each student set off on her own.

This poem was a great jumping-off point because it gives an insincere apology for doing something deliciously wrong. Many students enjoyed "confessing" to not doing homework, wearing older siblings' clothes, taking things without asking, and eating food that wasn't theirs. For most of the students, this was a totally new experience in writing poetry.

This Is Just To Say

This is just to say
I have flooded the school
And gone scuba diving through the halls.
If I say I'm sorry you won't believe me;
Besides, I have always dreamed of doing it.

　　　∼ Craig

This Is Just To Say

This is just to say
I have eaten your dog's food,
I am sorry
It tasted different,
So crunchy and hard.

　　　∼ Ryan

Williams's "The Red Wheelbarrow" provided a similar opportunity for some more poetry baby steps.

The Red Wheelbarrow

so much depends
upon

a red wheel
barrow

glazed with rain
water

beside the white
chickens.

　　∼ William Carlos Williams

Natasha used her parallel poem here to poke fun at Williams's original. While she closely follows the form, she clearly makes her feelings known when it comes to "The Red Wheelbarrow." For our students, this represents another new use of poetry, and a baby step toward parody.

Mental Hospital

So much depends
Upon

Being able to write

And not selling
stuff

You wrote during
your

Stay in a mental
hospital

> ~ Natasha

In this parallel poem, Elizabeth shuns the form of the Williams poem but keeps the red wheelbarrow.

Silence Broken

In
the
silence
of
the
night
I
slept
A
red
wheelbarrow
fell
through
the
ceiling
I
slept
no
more.

> ~ Elizabeth

It should be noted here, Elizabeth was delighted with her ending, "I slept no more." She also felt that she perfectly mimicked what she felt was a surprise appearance of chickens in the original by having the red wheelbarrow crash through her bedroom ceiling.

We then arrived at Robert Frost's poem "The Road Not Taken." As we read the poem, we noted poetic devices, discussed interpretations, placed a copy in our notebooks, and bathed in the beauty of the words, as in these few lines:

Two roads diverged in a yellow wood,
And sorry I could not travel both
And be one traveler, long I stood
And looked down one as far as I could
To where it bent in the undergrowth . . .

At first, Frost's masterpiece suffered the same treatment as Williams's works as the students wrestled with another new piece to parallel.

The Idea Not Taken

Two ideas converged inside my head
I'm sorry I don't know which one to take
As a writer there I thought
And thought for as long as I could
To see so many ideas light up in my head
So I thought and thought

And perhaps choosing the better idea
Since it sounded easier to write

I am telling this with disappointment
Tons and tons of thought wasted
I chose the easy way out
And that has made all the difference!

$\sim$ Caitlin

A pair of students saw a different kind of parallel between Frost's poem and a book they had recently read. Below is an excerpt of their work:

Harry Potter

Two worlds converged at one train station
And sorry I could not live in them both
And being one person, long I stood
As I looked between platform 9 and 10
I could not see platform 9 and 3/4

Then the other I could see so clear
Which in I was hated by the Dursleys
Because Dudley was a spoiled brat
I shall start a new life in the wizard world
And that very first day I belonged to Gryfndor . . .

    ~ Jason and Sarah

While not perfect in convention, this piece demonstrated that not only were the students able to mimic the pattern of a poem, but they also could build in some sort of personal meaning. We knew we were on the right track. It was clear that lurking beneath the surface were some real topics and issues to explore.

The Friend Not Taken

Two friends diverged in my mind,
And sorry I could not be friends with them both
And being one person, not two
And I looked at them both finding
their special qualities.

So I thought just as fair
And having perhaps choosing the
wrong one
Because of my choice, they would
never forgive me.

I shall choose with a sigh
Friendship and memories with this person
Two friends diverged in my mind
I took neither one, I'll be on my own
And that has made all the difference.

    ~ Sarah

Taking the next step, students wrote parallel poetry based on "Five Versions of the Icicle" by Nancy Willard. As the title suggests, this poem presents five impressions of an icicle as expressed by five different characters: a mother, a laundress, a cook, a gardener, and a widow.

This poem forces students to experiment with perspective. While the pattern of the poem is simple, expressing a number of perspectives concerning a single object requires the students to do some linguistic and mental gymnastics. We dared the students to rise to the challenge.

Water: From Five Different Perspectives

It is what nurtures my crops,
said the farmer,
to help them grow so I can sell.

It is what quenches my thirst,
said the aerobics teacher,
to cool me down after a hard workout.
It is my home,
said the fish,
to live and swim in.

It is my hobby,
said the swimmer,
to have fun splashing in it.

It is the dangerous tide,
said the beach's lifeguard,
to become stronger than and overcome everything else.

~ Maria

Maria's piece illustrates a clear understanding of perspective and the form of the original "Five Versions of the Icicle" poem. Adam, in his piece, used the form to express his adolescent angst.

Five Versions of Nothing
It is what I see, said the blind man,
black, just black

It is what I hear, signaled the deaf man,
blank and cold

It is what comes out of my mouth,
signaled the dumb man,
just breathing my mouth is for

It is what I remember, said the lady
with Alzheimers disease,
holes in my memory

It is what I am, said the man with no
hopes, no future, no goals, and no
motivation,

No one
Nobody
Nothing

      ~   Adam

Writing parallel poetry is a valuable exercise, we found, but it was time for our student-writers to strike out on their own. We knew, however, they still were in need of some guidance. To provide needed structure in a more open-ended format, we worked with some poetry we called "template poetry." In template poetry, students are given a series of line starters and are asked to fill in the rest of the lines. The result is close to an original poem, with the obvious exception of the line starters. One example of this, picked up in a sharing session in a 1998 PAWLP seminar, was an "I Am" poem. We provided the first few words of each line.

I Am Poem [Template]
I am (describe yourself as you dream or as you wish you could be)
I wonder . . .
I hear . . .
I see . . .
I want . . .
I am (repeat same as above . . . I am)
I pretend . . .
I feel . . .
I touch . . .
I fear . . .
I am . . . (repeat)
I understand . . .

269

I say . . .
I dream . . .
I try to . . .
I hope . . .
I am (repeat)

After guiding the students through this once as a group, we asked them to fill out this template on their own. We were surprised by some of the results.

I Am

I am who you want me to be
I wonder what kind of person you'll
make me be
I fear you'll make me a nobody
I cry when I don't know what I'll be
tomorrow
I am who you want me to be
I understand I might be crazy
I say I don't know who I am
I dream I am a famous person
I try to think I'm not strange
I hope I'm not insane
I am who you want me to be
I hear what you say about who I am
I see you talking about who I am
I want not to be dull
I am who you want me to be
I pretend I am energetic
I feel nothing
I touch nothing
I am who you want me to be

$\sim$ Edward

I Am All That I Can Be [excerpt]

I am all that I can be
I wonder why I always try to be like others
I hear voices saying that I can be better

I see others that I feel are much more sophisticated
and more mature than me
I want more to say to me "I like your shirt," instead
of saying "I did better than you!"
I am all that I can be
I pretend that I am someone or something other than myself
I feel depression and that I could've done better
I touch pictures of things that I'm not and wish to
myself that I am what's on the picture
I fear that if I do change I'll want to change back
I cry when I stare in the mirror and picture
something other than my face
I am all that I can be
I understand that I can't be everyone that I want
and that life is dependent on choices
I say to myself that I can make my own choices . . .

      ~ Courtney

Both Edward and Courtney were surprised by the power and revealing nature of their template poems. Both were struggling with a sense of insecurity, yet both volunteered to share these with their classmates. When they finished, there was a pregnant pause, and then one student simply sighed, "Wow!" The performance served to raise the bar for the others.

Another type of template focused on nostalgic memories. We called it a "That Was . . ." poem. This template encouraged students to draw on meaningful memories to convey the circumstances as well as the essence of that time. Memories of several teachers and the deeds that touched her heart joined to form Kathleen's poem "That Was My Teacher." See if you can find the template.

That Was My Teacher

Have you ever met my teacher?
Sure you have.
Remember that time
When you got a hundred on your test
Or when you got a fifty
And you cried on your desk?
Remember how she handed you a tissue

271

And the retest
That was my teacher.

Remember that time
When you got in a fight with your friends
And you sat alone at lunch
And you didn't talk to anyone
And when she found out
You sat in the corner of the room
talking to her,
The quietness of her voice?
Remember how she helped you and
your friend get back together
All joyful and relieved
That was my teacher.

Remember that time
When you were trying to correct
Mistakes on your worksheet
And you didn't know what you did wrong
And your head was starting to hurt
But when your teacher said,
"Don't worry, I'll help you."
Remember how her words made you understand
All firmly held, but nice?
That was my teacher.

If you try very hard,
Can you remember that time
When you forgot to wear a cartoon
shirt for spirit day
And you were the only one
And you found me an extra one right away?
It took you a long time to find one
Do you remember it was her shirt you
were wearing?
That was my teacher.

~ Kathleen

HANDING OVER THE KEYS TO POETRY

Now the meaning had become the focus of student poetry. Rhyming, for almost all the students, took a backseat. "It's okay to rhyme," they seemed to understand, "if I say everything I want or need to say." Most students abandoned the idea of rhyming altogether at this time.

By this point, the writers' workshop was alive with poetry. It was satisfying to see what Bruner would call "hand over" taking place, as each day the students became more competent and more independent poets. To describe the process of hand over, Nancie Atwell tells the story of teaching her daughter how to brush her teeth. At first, Atwell did it for her. The next step was for both mother and daughter to have a hand on the toothbrush, brushing away. Next, she watched her daughter, offering encouragement. In the end, Atwell's daughter was able to brush her own teeth with no input or intervention. Thus, the hand over was complete.

The students were eager to compose and revise; they were better equipped to create original poetry and take risks. Some students were eager to work from favorite poems hidden in their special poetry notebooks. Others wanted to develop themes that emerged from template exercises, trying out their own voices.

One student, Caitlin, loves horses; all her written pieces in some way return to the theme of horses. Daydreaming one day in class, Caitlin noticed the poster-sized version of Carl Sandburg's "Fog" on a bulletin board. There was an illustration of a lighthouse and a catlike cloud of fog. She had been working on a poem about Assateague Island and its famous ponies. Click. Suddenly the lighthouse and its flashing light made its way into her poem.

The Island's Guard Tower
It stands tall and proud,
Guarding the gleaming, moonlit channel,
Guarding the wild ponies sleeping in a
warm, comfy crowd
It keeps watch over the friendly passing boats.
As the two tiny islands sleep peacefully,
The beauty of the moon in the sky seems as
though it floats.
One, two, three. Flash. Flash.
The ponies go to sleep.

273

The children go to rest.
The island makes but not a peep.
One, two, three. Flash. Flash.
What's this tower that guards boats from
shores ever so crude?
What's this tower that watches over the
sleeping town?
To which your mind it shall not delude,
A lighthouse that turns my frowns upside-down.
One, two, three. Flash. Flash.
Assateague Lighthouse.

> ～ Caitlin

Caitlin purposely used repetition and personification in this piece. She even worked in a subtle rhyme scheme. She wanted to use her words to make the reader see the flashing lighthouse. One way or another, she managed to work in some alliteration and vivid sensory imagery.

Natasha, new to the school district from Russia, released a flood of feelings comparing her old home versus her new one. She first had written about this subject in prose. Poetry gave her a means to explore her feelings.

Between Worlds
Caught between worlds
Don't know where I belong
One side I long since left
The other side my new home
If someone's saying something
About life over there
They criticize my birthplace
Oh, this I just can't bear
If someone dares to mention
Some fault of this country
Then suddenly all that I left
Is a distant memory

Who knows where life shall take me
But this one thing I know
I will never go back to

What used to be my home
Yet I am so uncertain
If my life I can lead
Not knowing where my heart is
Only knowing that it bleeds.

　　　～ Natasha

Note that this poem about being caught between worlds is in two stanzas. The desperation she feels trying to fit in is powerful, as evidenced by her strong word choices. This piece is clearly far from puny.

Charles is a mild boy. He has a wealth of knowledge but has never really seemed interested in sports. However, he found himself getting caught up in all of the hockey discussions brewing around him. Although he has never played himself, he chose to use poetry to put on the mask as if he had.

Goalie
I hear the swish of skates
As the players come closer
Sweaty breath above the ice
Clashing sticks like swords
Fighting for the prized puck
The ice ripples like my tense muscles
Stretching my nerves like strings
Suddenly, the little puck tries to rush past
Crash! I stop its course
Swish! I repel it back to the ice fighters
The game is over
My post is safe
Victory is ours!

　　　～ Charles

Anthony, a classmate of Charles, is an ice hockey goalie. When asked if Charles had found the mark with his imagery and quickly paced lines, Anthony replied, "Yeah, even better than I did!"

Erica shyly slipped this poem on the teacher's desk with the simple request, "May I hang this on the art teacher's door?"

A World of Art
The sky is the easel
Hovering over the world

The water is the paint
Giving adventure and life

The air is the paintbrush
Flying lightly
Swiftly
Through the trees
It's a breeze

And we the people
Who have created
So many features
Cannot be described
As any art utensil
But only as the main illustrator.

      ~ Erica

Erica was finding another use for poetry. True, we had been hanging poetry throughout the school for some time, but this tribute represented a gift of writing. Other students saw what Erica did—as well as the complete and utter delight of the recipient—and began to follow suit. What a difference from "Bubba in Da Tubba"!

"THE BEST WORDS IN THE BEST ORDER"

This is not to say that every student's poetry transformed into soaring triumphs of literary genius, but the vast majority of the poetry produced was of a much higher quality. For example, remember Katie's poem about the beach? She stuck with it and applied what she learned in the many craft lessons. We had a conference about word choice and using specific details. Also, we discussed the use of white space and word placement to suggest movement, such as the kite flying. Katie wanted the ending to be more powerful, since leaving the beach is often very sad. We spoke about how, when she leaves the beach, she watches out the rear window as the beach gets smaller and smaller the farther away she goes. How could we make what had been her last line suggest that? Did her lion emerge?

The Beach

Wind brushing through your hair,
Flying
a
kite
in
the
air.
Swimming in the cold water,
While on the sand it gets hotter.

As I watch the sun go down,
I'm glad to be at the beach.

We pick up our stuff,
Without a sound

and we leave the empty beach,

Sighing
as
we
go.

     ~ Katie

Past attempts at improving student writers' poetry by only teaching lessons on writers' craft were doomed to failure. It's possible that the many lessons on the craft of poetry had actually done the opposite of what was intended. We hoped that these lessons would define poetry and help students write it. The standard "poetry unit" fare turned out to be more of an anchor than a sail. It seems that all of that "learning" forced the student writers to retreat to that safe world of poetry they knew and recognized: Seuss, Prelutsky, and Silverstein.

A first step beyond that is creating an atmosphere in which children gather, select, share, and enjoy poetry. Next, budding poets must be allowed to play with words, experiment with meaning, and safely take risks. As the writers become more confident through the scaffolding of parallel and template poetry, it's time to hand over the keys of creative control to these now-blossoming poets.

To be sure, we still see signs of struggle: Ken is still mulling over where to go with a new piece about Jeff. His struggle is encouraging, however. It's now over how to best say what he needs to say rather than what might rhyme with *skateboard*. That's a big jump.

At the same time, by expanding our own vision of teaching poetry, we have come to accept that Bill has as much right to love "Bubba in the Tubba" as Natasha has to love "Between Worlds." In the final analysis, through our work, we managed to spare ourselves and our students another crash-and-burn attempt at teaching poetry as a writing genre. Credit for this is due, in part, to lessons gleaned from our work at the PAWLP Summer Institutes, which led us to re-examine and reopen our thinking about poetry "as we'd always done it." In re-thinking our process, we were freed to figure out where the kids were, then lead them—at least most of them—toward greater self-expression through poetry. Now, everyone from Bill to Natasha seems to see what Coleridge meant when he defined poetry as "the best words in the best order."

REFERENCES

Atwell, Nancie. 1998. *In the Middle: New Understandings About Writing, Reading, and Learning*. 2nd ed. Portsmouth, NH: Boynton/Cook.

Bomer, Randy. 1995. *Time for Meaning: Crafting Literate Lives in Middle and High School*. Portsmouth, NH: Heinemann.

Fletcher, Ralph J. 1993. *What a Writer Needs*. Portsmouth, NH: Heinemann.

Frost, Robert, and Edward Connery Lathem, ed. 1979. "The Road Not Taken." In *Poetry of Robert Frost: The Collected Poems, Completed and Unabridged*. New York: Henry Holt.

Graves, Donald. 1994. *A Fresh Look at Writing*. Portsmouth, NH: Heinemann.

Heard, Georgia. 1989. *For the Good of the Earth and Sun: Teaching Poetry*. Portsmouth, NH: Heinemann.

———. 1999. *Awakening the Heart*. Portsmouth, NH: Heinemann.

Koch, Kenneth 1990. *Rose, Where Did You Get That Red?* New York: Vintage Books.

Tucker, Shelley 1992. *Writing Poetry*. Glenview, IL: GoodYearBooks.

Willard, Nancy. 1987. "The Five Versions of the Icicle." In *Household Tales of Moon and Water*. Florida: Harvest Books.

Woolfolk, Anita. 1993. *Educational Psychology*. 5th ed. Needham Heights, MA: Allyn & Bacon.

Behind Their Backs: Proximity and Insult in Student Response

Roger Green

*Written by Roger Green about his teaching experi
ence with ninth grade students in Fairfax County,
Virginia, this article was originally published in the
winter 2000 issue of* The Quarterly.

The research described in this article grew out of a teacher research
course sponsored by the Northern Virginia Writing Project. As a result
of the course I became able to see past what I wanted to happen all
the way to what might really be happening. Lessons that went awry and
students who weren't quite getting it became clues about what was really going on, and I learned to collect, analyze, and use what students
were telling me—through their body language, stray comments, journal
writings, and other bits of data—to improve my practice. I began to
look forward to that little itch of irritation that told me things weren't
quite right because I knew that moment would give me a starting point
for research.

In this research project, my breakthrough moments came as I was reading the students' journal responses to my questions about their work
in reading-writing groups. Looking back, I see clearly that I was largely
oblivious to the social undercurrents that ran through reading/writing
groups in my class. As I began to take my students' situation more seriously, guided by their writing and comments, I began to understand the
complexity and personal nature of their work in reading/writing groups.

That understanding in turn made me both more patient with their work in reading/writing groups and more determined both to model how the groups should work and to provide extensive guidance through the initial stages. This article details the surprises that initiated this journey.

~ *Roger Green, 2002*

*T*he response group has become a staple of language arts classrooms. Many teachers have observed that writing drafts that have been subjected to the talk therapy of student response are clearer, more orderly, more full of voice, and less error afflicted than pieces seen only by the teacher. However, many teachers, including me, have kept a distance from these groups as they meet, believing that to intrude will have the effect of damaging the delicate chemistry that is emerging among the writers. But at the beginning of this school year, I decided to take a step closer to these groups. I wanted to know more about what goes on in the minds of my ninth grade students as they work together on their writing. I gathered information by observing groups as they worked and by asking the students to write to me about their experiences. I thought I knew what happens in reading/writing groups, but I have been surprised by what I learned. In fact, I did not fully appreciate the intellectual and social challenges reading/writing groups pose.

PREPARING STUDENTS TO WORK IN READING/WRITING GROUPS

For the last seven years, my students at the magnet school for science and technology where I teach have been writing and sharing in small groups. In recent years, my students have commented on one another's writing in two ways: with the author of the piece present in "reading/writing groups," and in the author's absence in "publication committees." In a reading/writing group, each author reads his or her paper aloud, takes notes on the group's discussion of the paper, and later revises. In the publication committee, since the author of the piece is not a member of the group, a student acts as an agent for the author. This person reads the story aloud, takes notes on the discussion, and then writes a letter to the author explaining the group's thinking, elaborating where appropriate. I had viewed these two types of groups as nearly identical because they followed such similar procedures. In my mind, a publication committee was simply a reading/writing group working on a paper written by a student from another class. I came to see that students work quite differently when the author is not present. To illuminate this difference, I need to explain how my students came to be working in publication committees.

My department has been using publication committees in a variety of formats for eight years. Some years, I exchange student papers with those from another teacher. This year, I rotated the papers among my own three ninth grade English classes. The students were primarily writing fiction in a variety of forms. They took the first drafts of their papers to their reading/writing groups in their own classes, and I gave the second drafts to publication committees in another of my classes.

Before the reading/writing groups met for the first time, I took extensive steps to prepare the students to talk with each other about their writing. All of this preparation also applied to their work in publication committees. The initial preparation consisted of several steps. First, the whole class commented together on a story written by one of the students in the class. I made extra copies of the story, and the whole class sat in a circle. The author read the piece aloud, and then we talked about it. As the students commented, I led a discussion about the comments they made. We noticed that the story had strong points. We also noticed that in some places, characters or settings weren't described very clearly, and some parts were not logical. I emphasized the need to phrase comments kindly. Then, each student wrote comments about the first draft of a story written by a student of mine several years ago. After everyone had written his or her own comments, we shared ideas about the story and identified the most significant problems of the piece. The whole process of drafting, followed by reading/writing group meetings and further revision, stretched out over twelve weeks. The students went through two revisions again later in the year, this time taking about five weeks since I did not need to repeat the initial preparation.

After the initial work as a whole class, the students met in reading/writing groups to talk about their own stories. I outlined a procedure similar to the one we had used working together. The students would read each paper aloud, discuss it, and take notes. Each group had four members and two copies of each student's paper. The groups met for four forty-five-minute sessions. After each session, I collected the notes the students had made during the discussion, gave the students a grade on their comments, and wrote notes to them about the quality of the comments. I also sat with groups and helped them comment.

The students revised with the help of the reading/writing group's comments. I collected the revised drafts and passed them onto publication committees in a different class. For example, I passed the drafts from my fifth-period class to groups in my sixth-period class. Students could also submit their papers anonymously if they wished.

TROUBLE AHEAD

As the students settled down to work in publication committees on the revised drafts, I scanned the classroom for problems. The students sat in tidy circles of four spaced evenly around the room. One student in each group read a draft aloud, and the others followed on copies, just as they had done when they met in reading/writing groups. The students had worked well in reading/writing groups on the first draft of their own papers, so I felt they knew what they were doing.

I was just about to stand back and congratulate myself for preparing the students to talk about writing when I detected an ugly, sneering laugh from a group by the windows. Are they off topic already? I wondered irritably. No, they were obviously involved with the story. A student resumed reading aloud as I casually strolled over. They looked up at me but kept working. I recognized the story they were reading. It was a sensitive reminiscence of a real-life, tragic experience. Under my stern gaze, the group stopped giggling and worked quietly. But then, across the room, a group broke into peals of derisive laughter. "And look at this sentence," I heard someone whisper, provoking more snickers. I moved in their direction. As soon as I moved away, the first group began to cackle again. Then another group started to howl. "This really sucks," a student in a third group hissed, his group nodding enthusiastically.

I could barely contain my frustration. I could not understand why my students would insult the work of other students. They had not been cruel when they worked in reading/writing groups on their own stories. Their arrogance truly caught me off guard. Fortunately, for the most part, I contained my aggravation. I was a researcher, after all, as well as a teacher. I watched in bewilderment over the next few days as groups of ordinarily mild-mannered students in each of my classes ripped through story after story from another class. I listened in on groups of barbarians as long as I could stand it, occasionally resorting to snide comments whispered under my breath. Rather than just canceling the publication committees, I decided to see if I could figure out what was going on.

FIGURING OUT WHAT HAPPENED

It wasn't until I read the students' final evaluations of the whole process that I began to understand what had been happening in the publication committees. Tom explained it this way in his log:

Being on a publication committee is slightly different from being part of a reading/writing group. The really "nice" difference is that the author is not present, so the group doesn't have to be quite so polite and cautious. Instead, the group is able to really dissect the story without having to worry about the author being offended. Later, comments can be "pacified" or censored somewhat.

Lisa put it even more bluntly in her log: "The publication committee was much more fun. If a paper really stunk, you could say so and not worry about hurting the writer's feelings."

Freed by the author's absence to speak honestly, my students delighted in brainstorming ideas about the story. When they saw something they didn't like, they said so, and the whole group felt free to agree enthusiastically. The process was exhilarating and creative. Student after student praised the freedom of the publication committee. Hannah put it this way:

Being in a reading/writing group and being on a publication committee were two totally different experiences. In one you are dealing with the author and in the other you're not. When you deal with the author, you are careful of the feelings expressed and of how you phrase things. When you aren't dealing with the author, you are down right blatant and say exactly what's on your mind. It is almost two totally different ways of looking at a story. Not that one is good and the other is bad. They just get you different results.

My students' comments about publication committees raised questions in my mind about reading/writing groups. Hannah's comment suggested to me that the reading/writing sessions required a different mode of thought from the publication committees. I realized that before making a comment in a reading/writing group, the student had to decide how the writer would react. The student not only had to figure out what to say about a piece but had to decide whether the comment would do more harm than good. The reading/writing group required a measured, sensitive, and necessarily self-edited response. The publication committee session, on the other hand, invited uninhibited brainstorming of ideas. Students felt free to say whatever came to mind without worrying about how it sounded. This seems to me to be an important observation about the way students look at the writing of their peers. Even in a near-ideal situation in which literate, well-intentioned students truly want to be helpful, they must struggle with how to phrase their comments kindly. Not only that, but they must be aware of their body language so the author does not guess their thoughts. At least, this is the way they felt. Nearly every student reported being sensitive to the feelings of the author if the author was present.

Each student in the publication committee wrote a letter to one author explaining the group's ideas about the story. I was worried about how the letters would sound, but when they came in, they were courteous and thoughtful. In a few cases, the letter writer was overzealous, but the vast majority of letters were models of decorum. In their final evaluations of the whole process, the authors praised the letters' seriousness and insight. It was clear that in most cases, the publication committees had been at least as helpful as the reading/writing groups, and in many cases more helpful.

So how did the letters end up being so sensitive if the groups had been busy dissecting the stories? Rachel pointed out that being able to shape the comments into a letter was helpful:

> It was hard reading a story and then immediately having to come up with ideas to make it better. But if I got to take a story home and look at it, comments were much easier to make and I think they were more helpful to the authors. . . . It was great being able to plan out exactly what I was going to say and how I wanted to say it.

Charlie put it a little more cynically:

> One thing I learned from being in a publication committee is that people don't always say what they mean. When my pub. committee and I wrote comments to the authors, we often disguised what we meant to make the letter sound nicer.

So, after the group brainstormed lots of ideas about a piece, the letter writer took notes home and quietly decided how to phrase everything and also decided which comments to omit. With this extra time, few of the students failed to write a letter that was both polite and helpful.

Some students noticed a difference in the kind of comments made in the two groups. Walter noticed that

> in a reading/writing group, comments tend to be about details, and if a general comment comes up, the comment is usually pretty vague. This is mostly because the comments are spur of the moment type things. The

287

commentor hasn't had time to think abort it yet. On the other hand, in
publication committees, the people have a week to think about the story.
The comments tend to be more meaningful and deeper than in the read-
ing-writing groups.

Walter meant that the letter writer had a week from the time he or she first
saw the story until the letter was due.

Even though my students reported advantages to working in publication
committees, they also recognized the strengths of reading-writing groups. Perhaps the most important advantage is that the writer can ask and answer questions. In the reading-writing group, work on the paper can be a conversation.
As Jack put it,

I think that what really influenced my revision the most was my reading/
writing group's comments. They seemed to be more helpful because I
actually sat down with them and could see exactly what they were talk-
ing about. When I got my publication letter I didn't know what they were
talking about in some places, and they weren't right there with me so
I couldn't get any comments in really great detail like I could with my
reading/writing group.

The conversational nature of the reading-writing group also lends itself to
follow-up questions. Linda noticed that

in a reading-writing group, the author is sitting right in front of you. You
can ask the author questions and listen to their responses. You can also
respond to their responses and any questions they have about their story.

Alan had an experience that could happen in a reading-writing group but
not in a publication committee. As his group discussed his story about a trip to
Czechoslovakia, he began to tell anecdotes that were not in his paper. The group
encouraged him to include these funny anecdotes.

Even though Louise appreciated the give-and-take of the reading-writing
group, she recognized the value of the objectivity of the publication committee:

I liked my reading-writing group better because I was able to defend
myself and my story and make "on the spot" corrections. However, I
think my publication committee helped my story more because they saw

it from an objective point of view and made judgments based solely on their . . . impressions and not my presence waiting to clear up and confusion.

Mary made a similar point:

In the reading-writing group, I could talk with the author and get answers to my questions. It was easier to explain how you felt and also give the writer information they needed. In the publication committee, it was possible to look at the writing objectively and give advice about overall impressions.

My students worked on the pieces in the reading-writing groups first and later submitted revised drafts to the publication committees. Thus, the publication committees were working on more polished drafts. It may be that the more distanced, formal publication committee lends itself to work on a more polished draft, but I'm not sure this is the case. I suspect that more important factors may be the student's relationship with the reading/writing group and the nature of the individual story.

Later in the year, the students went through the whole process again. This second time, I gave them a choice of whether they wanted their first drafts evaluated by their own reading/writing group or by a publication committee from another class. In spite of the high praise the publication committees had received after the work on the first paper, only ten out of seventy-six students requested a publication committee. Thirty-three students requested that a publication committee evaluate their second draft. In conversation, some students said they chose the publication committee to get more-objective opinions; others because they didn't want to have to face their group with a story they didn't like. Still others chose to bring the story to a reading-writing group because they didn't want anyone outside the class to see it. Students continued to be more openly critical in the publication committees than in the reading/writing groups, though the difference was less pronounced. I gave the students the option of changing to a different group for the second paper, and a few students chose to move. During work on the second paper, I observed that the reading-writing groups seemed more comfortable about talking to the writer, and the publication committees seemed less gleeful in criticizing the absent author.

CONCLUSIONS

After examining writing groups this year, I'm wondering about the implications of what I have noticed. Hannah may be right that the thinking process is different if the author is present. The thinking process in the reading-writing group is more compressed. Students have to come up with comments and self-evaluate the comments at the same time. In the publication committee, the students brainstorm the comments first and later analyze the comments, deciding what to keep and what to leave out.

The students take the issue of confronting an author face-to-face seriously. The students in the reading-writing group were as worried about offending the author as about helping with the story. This sentiment was reported independently by nearly every student. This was true even when the group members simply had questions about the story. Certainly this feeling will diminish with time and positive experiences, but it should not be taken lightly by the teacher introducing students to writing groups.

The reading-writing group requires on-the-spot analysis that lends itself to producing a mixture of helpful and unhelpful comments. Students reported that about half of the comments their reading-writing groups made were useful. They reported that nearly all of the publication committee's comments were helpful. The publication committee had several advantages: time to reflect on the comments, time to evaluate and then eliminate comments that seemed useless, and time to organize the comments logically. I suspect that the publication committees produced many silly, extraneous, or trivial comments that were omitted from the letters.

The conversational nature of the reading-writing group was an enormous advantage, especially if the writer did a significant share of the talking. If the writer used the time to ask questions of the group and to answer the group's questions, then full advantage was being taken of this strength of the reading-writing group.

Communication about writing is difficult. In the reading-writing groups, some students worded their comments so diplomatically that the author didn't fully understand the point. As Jack mentioned, the letters from the publication committee were not always clear. Students did report that hearing the same comment from more than one source was very convincing. Sometimes a student had to hear the same comment from the reading-writing group and then later from the publication committee and from the teacher before it finally sank in.

The students learned as much about writing by reading other students' papers as they did by getting comments on their own work. This was especially true in the publication committees, where the students felt free to talk about what really worked and what didn't in a story. I did notice that students were quite capable of deriding a piece for the same faults their own writing exhibited. And, actually, they noticed this fact themselves, which is, I suppose, the point.

In the future, I will continue to use both reading-writing groups and publications committees with student writing. Through my teacher research project, I have come to understand that giving students the opportunity to talk about writing without the writer present sharpens their commenting skills by simplifying their task. With the writer missing, the commentors can concentrate on the writing without worrying about the complex social skills required to talk directly to a writer. However, publication committees can't replace reading-writing groups because authors need the experience of hearing directly from commentors, and more important, authors need to talk about their work, responding to questions and suggestions. With practice, commentors can master the skills they need to explain their ideas to an author in person. As I continue to work with student writing, I will be sensitive to my students' hesitancy to speak honestly with authors. I will spend more time modeling commenting skills as the teacher, and I will provide more structured activities in which students can practice commenting on writing. Teaching students to talk about their writing is a rich and complex undertaking and one that is well worth the necessary investment of time and energy.

Revising Revision: How My Students Transformed Writers' Workshop

Jan Matsuoka

Jan Matsuoka wrote this article about her teaching experience with a third and fourth grade combination class in Oakland, California. It was originally published in the winter 1998 issue of The Quarterly.

Revision has always intrigued me because so many students resist this pivotal part of the writing process. For some, the fact that I require extensive revision before a piece of writing can be published has discouraged them from writing at all. Some teachers also seem to have an aversion to—or at least a lack of knowledge about—teaching revision. When I was co-director of the Bay Area Writing Project and in charge of inservices in the schools, I noticed that very few teachers gave presentations on revision although there was a clear demand for such workshops. I was unwilling to give up my insistence on revision, but I was not getting much help from anyone else. So when I had a chance to do a teacher research project, I decided to work through my concerns myself.

As readers will see, the techniques I advance here could not have been developed without significant help from my students., Even though I am now retired, I continue to share strategies for revision with teachers in my Bay Area Writing Project presentations on writers' workshop. In this way, the contributions of the children in my classes continue to live on in classrooms throughout the area.

~ Jan Matsuoka, 2002

*T*he revision of writing is bittersweet, pleasure coupled with pain. Eric, my fourth grade student in a third/fourth grade combination class at Joaquin Miller Elementary School in Oakland, California, described this condition well when he wrote the following:

> When the teacher said we had to do a revision to publish a story, I said "Aw man" moaning in my head, but after my revision, I said it sounds better and then I did more revisions to make the story better.

For another student, Emilene, however, the process was pure agony:

> I don't like revision one bit even though it helps. I don't like it because it takes too long, and I can never think of a better story. I actually hate to revise.

Yet despite feelings such as Emilene's, revision is a requirement in my class if a child wants to publish a piece of writing. Over time, many students pick up on what needs to be done between first- and second-draft writing:

> I think that the difference between my first and second drafts was that in the middle of the story, I put more details in like what type of dog I had and what color. Jojo is a blondish brown collie and has sad brown eyes. You know more what he looks like.
>
> ~ Lena

> Whenever I rite something during Writers' Workshop, I always take my writing home, and I read it over and over to myself. I even read it again to my mom, my grandma, and my dog. In my story "My Grandma is the Next Michael Jordan," I noticed that I used the words then and said too much so I took out the thens and rote something esle besides said like screamed, announced, and whistpered.
>
> ~ Mareesha

> In my story "The House of the Dreaded Unknown" I put an arcade in the first draft because I liked that one espicialy. In the second draft I put chess in there instead because at the time I just beat my dad in chess. I loved that the whole ending depended on the guy winning the chess game. Otherwise he was doamed. I feel sort of weird about revision because you can think about one thing and do another.
>
> ~ Sean

But getting students to this point has not been easy. Revision is a difficult but inevitably necessary part of the writing process. A writer refining a piece of writing to uncover its essence is like a jeweler buffing a diamond to expose the luster within. Yet many students do not see it that way. They approach their work with such feelings of ownership, so sure that it is perfect the first time around, that they resist making any changes. Even after participating in countless minilessons on revision, watching others model revision, and conferencing with other students and me about an early draft of a piece, some students still recopy the original story over again, word for word.

For the teacher too, because of some students' resistance to change, revision is a difficult skill to teach. Even after over thirty years of teaching, on days when revision is the focus, I often need to go home after school and take a nap before dinner, sometimes never waking up until the next day. Nonetheless, the results that spring from successful revision are worth the struggle. Listen to Melissa's ebullience:

> I feel great that I revised it because now I have a great story. I feel like a
> real published author. I feel like Melissa, author from the outside world!

But we are hearing from Melissa at the end of the process. Along the way, many students resist revision, and when they are willing to revise, they have no idea where to start. Because I find so much value in revision, I am continually working to make the process easier and clearer. Thus, when I joined a teacher research group at University of California-Berkeley, I was naturally drawn to the question: What revision strategies help students improve their writing during writers' workshop? In this article, I want to highlight those strategies that proved successful as I collected data for two years, working first with my fourth grade class and most recently, with a third/fourth grade combination class.

DEFINING REVISION

In my research, revision has a two-pronged definition. The most common definition of revision is improving the first draft of writing and producing a final draft by subtracting, adding, or replacing words, phrases, sentences or paragraphs. Using this definition, however, the amount and nature of the revision will vary from student to student according to the ability and/or the interest of the writer. My third-graders and even fourth-graders with poor motor coordination make revisions directly on a first draft; if I were to ask these students to rewrite each paper, they would be overwhelmed by the task, and they might even learn to dread writing. Most of my fourth-graders, however, can write two drafts. But in any classroom, there are exceptions. One overachiever, a bright third-grader and an English language learner named Alejandra, ended up with five drafts of her story, "The Dracula Puppy Who Loved Candy Instead of Blood," each draft quite different from the previous one. Passing her desk during Writers' Workshop, I rarely saw her face, only the top of her head, as she labored, pencil in hand, writing one page after another. During our conference, she noted parts she loved in different drafts, and later on, cut and pasted them onto her final draft.

The second definition of revision involves a larger vision: the improvement of writing from one final draft to another, a growth over time. That's the kind of revision I was hoping to trigger in a conference with Sandee, another English language learner. I saw that her story, "My Trip to L.A.," was little more than list of events that had taken place over two weeks, all described on one page. I shared the parts of her story I had enjoyed, including the way she showed her excitement by reporting her inability to sleep the night before the trip and the certain types of cars her family had counted in order to kill the boredom of travel. As we talked about her goals for her writing in the future, she told me that she needed to be more careful about her capitals, using them at the beginning of sentences and with names.

I, however, was interested in more than cosmetic changes. I told her I wanted her to have more focus in any story she wrote. She gave me her "worried-Sandee look." I could tell she was puzzled, so I made rough sketches representing events of her trip to Los Angeles, drawing chuckles from her—she never knew how poorly I drew. Making a small frame out of another piece of paper, I placed it down on one of the drawings, a sketch attempting to show Sandee as she visited her grandmother. Focus, I told her, means I want her to only tell me all the details about this memorable meeting with her grandmother and not all the other things she did on this trip.

"Oh, I get it," she smiled, "like just one cartoon, not a whole bunch."

There were several pieces in between before she finally wrote a masterpiece focused on a snake her family found in the backyard and the way they finally got rid of this dreadful creature, reporting in the process her family's superstitions about snakes. She received an enthusiastic ovation as she shared this story in author's chair. I trace triumph on this occasion back to our discussion of how "My Trip to L.A." could be revised.

REVISION IN THE CONTEXT OF WRITERS' WORKSHOP

I have adapted the work of Donald Graves and Nancie Atwell to create my own version of Writers' Workshop. The minilesson is a featured part of this process. I give these lessons at the very beginning of the writing hour. They are lessons dealing with all aspects of writing. I might read aloud from a picture book to generate ideas, talk about "places in the room to go when you want to read your writing to someone," or present a lesson on how to use quotation marks when writing dialogue. I make certain that these lessons are no more than ten minutes long. I know it's time to stop when I get clear clues that students are itching to write: they toy with their pencils, rustle papers, wiggle in their chairs. Many students leap to their writing once the lesson is over.

Lessons on revision are an important part of my minilesson plan. In these lessons, I often effectively use transparencies or copies of first- and second-draft writing of former students. Students note the writer's strengths and needs for improvement in the first draft, and the next day, observe what the author did to revise in the second. They can see strategies used successfully and sometimes unsuccessfully. At times, they see that a writer's first draft is better than his second. Mareesha shares her thoughts on minilessons in an interview:

I personally like minilessons because it is interesting to know how someone else might have written. Then I think to myself, "Wow, I could use that idea in my own writing!" It really gets my mind going and also my thinking and adds to my writing. I might even trash a sentence or two and replace it with something else.

At the beginning of the school year, one of the more successful minilessons was on leads with examples of different ways an author might start the same story. I asked the students to choose a recent piece of writing and to compose another beginning. Jake made this revision:

FIRST DRAFT: *About two years ago we bought a house in Northstar at tahoe. We go up there every chance we get. It's a big house. It's got a loft on top in case you don't know what a loft is its something I can't explain.*

SECOND DRAFT: *Two years ago my mom brought up about getting an-other house. "But where?" we all said. Then my dad said, "I know a place. Where? We all exclaimed. At Lake Tahoe. It's a beautiful place. OOOOHHH, yaaaah we said. And we jumped around, hugging each other. So we went and looked at lots of houses.*

Interviewing Jake about the differences between these two leads, he said: "After your minilesson, I tried writing the second beginning. I like the second one because it's more interesting. It shows our excitement over getting a house at Tahoe. And we were really excited, you know. Hey, yeah, it has more showing than the first one. The first one is just a boring, like booo-ring. I don't know if anyone would read my story if they read the first one."

Minilessons that involve my students are certainly my most successful. Often I ask students to take out a recent piece of work and make revisions right on their paper: between the lines, in the margins. I require my students to skip lines when they write during writers' workshop to facilitate these kinds of changes. I might even request two changes. Because their writing is freshly done, they have a vested interest in a minilesson as they practice the new skill, revising on the spot. I collected the following sentences after several lessons on sentence expansion, the italicized verb phrases added during the lessons:

"He jumps on my mom's lap, *meowing for her to pet him*."
~ Jesus

"Then he left, *debating if he would like the job*."
~ Eugenia

"We screamed and screamed and screamed, *trying to get away*."
~ Lucy

"The two cats lay in front of the fireplace, *licking their paws*."
~ Jake

MINILESSONS REVISED

With results such as these, I thought everything was going great until two months into school when I asked my students to rank which writers' workshop activities they found most helpful. Minilessons received the lowest score. I was shocked—no, devastated. How could that be? I spent so much time and thought preparing for these lessons! I have a couple of students who are especially reflective about writing, so, as I had lunch with them, I showed them the survey and asked them why they thought minilessons rated so poorly. Here are portions of that conversation:

J: Not to hurt your feelings, Mrs. M., but we do like your minilessons, but when I'm writing a story, I want to get to my story. I am only thinking about what I am going to write. Umm. Sorry, but sometimes I don't hear you. (We all laugh.)

ME: Really, that's okay; don't apologize.

C: Yeah, no offense, but I kinda get ideas to make my story more exciting outside of school. Like I might see a TV program and think what a great ending and kind of go from there.

J: Umm. He's right. You don't stop thinking of writing when school stops because you're always thinking of how you can make it better so that the kids in class would love it.

ME: So are you both saying that once you become a writer, you are even thinking about writing outside of school? You become observant about what you see, hear, and read?

C: Like me, like I really am serious about my writing. If I write, I want something really great. I don't think everyone in our class is serious, if you know what I mean. Don't get me wrong, I'm not trying to put the other kids down. Most of us like writing a lot.

ME: No, no, I don't see your comment as a put-down. You're just being honest. That's why I am interviewing you two.

J: Yeah, I want to be a writer someday. But when I was writing about my younger brother being a brat, I kinda looked at him at home to see how I could improve how I wrote about him being stupid about looking at *Power Rangers* and karate stuff on TV and stuff. Mrs. M., you can't give a minilesson on that. (He laughs.)

I learned a great deal from this fascinating conversation. Becoming a real writer, a child looks not only to the classroom, but to the richness of the world. After that, minilessons became less frequent. I spent more time conferencing with individual students and instructing small groups. But of course, I did not give up altogether. Before one minilesson focusing on a different kinds of genre, I blurted out something about how tired I was of giving these lessons. Wouldn't it be wonderful, I said, if one of the students gave a lesson instead!

Spontaneously, Ludvig, a student from Sweden whose second language is English, raised his hand and said, "I'll give one now, Mrs. M." He raced to the front of the class.

"Today, I am going to talk about the word *said*," he began. "When your father is mad at you, you don't use the word *said* when you write about what he said. You use words like *yelled* or *screamed*. They go better with him being mad. And when you tell someone, 'I love you,' you don't say, 'I said.' [The class giggled]. You use *whispered* or *moaned*. [The class howled.] Are there any questions? Now I want you to look at your writing and change one *said* to a more exciting word."

Ludvig bowed as he received a standing ovation. The children combed their papers and struck out the many *saids*, replacing them with powerful verbs. We had a wonderful time as students shared their changes. True, I had given this lesson on *said* before, but this was a voice other than mine; it was a fresh challenge from a peer.

Right after this lesson, Kaneesha ran up to me. Showing me her paper and pointing to a sentence, she whispered, "Mrs. M., I use the word *said*, but I use it like this: '*I am so tired,' he said with his head hanging down.* Sometimes, isn't it okay to use it like this?"

"Of course! You're absolutely right!" Excited, I asked, "Do you want to give the next minilesson? Let's meet and talk about your lesson!" And so the idea of student minilessons caught on. Students signed up for times to be coached and to present to the class, some of the students even in pairs. The list of student topics looked like the following:

JAMAL: "How to Write a Longer Story"

DANA: "Getting Ideas Right from the Classroom for Stories"

MATT: "Handwriting"

KATELYN: "Draw First, Then Write"

JASON and EVAN: "Writing a Story with Someone"

EMMA: "How I Check on My Spelling"

I realized that the format of my minilessons became a model around which the students framed theirs, even down to those revisions on the spot. But most importantly, I noticed how attentive the students in the audience were to the minilessons given by their peers, the variety of voices enabling them to look at their work anew. Once reluctant to revise at my direction, students were now being pushed by their peers to make changes.

THE TEACHER-STUDENT CONFERENCE

One spur to revision that has proven successful year after year is the conference my student teacher and I have with individual students, each of us averaging three conferences per day. We focus on student work in process or on final drafts. Because the form below (figure 1) wasn't one that I created, I don't know who to credit for it, but nonetheless, I have found it invaluable in keeping a record of our conferences.

I staple this form to the right side of a writing folder with current work as a reminder of the goals a student has set for his or her writing. During

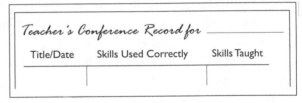

Figure I

these conferences, especially by the end of the first semester, we want to see the writer articulate the strengths and weaknesses of each piece. By becoming more reflective about the craft, a writer begins to internalize those skills that will allow revision throughout the writing process.

In figure 2, I show the form I used with Michael. We see that after Michael's first publication, "The Bloody Eye," he began to use dialogue with success and became quite adept at writing with show-not-tell (descriptive writing). In the second conference, Michael could point out the strengths of his writing, although I had to help him with areas that needed attention. Although Michael is a good writer, he is easily distracted, becoming more social with time. And thus, I needed to have more than one conference with him on "The Kidnapper" to keep him on track toward a final draft. When we directed him to use the computer, he was able to finally revise and publish this piece. It should be noted, however, that the form does not show the many times parent volunteers and I checked in with him, keeping him accountable for his time and work—what we call "putting on the pressure."

Teacher's Conference Record for Michael		
Title and Date	**Skills Used Correctly**	**Skills Taught (1-2)**
The Bloody Eye 10/1/96	1. Character's thoughts "How could he miss dinner?" 2. Tight story—good beginning, middle, and end	1. How did you feel? Show-not-tell dialogue (SNT)
Adven. of Mohawk Man & Super Cat 11/6/96	1. Good dialogue 2. SNT—"So scared…" "stung so hard that…"	1. Capitalize names 2. Other words besides "then"
The Kidnapper 1/15/97	1. Strong verbs—"threw," "plunged" 2. Other words besides "then" 3. SNT—"So scared…" "screamed so loud…"	1. Capitalize names 2. New lead besides "Hi! My name is…"
The Kidnapper 1/23/97	1. Verbs 2. Sense of humor shows through 3. Some names capitalized 4. New lead	1. Periods at end of sentences 2. More details in one scene

Figure 2

AUTHOR'S CHAIR

Author's chair gives students a chance to read completed first and second drafts to the class. The writer receives positive comments and may solicit questions. Some students are eager to read in author's chair; others must be strongly encouraged if not exactly bribed. By circulating around, listening to writing read aloud, and also by investigating writing folders after school, I find many examples of superb writing that need to be shared with the whole class. I want these presented as models, but I also, of course, want to hear from students who are struggling. The purpose of author's chair is both to show off accomplishment and to get help with revision. When students are not getting useful and appropriate comments from their response groups, author's chair provides a chance for a second opinion.

This second use of author's chair evolved from a conversation I had with Rene one day. He approached me, livid that he wasn't receiving helpful response on his writing from his peers. "How can I revise when I get dumb responses like these here?" he scowled, tossing the response sheets my way.

The suggestions for improving his piece included: "Rene, you need to spell better." "You need to have more show-not-tell." "Tell what was your mother's boyfriend's name." I told him I agreed that these comments were not helpful; they were either unspecific and unconnected to the content of the piece or too specific. To appease and support Rene, I decided, right then, to put him in author's chair. Rene then shared this writing:

> FIRST DRAFT: *one weekend I was learning how the bikeride. My mom's boyfriend was tecting me how to ride my Bike But I know how to ride my bike safer a wihl and I feel of my Bike and I hert my knie. It is fun to ride. I like ride my Bike at jaquin milar park and at my gradma's house and at Mrarit Collige and to Skyline Make and one more place is roberts park like to ride my Bike at Yosemite to. I can go Blasing than a speeding boolit on my Bike at Yoseite.*

His classmates proceeded to tell what they liked about the story and what he did well. Lastly, they asked questions and suggested improvements he could make, all of which I copied down:

Tell what the boyfriend's name is.

When did you fall?

You need show-not-tell.

How badly did it hurt when you fell?

What did they say when they were teaching you to ride the bike?

How old were you?

What does your bike look like?

How did you feel when you were riding your bike?

How many days did it take to learn?

I had Rene think overnight about what he wanted to do with all of this feedback. With the permission of Rene and his responders, I then showed an overhead transparency of this list of responses with Rene again on author's chair. I reminded everyone that as the author, it was totally Rene's decision as to which questions and suggestions he wanted to address in his second draft. Realizing he had such power, Rene now seemed to sit taller, basking in the attention. He then responded to his classmates: "I don't think it is important what my bike looks like although it was blue. Umm, I don't remember exactly what my mom and her boyfriend said or when this all happened. I will try to do the show-not-tell; that isn't hard. I have to think about the rest." Equipped with the contributions of his peers, Rene then wrote:

I'm Learning How to Ride My Bike

One weekend I was learning how to ride my bike. My mom's boyfriend Steve was teaching me how to ride my bike. But I know how to ride my bike a wihl. But I fell off of my bike and hret my knie reely bad. My niey hite so bad I felt like crying. My bike is blue. It is fun to ride. I like riding my bike at Joaquin Miller Park and at my gradmas house and at marit college and at rabers park and yseite. I can go faster than a speeding boolit on my bike. When I ride my bike I feel like I can ride my I bike all my life.

From that day on, the author's chair took on a new complexion as more and more students, like Rene, requested input from the whole class. Before they took the chair for this purpose, however, I required that they receive at least two peer responses. Seated there, they would ask specific questions about a work in progress: "What should I do with my writing now?" "What title should I give my story?" "How should I end this story?" "Where should I put show-not-tell?" "Do I have too much dialogue?"

In a reflective piece, Narami, a fourth-grader, expressed well the value of bringing an unfinished work to the author's chair:

It helped to be on author's chair because other people have more ideas than one person. The class had better ideas.

Thus, author's chair eventually became a richer pool from which students could draw ideas for change in their writing.

But my encounter with Rene lay bare another revision-related writers' workshop problem. Rene was getting "dumb responses" from some other students. This should not come as a surprise to most experienced teachers. We have noticed that the quality of response varies greatly from one student to another. How then are we to prevent the student who depends on response from others from feeling short changed?

I came upon a partial answer to this question when I read an article by Donald Graves in *Instructor Magazine* entitled "Experts in Writing." Graves suggests that there are students who have expertise in different aspects of writing in any classroom community. I was interested in this notion, as I thought it might help with the problem of inexpert response that plagued many students working on a revision. If each student had an expertise, then others could go to that person for assistance in a specific skill.

We began by generating a list of such proficiencies, using only about half:

show-not-tell	*similes*
using complete sentences	*metaphors*
words besides said	*using quotes in dialogue*
other words besides then	*sensory details*
using quotation marks	*poetry*
feelings of a character	*capitalization*
letter writing form	*character building*
vivid verbs	*leads*
possessives	*paragraphing*
setting a scene	*great endings*
dialogue	*catchy titles*
spelling	*humor*
transition words	

One day, I announced that I would be interviewing students to see if they qualified to be experts. I focused on only two proficiencies that morning. They were to sign up for conferences throughout the week and bring writing samples that proved they knew a particular skill. A buzz spread around the classroom, even a "Yes!" here and there, giving me clues that they were excited about this opportunity to prove their worth; quickly students began poring over their work, making corrections and additions. Revision was happening before my very eyes!

Sections like "show-not-tell" and "words besides *said*" quickly filled up, and with time, the experts then began interviewing their peers, freeing me to work with students in other areas. The experts were much more stringent about qualifying their peers than I would ever have been. When one interviewee was reduced to tears, we had to have an emergency meeting of experts to talk about being supportive while still testing. They learned a new word that day: *tact*.

What then were the results of such a venture? The more competitive and competent students tried to qualify for as many areas as possible so they also became risk-takers in their writing, plunging into areas like "thoughts and feelings of the character," "setting," and "character building," around which they previously tiptoed. Ironically, proofreading and revision became natural byproducts as students read, reread, and rewrote portions of their papers to perform well.

Becoming an expert was also a booster for those quieter students like Leona and Jesse who were superb spellers. They were very much in demand when students needed to edit their papers for publishing. They helped each student generate a list of words that he or she misspelled often. We depended less on parent volunteers for editing purposes as the students went to each other for help. Talk about building a classroom community!

To keep the experts from backsliding and falling into bad habits, I periodically asked for evidence that they were maintaining their skills. I put stars by their names on the "expert list" when they passed—more stars proved you were "too-good-to-be-true."

I met with the more reluctant students, offering them another pair of eyes with which to comb their papers to see areas where they were strong. Sean, almost afraid of his own shadow, was thrilled to see that he always got possessives correct, a skill mastered by very few students. Sandee, like several of my English language learner students, used *said* and other mundane verbs too often. With instruction from her best friend Katy, she began using the thesaurus and experimenting with word choices. Two weeks before the end of school, she became an expert in the category of "words besides *said*." Because students were motivated to qualify as experts, they were more attentive when I gave my minilessons. They now had ears to hear and the courage to try new strategies in writing. I had to chuckle when I saw Melissa even taking notes as I spoke.

There was, however, a downside to this generally successful technique. By definition the term *expert* is exclusive. Benjamin tried again and again to qualify for "catchy titles," but he just did not seem to have the catchy title gene, producing titles like "My Cute Dog" and "My Trip to San Diego." We looked at book titles and tables of contents to see if he could understand the gist of interesting titles. We brainstormed words he could add to "My Dog" to make it more exciting. Sadly, he didn't seem to understand. I tried to find other areas of expertise for him without much success. I still feel badly whenever I greet him in halls this year.

WRITING HALL OF FAME

As a way of showcasing writing that other students might admire and use as models for revision, we put together a flashy bulletin board titled "The Writing Hall of Fame," which was made up of snippets from such writing:

From Angela's "Home Alone": *He ran down the stairs and hopped on the couch and curled into a ball because he was so scared."*

Dennis from "The Abduction": *It was really weird. There were different lights from green to red to purple. It looked like Christmas. All they needed was a tree.*

Erica from "The Haunted House": *The porch steps creaked when I stepped on them. The door screeched when I pushed it. I felt something brushing the side of my head.*

Jesus from "Meow, Meow": *What's weird about [my cats] is Tippy meows like a lion and purrs like the pitter patter of a mouse's run. Mittens meows like a mouse and purrs like a volcano ready to erupt."*

Somehow, like some teacher-generated plans, the idea was easier to conceive than to carry out. Soon the board looked pathetically sparse. Before killing this project, I decided to ask three students, choosing those who were competent writers and already in the Hall of Fame, to form a committee responsible for finding treasured morsels of student writing for our Hall of Fame, whether they heard them during author's chair, while responding to writing, or merely through the grapevine. Ashley, one of the committee members, announced that they would be interviewing interested applicants for the Hall of Fame. Within weeks, we started to see students taking care to write with specificity in their pieces, even rewriting, to qualify as a Hall-of-Famer.

Committee members like Jake would occasionally ask my advice:

J: Mrs. M., do you think that Eric's paragraph should qualify for the Hall of Fame?

M: What did he write?

J: He wrote, 'The boy ran as fast as a cheetah across the school yard.' The rest of us on the committee feel that it is a sentence a lot of people write. It is kinda not a new idea.

M: Well, I will go along with the committee's opinion, Jake.

J: Yeah, we got a lot of those kinds of sentences lately: We just tell them go back and change that sentence. 'Try again,' we tell them.

M: Wow. You people are tough!

Soon after this conversation, I noticed Eric revising his cheetah sentence to give it originality or, as the kids say, "make it fresh."

After turning it over to the children, the Writing Hall of Fame generated renewed interest. Some children even gave up their recess to meet with the committee. Before each writing period, one committee member announced the new Hall-of-Famer, who then read his/her qualifying sentence or paragraph. A certificate designed by a child in our class was then awarded to the new member, followed by enthusiastic applause.

CONCLUSION

I have presented here some specific revision-related strategies that have evolved as I have done my research. It is my hope that teachers will be able to adapt some of these to serve their own classrooms and students. But I believe I learned more from my research than some specific classroom techniques. Reviewing what I have done over the past two years, I am struck by the fact that every time I got in a jam, it was the students who helped me out of it. I learned from them and with their help found better ways to do minilessons, author's chair, the Hall of Fame board, and more.

As I increasingly involved my students in the teaching of writing, asking them to help me find answers to sticky pedagogical problems, they responded with enthusiasm, generosity, and wisdom. In essence, they taught me as much as I did them—teaching turned full circle.

REFERENCES

Graves, Donald. "Experts in Writing." *Instructor*.

Energy Conversion: The Evolution of Experimenters' Workshop

Alexa Stuart

This article was written by Alexa Stuart about her teaching experience with fourth grade students in San Francisco, California. It was originally published in the summer 1996 issue of The Quarterly.

As a teacher, you know in your gut when something is not working in your classroom. You see it in your students' faces. And with any classroom problem, I, like many other teachers, often look in one of two directions for an explanation: either it is the students or it is my teaching.

In this case, I knew that the students were not enjoying my laboratory science class, and neither were they gaining a deep understanding of what makes the field of science so amazing. One afternoon, cleaning up vegetable oil vials after a step-by-step density experiment, I formed an explanation based on my students. "They don't appreciate how hard I am trying," I thought. "They don't realize how very boring it would be if I just used textbooks as my teachers did."

I might have stayed in this frame of mind if an image of one of my students hadn't flashed through my mind at that moment. During writers' workshop the day before, one of the fourth grade girls, Lizzie, had been drafting an outline of an upcoming chapter book on the dry erase board. She was drawing pictures and writing words, and she could barely keep her arm moving fast enough to capture her thoughts. Her cheeks were flushed with excitement, and her voice stammered as she tried to slow down to explain the plot to me.

"These are students who love to learn," I thought to myself, "given the right circumstances." I shifted to think about my teaching. My students love writers' workshop because they are treated like real authors. How could I treat my students like true scientists? How could I allow them to peek behind the curtain to experience the work that keeps scientists absorbed for years on a single problem? "The heart and soul of science is experimentation," I thought to myself. "Why not model an experimenters' workshop after writers' workshop?"

At that moment, I stopped trying to scrub out the oily, sticky vials and sat down at a student desk to draft my plan for experimenters' workshop. Instead of writing books, the children would create experiments during experimenters' workshop. Instead of having featured authors for students to present their stories, we would have featured scientists at the end of the workshop. Students would share what they did, what they noticed, and why they thought it happened.

This was a breakthrough, certainly, but it was also the culmination of all the training I had had thus far as a student of life and as a teacher.

Since that time, when teaching problems arise, I have wasted less time faulting the students and more time experimenting to make the classroom work. Rather than blame the children, I look deeply into their worlds and into my teaching, and there I find endless, if tentative, answers.

~ *Alexa Stuart, 2002*

*O*ne day, in the last year of my training to become a teacher, Dick Rezba, my instructor in a science methods class, set a bag in front of each student. The bags contained a collection of objects that inspired no particular excitement: wires, coils, batteries, and magnets.

"I want you to experiment with these for about thirty minutes," Dick said, "and then we will share what we discovered."

I opened my bag hesitantly, almost frightened to touch anything. I had rarely touched things in science class, except on command. Hands-on-science in my education usually meant watching demonstrations and conducting experiments to the rhythmic mantra, "Okay, don't touch until I tell you. Otherwise, it might not turn out right." Now I was invited to touch without restriction. In the classroom, the excitement was palpable.

"Wow, look at this!"

"Does yours do that when you put the magnet close?"

"Let me see if it does that again."

"What did you do to make yours do that?"

"I wonder why it does this?"

"I wonder if it's because the magnet affects the electrons' flow?"

"Let's see: if the current is flowing because of the magnet, then this should happen when I try this."

At the end of thirty minutes, we had a lively discussion about what we had observed and why we thought it had happened. I realized that in sixteen years of science education, this was the first time I had been allowed to truly experiment.

Dick went on to encourage us to create experiments based on our interests. I liked to make chocolate chip cookies, so he encouraged me to brainstorm cookie experiments. For example, I compared the taste of cookies made with margarine to those made with butter.

I came to realize that, outside of science class, I had been doing the work of a scientist over much of my life. Years earlier, for instance, when my brother and I had raced home from the neighborhood store, each using a route we believed was shorter, we were conducting experiments. Our argument about whether one of us was running faster than the other was an argument about controlling variables. When our mother tried to help us settle the dispute by driving the two routes, odometer running, we were left—because no automobile can cut corners like a kid in full flight—with a dose of the uncertainty that drives scientific work. I had also been conducting experiments during my student teaching when I tried a new approach to quiet a noisy class, reflected on the results, and used this information to inform my next approach.

I was excited by my new understanding of the purpose of science and experimenting. Experiments moved from the pages of the science fair books into day-to-day reality. However, when I began teaching, the demands of the curriculum, the pressures of the job, and my own insecurities about trying something new made it difficult for me to change my science program from the way I had been taught in elementary school.

As a new teacher, I became involved with the writing project and was exposed to the concept of writers' workshop. It made so much sense to me. Of course, students learn to write by actually writing instead of by filling out worksheets. In writers' workshop, I had children craft pieces according to their own interests and experiences, hire editors, and publish their work as they became "featured authors." Students begged for more writing time. They dedicated themselves to the task of producing quality work they could share with others. They constantly surprised me and themselves with fresh insights.

Science class, however, had no such flow to it. Even though I prepared for hours trying to make the curriculum goals clear—for example, teaching the relationship between mass, weight, density, and volume—my science teaching left me feeling strangely empty. I often used writing to test the students' understanding of a science concept, but the unspoken reality was that students were often writing for me and not their classmates, and it showed. The writing lacked depth and enthusiasm. And to be honest, I didn't look forward to reading thirty explanations of how photosynthesis works.

My other goal was to use hands-on experiments, so I led the class through experiments I found in books. It was a constant struggle to keep the children following the prescribed steps. When I had the class respond to questions about experiments, again their writing was rote and predictable.

Demonstrations could be equally frustrating. I worked hard to prepare them, spending time prepping and getting everything just right. Then came the "wow," and then it was over with lots of cleanup ahead.

I became particularly aware that my science class lacked purpose when I contrasted it with the excitement and energy of the writers' workshop. When I had children write their thoughts about writing, they wrote:

Writing is a wondrous thing. Whatever you're thinking ends up on your paper before you even finish thinking about it.

Writers' workshop is like blossoming into a new flower.

When I had them write about science they wrote:

Science is like a pencil. It begins and soon it's gone.

Science is like learning about one topic after another in a lot of detail.

Science is like . . . I couldn't think of anything.

This writing exercise affirmed what I had noticed. How could I explain the difference between students' clear and joyful statements about writing and their foggy, uninspired statements about science? And what was I going to do about it?

After a great many false starts and days when I put in more time hoping that things would feel different, I thought back to my experience in college. Maybe I could create a science workshop much like my writers' workshop. Just as students in writers' workshop became engaged as writers, students in experimenters' workshop could become engaged as scientists: constructing hypotheses, experimenting, and sharing findings. I would start with a minilesson and then, just as students in writers' workshop designed their own pieces, students in science workshop would design their own experiments. In both, students would write, share, respond to each other, and publish their finished work.

I decided to give it a try. Since we had been discussing states of matter, I gave each child a cotton ball dipped in rubbing alcohol and a cotton ball dipped in water, and I threw in a piece of recycled paper for good measure. I explained the basic structure for what we would be calling "experimenters' workshop." I made clear that the process would be similar to writers' workshop. I told students they could use any tools on the science shelves, such as scales and thermometers, and that they should write down their observations and explanations so that we could share them. My biggest fear was that when I said, "Now, experiment," they would not know what to do.

I was surprised that my brief guidelines were not followed by a barrage of questions. The students seemed to know exactly what to do.

Of course, a part of me was hoping that within the context of their new-found freedom students would still do what I wanted them to do. That is, since

315

we were studying states of matter, they would compare the evaporation rates of alcohol and water. Some students did. One student was glancing back and forth between the clock and the streaks of rubbing alcohol and water she had made on her recycled paper. When the alcohol streak disappeared, she recorded the time in her learning log and then recorded the time when her water streak disappeared. She subtracted, calculating the difference.

But most students went in directions that would not have occurred to me. One student dropped her two cotton balls from above her head to the recycled paper on the floor to see if one dropped faster than the other. One child was weighing each cotton ball to see if one weighed more than the other. Suddenly, the students cared if their measurements were accurate, and they put me to work with tasks such as showing them how to recalibrate a scale.

They were completely absorbed in their work and talking like scientists. I heard conversations like this one:

"Wow, look at the different color the alcohol makes on the paper compared to the water."

"Does yours do that, too?"

"I wonder if the same thing happens on a different color paper? I think I'll try it."

I was no longer on center stage. Rather, I moved about the room, prodding students with questions they were probably already asking themselves: "Why do you think that happened?" "How can you test that theory?"

For the first time in my science class, everyone wanted to share, to be the featured scientist. We ran out of time to share findings, and children were disappointed. But I was very excited and wrote in my journal that night all about experimenters' workshop and how I could improve it.

As I modified the structure for experimenters' workshop, I kept in mind the elements that made writers' workshop run smoothly. In writers' workshop, I started with minilessons that introduced students to everything from story starters to the conventions of capitalization. For experimenters' workshop, we had science minilessons: lessons on content provided in our science curriculum (for instance, how photosynthesis works); lessons on how to better use scientists' tools, such as scales and thermometers; lessons sharing exciting stories behind discoveries; lessons about current puzzles in science, such as how life began.

Next came experimenting time and writing time. I provided materials based on the content area we were studying. For example, when we studied heat energy, I supplied ice. When we studied plants, I brought seeds, flowers, and leaves. I tried to find cheap items and encouraged students to use creative materials: heat from their bodies during our study of heat, leaves they themselves had collected as we studied plants. The class was told to use the materials to learn about the subject we were studying, but the rest was up to them. Sometimes I would pose a specific problem for the whole class. I'd ask, for instance, "Which is denser, vinegar or water?" and let them create different experiments to find out.

When children wanted to meet with me, they signed up on the chalkboard. They usually wanted to show me something. If I saw something creative, I'd say, "You really ought to publish that. The class will love it." To publish their findings, the students had to write about what they did, what happened, and why they think it happened. I also wanted students to assess the chances that their speculation was, in fact, correct.

They were then expected to work with another student who served as a content editor to comment on their work, and if they wanted to present as a featured scientist—a role similar to the featured author in writers' workshop—they were required to hand in a checklist certifying they had completed all the necessary steps.

Featured scientists received feedback on their work, both strengths and suggestions. One featured scientist, Jessica, presented her experiment to discover whether vinegar or oil was denser. As the room settled, she began reading her paper while standing behind a desk on which were placed bags of oil and vinegar and a scale.

Vinegar Is the Key

My experiment shows that vinegar is more dense. I have complete confidence in my experiment because I was as accurate as I could be.

What I Did

To prove that vinegar is more dense I did an experiment. I put some vinegar into a plastic bag. Then I put the exact same amount of oil in another plastic bag the same size. Then I put both bags on the scale in our classroom.

What I Observed

When I put the bags on the scale, the side with the vinegar automatically dropped. That shows that vinegar is more dense.

317

Then Jessica put the bags on the scale, demonstrating what she had just reported.

Hands shot up. As with writers' workshop, students have been encouraged to make positive comments: "I like the way you made up your experiment," one student said. "I think that was a good test."

"It was clear and easy to understand," said another.

Other students had questions. "What if the scale is just wrong?" one asked.

Jessica said, "No, I thought it was at first, so I tried it on two different scales. Look." And she was off to the back of the room to grab another scale to weigh it again for the class.

"Are you sure you put the same amount in each bag?" another student wanted to know.

"Yes, Ms. Stuart was there when I measured it. Weren't you?" said Jessica.

When Jessica was finished with her presentation, she put her paper in our published science discoveries binder.

Students love to be featured scientists, so sometimes they write quickly and ignore their editors. For instance, when we were studying heat, I made ice cubes and thermometers available to the class. Two students decided to see if they could find something to melt ice quickly. At the end of class, they published their findings called "Which Ice Cube Will Melt First?" They read:

We have three containers. In one container, there is just soap. In another container it is water. In the last container it has water and baking soda. We are going to find out which ice cube melts first.

After a few minutes . . .
1) baking soda
2) plain water
3) soap

They found that the ice cube with the baking soda melted first, then the ice cube with the water, and then the ice cube with the soap. That's all there was to it. The students liked this experiment, but because the write-up had been cursory, the questioning was also cursory. I thought this would be a good experiment to take farther, so I photocopied the experiment and the next day asked all the students to try the same experiment to see if it turned out the same.

At the end of that next class, many students were racing to find editors, eager to publish findings that differed from the results of the original experiment. Two students published a write-up called "Ice":

> We did the same experiment, but we did things more correct. First of
> all we made sure that each ice cube was exactly the same size. Second
> of all we put the same amount of everything so that there wouldn't be
> more baking soda etc. We put baking soda in first, then soap, then water.
> Answer: The ice with the water melted first. The ice with the soap melted
> second. The ice with the baking soda melted third.

> List (to make sure you do it right)
> 1) You have to have the same size ice cubes.
> 2) You have to have the same amount of water, soap, and baking soda.
> 3) You have to have the same size containers.
> 4) The ice cubes have to be the same temperature.
> 5) If one container has a top, all the containers have to have a top. If
>   one container doesn't have a top, all the containers have to not have
>   a top.
> 6) One container can't be closer to the window than the others.
> 7) Don't do anything to one and not all, like mixing.

Not all students had the same results, although, surprisingly, water melted the ice first overall. After this presentation, the whole class started to pay more attention to variables, although they didn't yet use the word. Neither had my brother and I when, at about their age, we were arguing about the "fastest" route to the store and yelling, "Yeah, well maybe you just run faster." And, like my brother and me, students began to struggle with the uncertainty of what they discovered. They began to realize all the things that can go wrong. Fewer announced, as had Jessica, "I have complete confidence in my experiment because I was as accurate as I could be." More papers were ending with conclusions like:

> Yes we are pretty sure [of our theory]. But not really sure. We could do
> many other experiments to be more sure.

I thought back on a comment a student had made when, a couple of years earlier, I had encouraged students to use a certain hands-on science book to try

319

some experiments over the summer: "If you know exactly how the experiment is supposed to turn out, what is the point of doing it?" Now, like working scientists, my students are not sure how their experiments are going to turn out, and they find that process thrilling.

This year, although we spent less time going over formal content such as density or photosynthesis, their working knowledge of basic content seems far stronger than it did last year. The students use science vocabulary frequently when they write and have many chances to use content to devise theories explaining why things happen. I have a much clearer insight into their understanding of concepts.

I learned from my experience with writers' workshop that school writing does not need to be divided into so many little parts that what students do no longer resembles the art of writing. When I applied the concepts of writers' workshop to science, I found a way to present science so it would not be diced into narrow activities that rob students of the joy of asking, "What will happen if I try this?" and then embarking on a journey of experiment and explanation to find out.

Now when I ask my students to complete the statement "Science is . . . ," the responses are dramatically different than they were a year ago:

Science is finding a problem and figuring out a way to solve it and then trying to solve it and seeing if it works.

To me it is trying to find out different things. You do experiments every single day. Sometimes you don't even know it. If you don't experiment that means you never try new foods, clothes, hair styles and you just don't try any new things at all.

Science is like jumping higher and higher until you find the things you were looking for.

Science is like being surrounded by many doors. Each door is a different experiment with a different answer. It all depends on which door you pick.

TWO WORKSHOPS COMPARED

WRITERS' WORKSHOP	*EXPERIMENTERS' WORKSHOP*
1. To learn to write, you must actually write.	1. To learn to do science, you must be engaged in the core activities of science: constructing hypotheses, conducting experiments, and sharing findings.
2. Authors need to design their own pieces according to their own interests and experiences.	2. Young scientists need to design their own experiments according to their interests and experiences. Young scientists need to learn that they can create their own categories and have the flexibility of thought to see the world in a new way if it is needed.
3. The purpose of teaching writing goes beyond preparing certain students to be published authors as adults. All children and adults grow from the joy of sharing their messages through their writing.	3. The purpose of science education is not simply to create career scientists. All children and adults benefit from using the core elements of science as a way of gaining knowledge in all areas of life.
4. Children need to recognize themselves as authors.	4. Children need to recognize themselves as scientists.
5. Although the process of writing can be sorted into clear steps, these steps take on individual life with each person and each piece.	5. Although the process of science (the scientific method) can be sorted into clear steps, these steps take on individual life with each person and each spark of curiosity.

321

Romance in the Classroom: Inviting Discourse on Gender and Power

Diane Waff

Diane Waff wrote this article about her teaching experience with high school students in Philadelphia, Pennsylvania. A version of it first appeared in The Voice of the Philadelphia Writing Project *and was later published in the spring 1995 issue of* The Quarterly.

This article grew out of my concerns about unequal power relations between boys and girls in a special education program in which the boys outnumbered the girls eight to one. This inequity in numbers influenced the program's curriculum content and pedagogy and privileged the boys in the school and the classroom. I became concerned about students' learning under these conditions and my own role in perpetuating hierarchies in classroom relationships.

Out of these concerns came my teacher inquiry question: "What happens when my students and I consider issues of gender and power in our racially and ethnically diverse special education English class?" Exploring power relations both inside and outside the classroom provided insights into students' words and interactions, particularly their participation in classroom talk about texts. As part of my teacher research, I listened closely to student-to-student talk, recorded classroom discussions, analyzed student talk in a line-by-line manner, examined student journal entries, and conducted focus groups with students to explore their views. My investigation revealed that the girls did not find school a safe place, that they were being abused by their male classmates, and that they did not see me, their female teacher, as an ally. This perception alerted me to acknowledge that my practice was inconsistent with my values and caused me to examine my own words and actions.

Exploring the ways in which students participated in classroom talk about gender and power issues became a conscious part of classroom discussion and inquiry. This helped me understand the complexities lying just beneath the surface of my students' social lives. These new insights indicated that incorporating the "evaded curriculum" into the classroom discourse has a positive effect on individual student lives and on the well-being of the wider classroom and school community.

~ *Diane Waff, 2002*

I teach in the Leadership House, a program for mildly learning-disabled special education students in a large comprehensive Philadelphia high school. I work with approximately eighty boys and twenty-two girls, mostly working-class African Americans, Euro-Americans, and Latinos.

The strong male presence in this program has overwhelmed the girls. Classroom discussions, book selections, and even our system of rewards and punishments have favored boys. Boys select the movie of the month—a reward for perfect attendance—and classroom discipline has typically been meted out with a "boys will be boys" attitude. For instance, a girl enters the room to deliver a message, and a boy makes a lewd remark about certain parts of her body. When I look to the administration in disciplining the boy, I am told, "That's what boys do."

This environment is one that has encouraged sexual harassment and victimization of weaker students. It is one that has sent a clear message that appropriate behavior includes power and domination over others. Misunderstandings between boys and girls have often erupted into violent confrontations, and often girls have faded into the background, overpowered by more aggressive male voices. These gender conflicts have cut across racial and cultural lines. At Leadership House, my colleagues and I decided we needed to act to confront this unhealthy situation.

"GIRL TALK" GIVES FEMALES A VOICE

Three years ago, with the assistance of two volunteers—an African American female attorney and a Latina engineer—we began "Girl Talk." These were voluntary sessions that at first took place during the school day twice a month and now are held after school. The purpose of these sessions has been to encourage girls to raise issues of concern to them. And that is what they have done. Girls have revealed their dissatisfaction with a wide range of practices, including school curriculum, discipline policy, and biased teacher-student interactions. They have said they were tired of reading adventure stories featuring only males in heroic roles, that they were fed up with being called epithets like "bitch" and "whore," and that they disliked having their desires sacrificed for the male "majority."

Perhaps not surprisingly, as girls began to take part in these Girl Talk sessions, the boys complained bitterly over the creation of a program for girls only. They were also anxious for their stories to be heard and wanted an exclusive time just for boys. Although we did not set up a corresponding boys' group, I did devise a way for all students to make themselves heard on the problematic male-female interactions—both in school and out—that interfered with our ability to get through the school day comfortably.

JOURNAL WRITING IMPROVES GENDER-BASED INTERACTION

My first act was to initiate a ten-minute freewrite journal time at the beginning of each class period in which students focused on these issues. At first, some of the entries were perhaps predictable. Boys, for instance, complained of having to pay for dates, of being called on to lift heavy objects, and of being expected to serve as a girl's protector when she stirred up trouble. But as students wrote more, the level of hatred, violence, and pain expressed in these journal writings became truly frightening. Girls wrote things like, "David keeps touching me. I want to get up and punch him in the face until he bleeds," and "I hate my body, the boys moo every time I come in the room." The boys' entries included some such as, "These female teachers—I'm going to kill Ms. Smith, if she gets in my face one more time," and "The hookers in this school are nothing but money hungry hos." I myself showed my feelings, writing in my journal, "I hate the way the boys treat me. I know they don't tell Mr. Brown they love him when he gives them a reprimand."

Our collective anger over what we perceived as harassment by the opposite sex fueled passionate writing for more than two months. There wasn't an idle pen in the class, as it became clear to us that the negative interactions had taken their toll on our ability to function as a community. Over time, we came to agree that men and women need to treat each other more respectfully.

WRITING FOCUSES ON MALE-FEMALE RELATIONSHIPS

Next, I began to introduce novels, stories, and poems that considered themes of romance, love, and marriage. We looked at traditional works like *Romeo and Juliet* and de Maupassant's "The Necklace," as well as nontraditional works such as Nicholasa Mohr's novella *Herman and Alice* and Walter Dean Myers's *Motown and DiDi*. I found that by making issues of equality, sexism, sexual harassment, abuse, gender, and power a conscious part of group discussion, class inquiry, and writing, we opened up entirely new interpretations of the traditional works and stimulated inquiry into the nontraditional ones.

When students began to write about this literature, there was a great deal of dissonance between male and female responses. The girls focused on feelings and had idealized views on love, dating, and marriage. The boys focused on money, sex, and the fleeting nature of romantic attachments in the context of the pulls of everyday life. The following excerpts from student essays and critiques on love and marriage reflect these diverse male-female perspectives. One girl, Alex, responded:

> *The reason why people get married is because they don't want to leave each other's sides. They want to be with each other, have kids and take care of them, and get really close to each other. . . . If I got married I would be so happy. I really would take care of my husband and take him out once in a while. He would take me out too. We would never leave.*

Gabrielle said:

> *Well as for me, I think people get married because they love each other. They are happy with each other and they want to be a part of each other . . . . If I were married I would be happy to be with my husband and we would be together forever. We would love each other for life.*

Howard demonstrates a less idealistic view:

> *"Bullship"* [sic]
>
> *. . . If I said it once, I said it a thousand times, love is nothing but a four letter word to try to score. I think when a girl and a guy like each other, they might do some things together but not all things—and that will come to an end. All good things must come to an end because god darn it, Eve ate the apple!*

(Note: Howard ended all journal entries, essays, and diatribes against some particular stance taken by girls or me with "Eve ate the apple." This view of the original sin as a female responsibility and a sign of feminine psychological weakness was strongly echoed by many of the African American males espousing church fundamentalist views.)

Howard, along with many of the males in the class, did not permit himself to accept the possibility of the kind of love detailed in Engle's poem. His doubts are underscored by his descent into the macho description of love as being just another word for sexual conquest.

The traditional sex role stereotypes reflected in these journal entries began to change only when students started reading reality-based literature that focused on relations between the sexes. For instance, after a discussion in which students contrasted the relationships in de Maupassant's "The Necklace" and those in Nicholasa Mohr's unconventional *Herman and Alice*, a story of a heterosexual woman and a gay man, students began to explore the reasons for the ongoing conflict between males and females.

James wrote:

When you like women, they think you are supposed to do everything for them. It's not like we can't . . . it's like we won't. Women make men do the dumbest things. It just ain't right! Can't we get along? Like and love are two different things. Just because we call you, doesn't mean we need you. Women want it all . . . love, money, cars, money, money, money, and more money.

Marta wrote:

Some men think that if they give women money, cars and jewelry that women think that means they love you. It's not that way, because we women see it a totally different way. Well they're not showing us they care by giving us money and a car, even though they do that. To express love all they have to do is say they love us. The meaning of love is strong affection for each other. That is what love is. . . .

When Marta read this aloud in class, her view shocked many of the young men, who had believed that most women expect money as a sign of affection. As the boys and girls talked, they began to realize they had many similar reactions to the characters' behavior in these two works. Both boys and girls objected to Mme. Loisel's failure to support her husband in "The Necklace," and both agreed that Alice in *Herman and Alice* had valid reasons to leave. When I asked students to think and write about the kinds of issues raised in this literature and in their lives, they and I had a chance to discuss our feelings honestly. Boys and girls began to share ideas, and they began to notice they had similar notions on many issues.

FOLLOW-UP TALK CONFRONTS GENDER ISSUES

Our commitment as a class to asking different questions began to have a positive effect. In one discussion, the girls and I challenged the boys' use of the phrase "booty calls," which signifies a phone call to a girl for sex. The girls were unanimous in their disapproval of a term that disparages all women. The boys grudgingly acknowledged our complaint and vowed to reconsider its use. Even when students went on to another class, they continued to discuss the pain the term evokes for girls. The female teacher in that class was so impressed that she came to me vowing to speak out against sexist remarks not only in the classroom but in the faculty room as well.

But even when we thought we were making progress, deep-seated biases continued to surface, as when we read the short story "Spilled Salt" by Beverly Neeley. The story, about the rape of a young woman by a man who offers her a ride home, brought out attitudes we thought we had overcome. The boys made statements like "Dress like a ho, you get what you deserve." They put forward the stereotypical male view of what constitutes a "good girl" and a "bad girl."

This stance was an invitation to the girls to become assertive. They stood up for themselves and actively challenged sexism and demeaning stereotypes. They asserted their right to wear anything they wanted without fear of getting groped or raped. They challenged the notion that a single woman without a man is sexually suspect or that someone is asking for trouble when she goes out alone. One male student's blame-the victim question, "Didn't her mother teach her not to get in the car with a stranger?" was decisively countered by the comment, "Didn't his mother teach him it's wrong to rape people?"

When I recounted this exchange to a colleague in a gender studies group run by the Philadelphia Writing Project, she pointed out that this comment points to the universal perception that it is the female responsibility to teach moral behavior. I took this back to my classroom and put it on the floor for discussion. Both boys and girls agreed that it is the duty of fathers as well as mothers to provide moral leadership. It was Howard—the "Eve ate the apple" boy—who had the last comment about the incident presented in the story: "I guess you can't put it all on the woman either."

There is now a growing will and commitment by my entire class to hear the girls' voices. Girls have been empowered by collective strength from their participation in Girl Talk, and journal writing and classroom conversations have created a space in which girls can now speak out when they see me favoring boys.

CONCLUSION

All of this experience has led me to look at my own behavior. I have become much more aware of my tendency to call on boys and to engage them in conversation. In the past, I did this to maintain classroom control by keeping the more vocal boys engaged, but the girls let me know through private conversations, journal writes, and open discussion that this practice was indefensible. Now, I work hard to make room for girls' talk and defend girls' space by constantly reiterating the norms for classroom behavior: "Talk one at a time and respect each other." Now I encourage the girls to be more assertive, to give their opinions, and to stand up for themselves. I actively challenge sexism and stereotypes, and I don't hesitate to question the subtle undercutting I get from male students who choose to give me compliments at inappropriate times.

I am committed as a woman teacher to model strategies of resistance to gender, racial, and cultural bias by asking students what they think and insisting they reflect on diverse perspectives. We call on a discourse of empowerment sustained by feminist pedagogy:

> *Public schools constitute a sphere in which young women could be offered access to a language and experience of empowerment. In such contexts, "well-educated" young women could breathe life into positions of social critique and experience entitlement rather than victimization, autonomy rather than terror.* (Fine 1992, 59)

We are on the road to building healthy classroom relationships that help students become conscious of fairness and equality both in school and out. My students and I work together as a team, and I no longer assume the total burden of maintaining classroom discipline. The students monitor negative interactions, and often just a "Be cool, man" from a peer is enough to get back on track. One of the students who most frequently expressed sexist attitudes and made unwelcome physical conduct recently wrote to me, "I don't know if I learned a lot of new information in this class per se, but it is making me look at things in a different way."

What's different is that I have incorporated into classroom discourse issues of gender and power—what has been called by the American Association of University Women the "evaded curriculum." I have done this by using traditional and nontraditional literature, discussion, and written reflection. The effect has been to improve the lives of individual students and the social well-being of the wider school community.

REFERENCES

American Association of University Women. 1992. "Executive Summary." *AAUW Report: How Schools Shortchange Girls*. Washington, DC: AAUW Educational Foundation.

Engle, P. 1987. "Together." In *Relationships*, ed. M. Spring. New York: Scholastic.

Fine, M. 1992. *Disruptive Voices: The Possibilities of Feminist Research*. Ann Arbor: University of Michigan Press.

A FEW WORDS ABOUT THE AUTHORS . . .

MYRON BERKMAN

Myron Berkman teaches English language development and social studies at Berkeley High School in Berkeley, California. He is a teacher-consultant with the Bay Area Writing Project, at the University of California, Berkeley. He is also the author of *Our Lives*, a reading and writing book for beginning English learners, published by Linmore Publishing. He was a Peace Corps volunteer in Thailand from 1973-1975 and has a wicked serve in tennis.

PEN CAMPBELL

Pen Campbell teaches eighth, ninth, and twelfth grade English at Lake Michigan Catholic High School in St. Joseph, Michigan. She is a teacher-consultant with the Third Coast Writing Project at Western Michigan University and, with Scott Peterson, has led Teacher as Writer Advanced Institutes. Her poetry has appeared in the *Language Arts Journal of Michigan, Home and Other Places: Voices of Southwest Michigan, Grass Roots Review,* and other magazines.

EDWARD DARLING

Edward Darling teaches at South Burlington High School in Vermont and is a teacher-consultant with the National Writing Project in Vermont, at the University of Vermont. He strives to teach Ken Macrories's principles of personal-public writing, as described in *Writing To Be Read*. Since high school, Darling's student Kyle Ransom (whose work is featured in Darling's article) has begun college where he is majoring in English. He continues to write, concentrating on short stories.

DINA SECHIO DECRISTOFARO

Dina Sechio DeCristofaro is a co-director of the Rhode Island Writing Project at Rhode Island College. She teaches fifth grade at Hope Elementary School in Scituate, Rhode Island.

ROGER GREEN

Roger Green is a teacher-consultant with the Northern Virginia Writing Project at George Mason University. He teaches ninth grade English at Thomas Jefferson High School for Science and Technology in Fairfax County, Virginia.

JEAN HICKS

Jean Hicks is the director of the Louisville Writing Project at the University of Louisville in Kentucky. Through school partnerships, she also works directly with teachers and students at three elementary schools and three middle schools to improve learning through better writing and reading instruction. She has co-authored two National Council of Teachers of English (NCTE) books on metaphorical thinking and has co-authored a manuscript with Tim Johnson on teaching students to write plays.

ROMANA HILLEBRAND

Romana Hillebrand currently teaches writing at Washington State University in Pullman, Washington. Prior to moving to the Northwest, she taught at the secondary level in the Los Angeles Unified School District for fourteen years. A board member of the Northwest Inland Writing Project (NIWP) at the University of Idaho, where she taught for six years, she has presented papers on rhetorical strategies at various conferences sponsored by NIWP and NCTE, among others. The first chapter of her thesis on collaboration in the writing classroom was published in *English Journal.*

DAN HOLT

Dan Holt, a co-director of the Third Coast Writing Project at Western Michigan University and a former Michigan Writing Teacher of the Year, teaches creative writing at St. Joseph High School, in St. Joseph, Michigan, where he is also the advisor for the newspaper and literary magazine.

JIM HORRELL

Jim Horrell teaches sixth grade language arts and social studies at Murray Avenue School in Lower Moreland Township School District in southeastern Pennsylvania. He is a teacher-consultant with the Pennsylvania Writing and Literature Project (PAWLP), where he is also a coordinator for PAWLP's young readers/young writers summer program. In his spare time, he is rewriting a novel for young adults.

CATHERINE HUMPHREY

Catherine Humphrey is a teacher-consultant with the Inland Area Writing Project at the University of California, Riverside. She has taught English at every level from middle school to university and currently works as English chair at Los Osos High School in Alta Loma, California. She works with the California Writing Project as part of a teacher-research team called Improving Students' Academic Writing. She is particularly interested in developing protocols for looking at student work publicly: a collaborative between teachers, students, and parents.

TIM JOHNSON

Tim Johnson is a co-director of the Louisville Writing Project at the University of Louisville, Kentucky, and teaches English and drama at Central High School in Louisville.

335

SUZANNE LINEBARGER

Suzanne Linebarger is the inservice director for the Northern California Writing Project at California State University, Chico. She teaches third and fourth grade at Pines Elementary School in Chico, California.

SARAH LORENZ

Sarah Lorenz teaches high school English and Christian studies at Franklin Road Christian School in Novi, Michigan. She is also the school's new programs director and works with school change and staff development. She is the teacher facilitator for professional development with the Eastern Michigan Writing Project at Eastern Michigan University, and has published articles such as "Professional Whining" in *KAPPAN*, as well as others in *English Journal* and *The Quarterly*.

JAN MATSUOKA

Jan Matsuoka retired from the Oakland Unified School District in 2000, where she had been teaching third grade. Her continued work with the Bay Area Writing Project (BAWP) at the University of California, Berkeley, enables her to stay connected to teaching through the periodic workshops she gives and the inservice series she has coordinated at school sites. Among recent ventures, she had the rewarding experience of coaching two teachers preparing to give their presentations for the BAWP Summer Institute, and she has helped organize a monthly poetry group where writers share poetry and exchange new ideas for writing.

KAREN MURAR

Karen Murar is a teacher-consultant with the Western Pennsylvania Writing Project at the University of Pittsburgh. She has taught secondary English for twenty-eight years at Gateway High School, Monroeville, Pennsylvania.

KATHLEEN O'SHAUGHNESSY

Kathleen O'Shaughnessy is a co-director of the National Writing Project of Acadiana at the University of Louisiana at Lafayette. She teaches sixth grade reading/writing workshop at Episcopal School of Acadiana, a small independent school in Cade, Louisiana. She is a National Board certified teacher in early adolescent English language arts and also works for the Louisiana State Department of Education as a mentor for National Board candidates.

SCOTT PETERSON

Scott Peterson is an Instructional Support Specialist in the Mattawan, Michigan, school district. He is a teacher-consultant for the Third Coast Writing Project at Western Michigan University and teaches writing classes for teachers at the university. He is co-author of the book *Theme Exploration: A Voyage of Discovery* and wrote one of the chapters for *Lessons to Share on Teaching Grammar in Context*.

BOB PRESSNALL

Bob Pressnall is a teacher-consultant with the Bay Area Writing Project at the University of California, Berkeley, and teaches at Albany Middle School in Albany, California.

ANNE RODIER

Anne Rodier teaches English and creative writing at Louisville Central High School, a demonstration site of the Louisville Writing Project at the University of Louisville, Kentucky. She is a National Board certified teacher and author of numerous articles and the book, *What Do You Say to a Man Who Is Dying. . . .*

GERRI RUCKEL

Gerri Ruckel is a teacher-consultant with the Pennsylvania Writing and Literature Project (PAWLP) at West Chester University. She has taught writing and literature in the Lower Moreland Township School District for thirty years and has been awarded the Lower Moreland Excellence Pin for outstanding teaching. Currently she teaches sixth grade language arts readers/writers workshop.

RAY SKJELBRED

Ray Skjelbred teaches seventh grade at the Marin Country Day School in Corte Madera, California.

PATRICIA SLAGLE

Patricia Slagle spent twenty-eight years as a public high school English teacher in Louisville, Kentucky. During that time, she taught all grade and ability levels but found herself most frequently teaching challenged students in upper grades. She also served as an English department chair during that period. Her numerous National Council of Teachers of English (NCTE) presentations have included various writing-related topics as well as her other interests: incorporating critical viewing skills in language arts instruction and classroom management. She has served on the NCTE Executive Committee and as a program and convention chair for NCTE. She currently works as a language arts consultant for textbook publisher McDougal Littell. She is affiliated with the Louisville Writing Project at the University of Louisville, Kentucky.

ALEXA STUART

Alexa Stuart is currently working to refine experimenters' workshop at an enrichment program in San Francisco. She is a teacher-consultant with the Bay Area Writing Project at the University of California, Berkeley, and is currently working with NASA to help primary students understand the Cassini mission to Saturn. Her two primary research focuses are: how to make experimenters' workshop work better for younger children, and how to create balanced writing programs. Stuart, who has taught first- through fifth-graders, has been known to say to her students, "Everything is an experiment!"

BOB TIERNEY

Bob Tierney is a teacher-consultant with the Bay Area Writing Project at the University of California, Berkeley. He retired from the classroom after thirty-two years of teaching high school biology and general science and coaching both football and baseball. He now lives in Poker

Bar, California, and spends most of his time trying to be the world's best unpublished writer of adventure stories.

PETER TRENOUTH

Peter Trenouth is now in his second year with the Whitman-Hanson Regional School District in Whitman, Massachusetts, where he is the language arts coordinator. He previously spent twenty-nine years teaching high school English. He still teaches one class of junior English and continues to stress to both teachers and students writing's potential for serving intellectual investigation and personal reflection. Since his work in the 1999 summer institute, he has participated in activities with the Boston Writing Project at the University of Massachusetts. Over the past twenty years, his articles have appeared in several publications, including *English Journal* and the *Newsletter of the Boston Writing Project*.

ANNA COLLINS TREST

Anna Collins Trest currently teaches reading courses at the University of Southern Mississippi. She has also taught high school English and drama as well as elementary language arts. Her article in this book was written during her experience teaching in a gifted elementary program. She is a teacher-consultant with the South Mississippi Writing Project at the University of Southern Mississippi.

DIANE WAFF

Diane Waff is co-director of the Philadelphia Writing Project at the University of Pennsylvania and a vice principal at Trenton Central High School in Trenton, New Jersey. She has written teacher research articles focused on adolescent literacy and was a co-editor of *Reconceptualizing the Literacies in Adolescents' Lives* published in 1998 by Lawrence Erlbaum.

ELAINE WARE

Elaine Ware is a teacher-consultant and coordinator of the advanced institute on teacher inquiry with the Western Pennsylvania Writing Project at the University of Pittsburgh. She is particularly interested in student collaborations now possible through technology with the availability of virtual classroom environments. She has taught college writing and American literature for twenty-five years and is currently teaching at Indiana University of Pennsylvania in Indiana, Pennsylvania. Some of her work on student literacy and technology can be viewed at http://www.english.iup.edu/eaware.

STEPHANIE WILDER

Stephanie Wilder grew as a writing teacher at Charlotte Country Day School in Charlotte, North Carolina, a warm and friendly climate for teachers and students. She has recently moved to more rugged terrain, teaching English to incarcerated boys in Asheville, North Carolina, and is finding that the ideas of the National Writing Project work, no matter what the setting.

A NOTE ON THE EDITORS . . .

Amy Bauman and Art Peterson are senior editors with the National Writing Project.

Index

T

V

W